Regional Dress

Regional Dress

Between Tradition and Modernity

Sara Hume

BLOOMSBURY VISUAL ARTS
LONDON • NEW YORK • OXFORD • NEW DELHI • SYDNEY

BLOOMSBURY VISUAL ARTS
Bloomsbury Publishing Plc
50 Bedford Square, London, WC1B 3DP, UK
1385 Broadway, New York, NY 10018, USA
29 Earlsfort Terrace, Dublin 2, Ireland

BLOOMSBURY, BLOOMSBURY VISUAL ARTS and the Diana logo are trademarks of Bloomsbury Publishing Plc

First published in Great Britain 2022
Paperback edition published by Bloomsbury Visual Arts 2024

Copyright © Sara Hume, 2022

Sara Hume has asserted her right under the Copyright, Designs and Patents Act, 1988, to be identified as Author of this work.

For legal purposes the Acknowledgments on pp. xiv–xvi constitute an extension of this copyright page.

Cover design by Adriana Brioso
Cover image: *Le drapeau alsacien* by Charles Spindler, 1909.
Coll. and photogr. BNU de Strasbourg.

All rights reserved. No part of this publication may be reproduced or transmitted in any form or by any means, electronic or mechanical, including photocopying, recording, or any information storage or retrieval system, without prior permission in writing from the publishers.

Bloomsbury Publishing Plc does not have any control over, or responsibility for, any third-party websites referred to or in this book. All internet addresses given in this book were correct at the time of going to press. The author and publisher regret any inconvenience caused if addresses have changed or sites have ceased to exist, but can accept no responsibility for any such changes.

A catalogue record for this book is available from the British Library.

A catalog record for this book is available from the Library of Congress.

ISBN:	HB:	978-1-3501-4798-0
	PB:	978-1-3503-2773-3
	ePDF:	978-1-3501-4799-7
	eBook:	978-1-3501-4800-0

Typeset by Integra Software Services Pvt. Ltd.

To find out more about our authors and books visit www.bloomsbury.com and sign up for our newsletters.

Contents

List of Plates	vii
List of Figures	ix
List of Maps	xiii
Acknowledgments	xiv
Maps	xvii

	Introduction	1
	Overview of Alsatian History	8
1	**Religious Performance**	15
	Relationship between Religion and Dress	16
	Processions and the Performance of Catholicism	23
	Performance of Protestantism	27
	Other Minority Religious Groups	32
	Exclusion of Minority Religions from Public Spaces	41
	Dress as Ritual	45
	Declining Link between Regional Dress and Religious Observance	47
	Conclusion	53
2	**Visual Representation**	57
	Field Guide to the Folk	58
	Photography of Regional Dress	66
	Realism and Regional Dress	69
	Book Illustrations	75
	Art Nouveau and the Alsatian Awakening	80
	Spindler as Photographer and Ethnologue	83
	Development of *l'Alsacienne* as a Symbol of Alsace	93
	Conclusion	95
3	**Material Goods**	97
	Basic Components of Rural Alsatian Wardrobes	100
	Shift to Coordinating Outfits	104

	Quantity and Value of Clothing	107
	Evolution of Special Occasion Wear	110
	Development of Retail in Alsace	112
	Introduction of Department Stores into Alsace	119
	Home-Based Industrial Production	121
	Education and Apprenticeship for Craftspeople	124
	Apprenticeships in the Interwar Period	129
	Tailoring and Dressmaking in Literature	131
	Conclusion	133
4	**Museum Objects**	135
	Roots of Folk Museums	136
	Founding of the Musée Alsacien	140
	The Collection and Its Acquisition	145
	Nature of the Early Displays	153
	Producing and Reproducing the Image of Regional Culture	157
	Kermesse: Masquerade and Commerce	162
	Conclusion	164
5	**Living History**	167
	Non-Religious Festivals	169
	Wedding Processions	173
	Turn-of-the-Century Festivals	174
	Folklorization of Fête-Dieu	178
	Folk Dress in Political Rallies	180
	Organization of Folk Groups	186
	Nazi Influence on Folklore	192
	Re-Emergence of Interest in Folklore	195
	Conclusion	198

Conclusion 201

Notes 211
Bibliography 233
Index 246

List of Plates

Plate 1   Members of the Groupe folklorique du Pays de Hanau de Bouxwiller perform in Strasbourg's Place Gutenberg in summer 2007. Photograph by author.

Plate 2   Fête-Dieu procession in Geispolsheim, 1908 from *Images du Musée Alsacien*. Coll. et photogr. Bibliothèque nationale et universitaire, Strasbourg.

Plate 3   Charles Emrich, "Paysanne de Kochersberg" [Catholic] from *Collection de six costumes nationaux alsaciens et badois*, 1834. Coll. et photogr. BNU, Strasbourg.

Plate 4   Charles Emrich, "Paysanne de Kochersberg" [Protestant] from *Collection de six costumes nationaux alsaciens et badois*, 1834. Coll. et photogr. BNU, Strasbourg.

Plate 5   Jan Lewicki, "Paysans du Kochersberg, jeunes gens" from *Costumes d'Alsace et de Bade*, 1834. Coll. et photogr. BNU, Strasbourg.

Plate 6   Louis Marie Lanté and Georges Jacques Gatine, "Paysanne alsacienne de Kochersberg" from *Costumes de divers pays*, 1827. Coll. et photogr. BNU, Strasbourg.

Plate 7   Gustave Courbet, *Burial at Ornans (Un enterrement à Ornans)*, 1849–50. Paris, Musée d'Orsay, accepté par l'Etat à titre de don de Mlle Juliette Courbet en 1881.

Plate 8   Gustave Brion, *Cortège nuptial*, 1873. Musée des Beaux-Arts de Strasbourg, Photo Musées de Strasbourg, A. Plisson.

Plate 9   Gustave Doré, *Soir en Alsace*, 1869. Musée d'Art Moderne et Contemporain de Strasbourg, Photo Musées de Strasbourg, A. Plisson.

Plate 10 Jean-Jacques Henner, *Alsace. Elle attend*, 1871. Paris, Musée National Jean-Jacques Henner. Photo © RMN-Grand Palais/Franck Rau.

Plate 11 Hansi, Pages d'Album, 1916, Gravure no. 53/150. Coll. et photogr. BNU, Strasbourg.

Plate 12 Bodice of wedding dress of Odile Schmitt, 1903. Collection of the Musée Alsacien de Strasbourg.

Plate 13 Purple silk bodice from Geispolsheim. Collection of the Musée Alsacien de Strasbourg.

Plate 14 Courtyard of Musée Alsacien. Photograph by author.
Plate 15 Gustav Kraus, Procession celebrating the wedding of King Ludwig and Queen Therese in Munich on October 4, 1835. Münchner Stadtmuseum, Sammlung Graphik/Gemälde.
Plate 16 Gustav Kraus, Procession celebrating the wedding of King Ludwig and Queen Therese in Munich on October 4, 1835. Münchner Stadtmuseum, Sammlung Graphik/Gemälde.
Plate 17 Frédéric-Emile Simon, Cultivators from the Industrial Parade in Strasbourg June 25, 1840. Coll. et photogr. BNU, Strasbourg.
Plate 18 Frédéric-Emile Simon, Inhabitants of the Robertsau from the Industrial Parade in Strasbourg June 25, 1840. Coll. et photogr. BNU, Strasbourg.
Plate 19 Fête-Dieu procession in Geispolsheim, 2009, Photograph by author.
Plate 20 Corpus Christi procession in Seehausen, Bavaria, June 2015. Photo by Carsten Koall/Getty Images.
Plate 21 The character of Frau Antje created to promote the dairy products in the Netherlands. Dutch Dairy Association.
Plate 22 President Barack Obama and German Chancellor Angela Merkel are welcomed by girls in traditional Black Forest dress in Baden Baden, April 3, 2009. Photo by Alex Grimm/Getty Images.

List of Figures

1.1. Théophile Schuler, Costume studies of Schleithal and Oberseebach, 1858. Cabinet des Estampes et des Dessins de Strasbourg. Photo Musées de Strasbourg, M. Bertola.   20
1.2. Théophile Schuler, Costume studies of Hunspach, 1858. Cabinet des Estampes et des Dessins de Strasbourg. Photo Musées de Strasbourg, M. Bertola.   21
1.3. Fête-Dieu procession in Schleithal, ca. 1930s. Photograph by Lucien Blumer. Archives de Strasbourg, 1 Fi 189.   25
1.4. Charles Spindler, Exiting the church, Oberseebach, ca. 1890s. Spindler Archives.   28
1.5. Exiting the church, Oberseebach, ca. 1930s. Photograph by Lucien Blumer. Archives de Strasbourg, 1 Fi 189.   28
1.6 Charles Spindler, Wedding procession, Hunspach, ca. 1890s. Spindler Archives.   29
1.7. Charles Spindler, Wedding procession, Hunspach, ca. 1890s. Spindler Archives.   30
1.8. Wedding procession in Oberseebach, ca. 1930s. Photograph by Lucien Blumer. Archives de Strasbourg, 1 Fi 189.   31
1.9. Jan Lewicki, "Paysans du Kochersberg, âge avancé" from *Costumes d'Alsace et de Bade*, 1834. Coll. et photogr. Bibliothèque nationale et universitaire, Strasbourg.   33
1.10. Jan Lewicki, "Anabaptistes" from *Costumes d'Alsace et de Bade*, 1834. Coll. et photogr. BNU, Strasbourg.   34
1.11. Alphonse Lévy, *Schulé klopfer* from David-Léon Cahun, *La vie juive*, 1886, p. 10. Hanna Holborn Gray Special Collections Research Center, University of Chicago Library.   38
1.12. Alphonse Lévy, Couple walking outside from David-Léon Cahun, *La vie juive*, 1886, p. 82. Hanna Holborn Gray Special Collections Research Center, University of Chicago Library.   39
1.13. Alphonse Lévy, Seder from David-Léon Cahun, *La vie juive*, 1886, p. 30. Hanna Holborn Gray Special Collections Research Center, University of Chicago Library.   40

1.14. Alphonse Lévy, Man wearing a kippah from David-Léon Cahun, *La vie juive*, 1886, p. 59. Hanna Holborn Gray Special Collections Research Center, University of Chicago Library. 41

1.15. Alphonse Lévy, Sukkot from David-Léon Cahun, *La vie juive*, 1886, p. 104. Hanna Holborn Gray Special Collections Research Center, University of Chicago Library. 42

1.16. Moritz Oppenheim, Seder, ca. 1867. Hanna Holborn Gray Special Collections Research Center, University of Chicago Library. 42

1.17. Embroidered bonnet with untied ribbon. Second half of the nineteenth century. Collection of the Musée du Pays de Hanau de Bouxwiller, Photo A. Mertz. 46

1.18. Bonnet with wide ribbon tied into a bow, nineteenth century. Collection of the Musée du Pays de Hanau de Bouxwiller, Photo A. Mertz. 47

1.19. Grand'messe pontificale held in Strasbourg July 21, 1935, auteur non mentionné. Archives de Strasbourg, 1 Fi 2 / 7. 50

2.1. Jacques Grasset de Saint-Sauveur and L. F. Labrousse, "Homme et Femme de Housberg, près Strasbourg" from *Costumes de Différent Pays*, ca. 1797. Collection of the Los Angeles County Museum of Art. 61

2.2. "Alsacien et Alsacienne" from *Les français peints par eux-mêmes: Encyclopédie morale du dix-neuvième siècle. Province. Tome Troisième*, 1842. Bibliothèque nationale de France. 65

2.3. Charles Lallemand and Ludovic Hart, Stereoscopic image of women from Blaesheim, Alsace, 1860s. Private Collection. 67

2.4. Charles Lallemand and Ludovic Hart, Stereoscopic image of family from the Outre-Forêt, 1860s. Private Collection. 67

2.5. Adolphe Braun, *Alsace*, ca. 1871. Boston Athenaeum. 69

2.6. Print that appeared in *L'univers illustré* based on the original painting by Gustave Brion, *Bible Reading. Protestant Interior in Alsace*, 1868. Louis Bertrand/Alamy Stock Photo. 71

2.7. Photographic print of Jules Breton, *A Great Pilgrimage in Brittany*, 1862–5 published by Goupil & Cie. Digital image courtesy of the Getty's Open Content Program. 73

2.8. Photographic print of Charles-François Marchal, *La foire aux servantes à Bouxwiller*, 1864 published by Goupil & Cie. Collection of the author. 74

2.9. Alfred Touchemolin, Detail of "Intérieur d'une ferme du Kochersberg," from Frédéric Piton, *Strasbourg illustré en panorama pittoresque*

List of Figures　　　xi

        historique et statistique de Strasbourg et de ses environs, 1855.
        Coll. et photogr. BNU, Strasbourg. 75
2.10. Gustave Doré and Adolphe François Pannemaker, *La cigale et la fourmi* (*The Ant and the Grasshopper*) from Jean de la Fontaine *Fables*, 1868. Bibliothèque nationale de France. 77
2.11. Gustave Doré, *L'Alsace meurtrie*, 1872. Copyright: Collectivé européenne d'Alsace – Sébastien Sutter. 79
2.12. Charles Spindler, Messti, ca. 1890s. Spindler Archives. 84
2.13. Charles Spindler, Shepherd and child in mended clothes. Spindler Archives. 85
2.14. Charles Spindler, Women at a river doing laundry. Spindler Archives. 86
2.15. Charles Spindler, Family in Steinselz. Spindler Archives. 86
2.16. Charles Spindler, Family in Steinselz. Spindler Archives. 87
2.17. Charles Spindler, Family in Outre-Forêt. Spindler Archives. 88
2.18. Charles Spindler, Photograph of young woman from Steinselz showing grid marks. Spindler Archives. 89
2.19. Charles Spindler, Illustration of girl from Steinselz copied from photograph. Coll. et photogr. BNU, Strasbourg. 90
2.20. Charles Spindler, Model dressed in costume from Spindler's collection. Spindler Archives. 92
2.21. Charles Spindler, Illustration from *Images alsaciennes* copied from photograph of model, 1893. Coll. et photogr. BNU, Strasbourg. 93
3.1. Odile Schmitt and Isidore Hartmann with their children, 1906. Musée Alsacien de Strasbourg. 98
3.2. Odile Schmitt and Isidore Hartmann, 1914. Musée Alsacien de Strasbourg. 99
3.3. Attached skirt and corselet. Collection of the Musée Alsacien de Strasbourg. 102
3.4. Charles Spindler, Girls in Geispolsheim wearing shirred sleeves, ca. 1890s. Spindler Archives. 103
3.5. Wedding of André Muller and Eve Irrmann in Berstett, 1904. From *Berstett: Un village pittoresque du Kochersberg* (Strasbourg: Editions Coprur, 1993), p. 161. 111
3.6. Charles Spindler, Woman in Hunspach wearing apron of jacquard woven textile. Spindler Archives. 115
3.7. Advertisement for Kaufhaus Modern, ca. 1913. Archives de Strasbourg, 5 MW 283. 120
3.8. Charles Spindler, Man weaving. Spindler Archives. 122

List of Figures

3.9.	Charles Spindler, Girls knitting in doorway. Spindler Archives.	123
3.10.	Charles Spindler, Girls outside while one knits. Spindler Archives.	123
4.1.	Bodice from Hunspach. Collection of the Musée Alsacien de Strasbourg.	152
4.2.	Bodice donated by Charles Spindler. Collection of the Musée Alsacien de Strasbourg.	153
4.3.	Room from Winzenheim from *Images du Musée Alsacien à Strasbourg*, 1912. Musée Alsacien de Strasbourg.	154
4.4.	Charles Spindler, "Diplôme de sociétaire." Musée Alsacien de Strasbourg.	158
4.5.	Late-eighteenth-century farm in Imbsheim from *Images du Musée Alsacien à Strasbourg*, 1914. Coll. et photogr. BNU, Strasbourg.	159
4.6.	Postcard from the Musée Alsacien showing exhibition. Archives de Strasbourg, 5 MW 275.	160
4.7.	Kermesse at the Musée Alsacien, 1907. Coll. et photogr. BNU, Strasbourg.	163
5.1.	Gustav Kraus, Procession of thirty-five wedding couples at Oktoberfest in Munich on October 16, 1842. Münchner Stadtmuseum, Sammlung Graphik/Gemälde.	174
5.2.	Parade of Alsatians greeting the Kaiser on his visit to Strasbourg from Bernhard Friedrich Wilhelm Rogge, *Kaiserbüchlein: 1797–1888. Zur Erinnerung an Deutschlands Heldenkaiser Wilhelm I*, 1888. Widener Library, Harvard University.	181
5.3.	Girls in Bastille Day parade in Strasbourg, 1919, auteur non mentionné. Archives de Strasbourg, 1 Fi 1 / 2.	183
5.4.	Allegorical tableau at Bastille Day in Strasbourg, 1919, auteur non mentionné. Archives de Strasbourg. 1 Fi 1 / 3.	184
5.5.	Visit of Maréchal Foch to Strasbourg, November 21, 1920. Archives de Strasbourg, 1 Fi 1 / 26.	185
5.6.	Nazi soldiers with women wearing Alsatian dress in Strasbourg, 1940. Archives de Strasbourg, 1 Fi 134.	194

List of Maps

Map 1   Map of Europe   xvii

Map 2   Map of Alsace   xviii

Acknowledgments

The completion of this book depended on the assistance, encouragement, and involvement of a large number of people. Once I left Chicago to begin my job at the Kent State University Museum, this project could have faced total derailment and the fact that it did not is thanks to a network of support spread across two countries. First and foremost I must thank my advisor, Leora Auslander, who provided the perfect blend of encouragement and criticism, and was always able to instill in me the sense that becoming a historian was a worthy endeavor. I only spent three years in Chicago, but my intellectual growth during that brief period was immeasurable. After having merely dabbled in history in college, I had a great deal of ground to make up before I could call myself a doctor. Jan Goldstein and Michael Geyer were both instrumental in guiding me through the daunting task of acquiring the necessary foundations. Christine Mehring provided her insights into a project that pushed the boundaries of history into areas more familiar to art historians.

I am also grateful for the opportunity to have presented work at the University of Chicago at the Modern France Workshop, the Modern Europe Workshop and at the Material Culture Workshop. These workshops were invaluable owing to the feedback of the attendees, particularly Eleanor Rivera, Jack Hight, Carolyn Purnell, Robin Bates, and Tyson Leuchter and Sarah Weicksel. Once I moved to Ohio I found an interdisciplinary network of support and intellectual discussion through both writing partners and groups notably Marie Gasper-Hulvet, and Ruxandra Looft who invited me to join her writing group at Iowa State.

In transforming this project into a book, I am grateful to the folks at Bloomsbury especially Frances Arnold for promptly responding to my steady stream of inquiries as well as Hannah Crump, Yvonne Thouroude, and Rebecca Hamilton. I am further grateful to Bloomsbury for allowing me to use sections of my writing that first appeared in the chapter "Between Fashion and Folk: Dress Practices in Alsace during WWI" in *Fashion, Society and the First World War: International Perspectives*, edited by Maude Bass-Krueger, Hayley Edwards-Dujardin, and Sophie Kurkdjian (London: Bloomsbury Visual Arts, 2021). I would also like to thank Duke University Press for allowing me to republish sections of "The Final Bows: The Evolution and Replacement of

Regional Dress in Alsace, 1870–1920" from *French Historical Studies*, 43, no. 2, (April 2020): 271–297.

Financial support from a number of sources was critical to the completion of my research and the production of this book including the Research Publication Grant from the Design History Society, the Pasold Research Fund Publication Grant, a grant from the Professional Development Excellence Pool at Kent State, the University of Chicago Department of History Albert Kunstadter Fellowship, Provost Summer Award, the Bourse d'échange de l'Ecole des Hautes Etudes en Sciences Sociales, and a grant from the France Chicago Center. My research was facilitated by the tremendous cooperation and resources of these institutions: the Archives départementales du Bas-Rhin; the Archives de Strasbourg; the Bibliothèque nationale et universitaire, Strasbourg; the Musée d'Art et d'Histoire de Saverne; and the Musée du Pays de Hanau. I would like to extend a special thanks to Malou Schneider and Andrée Schneider at the Musée Alsacien for their insights and access to the collections, to Jean-Charles Spindler who afforded me liberal access to the remarkable collection of photographs by his grandfather as well as other papers and correspondences and Nicolas Stoskopf who was so generous with his grandfather's papers, letters, and newspaper clippings. I also want to extend my appreciation to the Office pour la Langue et la Culture d'Alsace (OLCA) and Bénédicte Keck who taught me the rudiments of the Alsatian dialect.

The support and cooperation of a number of individuals in Alsace was as critical to the completion of this book as the availability of institutional resources. In large part, my determination to complete this book after finding full-time employment in the United States was motivated by the sense of obligation for the generosity and hospitality shown to me in Alsace. First and foremost I would like to thank Georgette Weber who opened her home to me, shared her extensive knowledge of Alsatian culture, and bent over backward to assist me in my research. Along with her family and the other members of the Groupe Folklorique du Pays de Hanau de Bouxwiller, she provided me with an understanding of Alsace that cannot be found in books. Hary Rabezandrina made Strasbourg feel like a home with her friendship and generosity. I also found a welcoming reception and invaluable assistance from a number of individuals and groups including Lucette Rudloff and the other members of the Coquelicots de Geispolsheim, René Scheisser, Armand Gar and the Groupe Folklorique de Hoenheim, Marie-Louise Hemmerle, Jean-Luc Neth, Anne Wolff, Raymond Matzen, Jean-Marc Schlagdenhauffen, Marie Rose Allard, Barbara Gatineau, Léone Prigent, Philomène Buntz, Lucette Rudloff, and Michel and André Ebersold.

Once I returned to the United States my progress in writing first my dissertation then adapting it into a book would not have been possible without the remarkable support of the entire staff of the Kent State University Museum. The two directors, Jean Druesedow and Sarah Rogers, granted me the time to dedicate myself to my writing despite the numerous other demands of my job. As I have straddled two worlds—as a historian working on my book and a curator organizing exhibitions—my colleagues at the museum have ensured the success of my work at my day job, especially Joanne Arnett, Joanne Fenn, Mary Gilbert, Bianka Hausknecht, and Jim Williams.

My task of writing has been made less lonely through the presence of wonderful friends and a supportive family. I hope that I have made it clear to you all long before I sat down to write up these acknowledgments how much your encouragement has meant to me along the way. Most critical to my completion of this book are my Chicago friends who provided timely intellectual and emotional support, most notably Erika Vause, Susan Stearns, Sarah Panzer, Taeju Kim, and Justin Glasson. Lastly I must thank my family for continuing to believe that eventually I would finish the dang thing. A special thanks to my mother and father who actually read my drafts and were full of helpful advice and to Renate Hume and Roy Henderson. Finally a big thanks to JJ for being my best friend through so many years of this endeavor.

Maps

Map 1 Map of Europe.

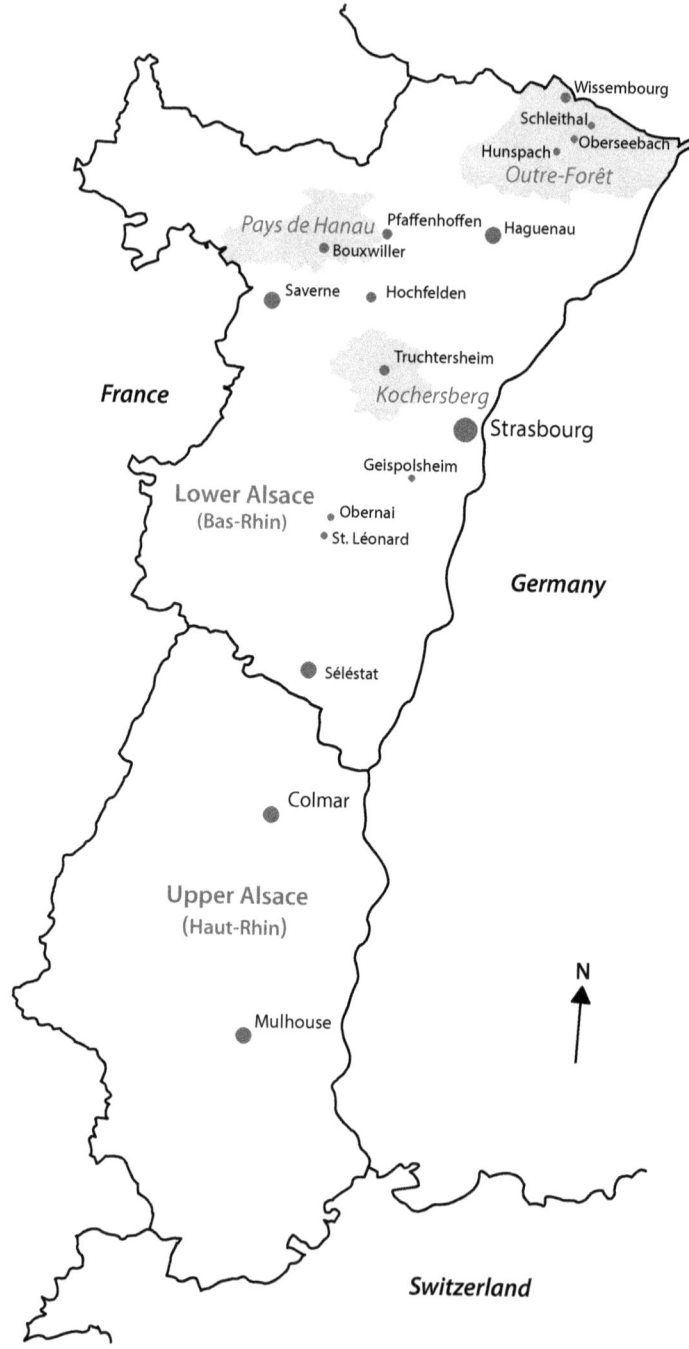

Map 2 Map of Alsace.

Introduction

On a Sunday afternoon in July 2007, a troupe of dancers dressed in regional Alsatian dress paraded into Strasbourg's Place Gutenberg and onto a stage. The women wore thick wool skirts, small bodices, and stomachers over white blouses with wide ruffled collars and enormous black bows on their heads. The men wore red wool vests with two rows of brass buttons and short black hats with wide circular brims (Plate 1). Just next to the stage, an orchestra played polka music to accompany the dancers. The members of the orchestra were wearing the same costume as the male dancers but without the hats. After a couple of dances, one of the performers stepped up to the microphone and provided an explanation of the costumes and dances for the assembled tourists.

A folk group has performed in the center of Strasbourg on Sundays in July and August since 1963. While the tourists may be momentarily entertained and appreciative of their brief immersion into Alsatian folkways, for the dancers and musicians in the groups, these performances demand hours of rehearsal and a significant investment in these elaborate costumes. Photos and illustrations of regional dress appear everywhere and on everything in Alsace: on beer bottles, postcards, cookie tins, and in store windows, but these performances throughout the summer provide visitors the chance to see actual costumes. The audience of tourists and the cartoon images on commercial products suggest that these costumes are simply kitsch. As the group performed their choreographed dances, it is natural to wonder whether this is what Alsatians really wore a hundred years ago or why these men and women are so dedicated to preserving these styles. Why do Alsatians hold so strongly to these practices and present themselves to visitors in this particular manner? The transmission of these stories and dances and costumes through generations is not simply a way of remembering, it is a way of understanding themselves.

Similar folk groups perform throughout Europe although the details of their costumes and headdresses are different. In answering questions such as why regional costumes have been worn and preserved, taking a specific region as a case study provides a detailed framework for understanding the general practices of regional dress more broadly. Regional dress is essentially local and yet many facets are common across localities from France and Germany to Scandinavia and Austria. The distinctiveness of Alsace, like any region, is the essential truth underlying the celebration of its particular culture. Because of this distinctiveness, understanding regional dress demands understanding the historical background and cultural context. In choosing Alsace in particular, this study by necessity becomes comparative owing to the region's situation at the border of France and Germany which has given rise to the two nations' competing political and cultural claims. While this comparison operates at the national level, the book also develops transregional comparisons between the developments in regional dress in Alsace with those elsewhere.[1] The comparative examples often focus on other regions in France and Germany, but other nations are examined as well. The depth of the examination of regional dress in Alsace is ultimately in the pursuit of understanding truths about regional dress more generally.

Regional dress emerged in rural areas across the continent. The societies that gave rise to its development in the eighteenth and nineteenth centuries are often characterized as traditional and defined in opposition to modernity. Eugen Weber's seminal text *Peasants into Frenchmen* describes at length the prevailing culture of rural France on the eve of its modernization, which he asserts occurred between 1870 and 1914.[2] Speaking local dialects, largely illiterate, believing superstition, the peasants are characterized by Weber as backward and crude. This proved a counterpoint to the introduction of modernization which he ascribes to such forces as railroads, education, and military service. The ultimate outgrowth of modernization according to Weber was the establishment of a sense of nationalism—a consciousness of being French.

Historians are fixated on defining the differences between past and present, and the notion of modernity as a break from earlier periods is pervasive.[3] Most literature on modernity places its emergence in cities such as Paris and London as early as the late eighteenth century. The French Revolution provides one point of rupture with its abolition of the feudal system and undermining of the authority of the Catholic Church. This growing secularization to the detriment of organized religion was a hallmark of modernity.[4] Weber emphasized another feature in his work on modernization: nationalism. The movement of people from the countryside to cities, which characterized the demographic changes of the nineteenth century and contributed to urbanization, served as another pillar of modernity. A fourth characteristic of modernity was industrialization. The transformation of how goods were produced enabled their distribution in large department stores which transformed the material life of people across the socioeconomic spectrum. These widespread social changes of modernization resulted in the well-established transformation of the lived experience of Europeans.

However, the traditional society so denigrated by Weber offered significant value to rural residents: strong social cohesion centered around shared religious faith. They bought their goods from artisans whom they knew personally. Small villages developed distinctive clothing styles which reflected their life. Created by local dressmakers or tailors, this regional dress was worn for special occasions which centered around religious observance and included weddings, first communion or confirmation, processions, and feast days (Plate 2). While rooted in this traditional society, regional dress persisted through the nineteenth and survived for different occasions into the twentieth and even twenty-first centuries. This book focuses less on the origins of regional dress in traditional villages than on its evolution in the face of modernization. In summarizing the response of the rural French population to rapid transformations of material conditions, Eugen Weber wrote: "Change is always awkward, but the changes modernity brought were often emancipations, and were frequently recognized as such. Old ways died unlamented."[5] The performances of the Alsatian folk groups, however, seem to belie Weber's assessment. Alsatians, like their counterparts in other rural areas, regretted and even resisted the loss of their distinctive culture and sought to preserve them in a number of ways.

The divide between traditional and modern society is not as clear cut as it is often portrayed. As David Harvey writes, "One of the myths of modernity is that it constitutes a radical break with the past."[6] The evolution of regional dress highlights the persistent tensions between these ostensibly opposing forces. The distinctive styles may have had their roots in the religious observances in local villages, but by the beginning of the twentieth century the occasions for their wear switched to secular, often political occasions. While there was a secularization of the meaning and performance of regional dress, this was not necessarily evidence of corresponding secularization of society. Alsace is a particularly useful case study in examining the encroachment of secularism as it is a region notable for the high degree of religious observance and strong representation of minority religious groups among its population. The legal status of religion in Alsace stands as an exception to the French policy of *laïcité* or the separation of church and state, which was implemented while Alsace was part of Germany. This exceptionalism proves enlightening in both understanding why Alsace, unlike much of France, developed distinctive dress but also the underlying linkages between modernization and declining religious observance.

As regional dress lost its function as an integral part of religious observance it increasingly became a political symbol and an element in political parades and demonstrations. The question thus emerged whether the dress signified allegiance to a region or to the nation, or more precisely what the proper relation between these two might be. While Weber equates nationalism with the elimination of regional distinctions, historians have sought to articulate a more nuanced relationship between regionalism and nationalism. Even in the French case that Weber addresses, historians have argued for the persistence of regional identity.[7] Stéphane Gerson, for instance, asserts that the cult of local memory directly contributed to modernity as he argues for the complicated interplay between attachment to the *pays* in the sense of the local as well as the national.[8] In Germany the attachment to the region or *Heimat* is much more widely understood as contributing to rather than opposing national allegiance.[9] Regional dress is one instance of local particularity that came to define and stand for people's identification with their region. In the case of Alsace it also came to stand for Alsace's loyalty to France. This complicated interplay between local, regional, and national belonging is at the heart of the story of regional dress.

Regional dress also highlights the tensions between rural culture and growing urbanization. While by and large the emergence of these distinctive dress styles occurred in the countryside, many of the men and women who worked for their preservation were based in cities. While this book seeks to explore the perspective of the rural populations who originally produced and wore the dress, many of the sources were produced by members of the bourgeoisie—the artists who recorded the styles, the notaries who inventoried people's wardrobes, the ethnographers who studied and collected the garments, and the founders of the museums that displayed these collections. Regional dress endured as a point of intersection between peasants and the bourgeoisie. In fact, as regional styles evolved, the visual representations by artists in turn served to influence how rural residents styled their clothing. The exchange between the socioeconomic groups went both ways. The folk performances in Strasbourg represent yet another stage in the ongoing performance of rural customs for an urban audience.

Industrialization and the resulting mass production of items including textiles and clothing had a clear effect on both the production and consumption of dress and the aesthetic changes in style. In this clash between traditional production and the introduction of manufactured goods, it is natural to assume that regional dress resulted from the former and was threatened by the latter. The reality is more complicated. Many of the elements of regional dress such as the ribbons or lace that composed the headdresses and the jacquard-woven textiles for the aprons were produced on machines often far from the regions where they were worn. In the early twentieth century, provincial department stores not only stocked cosmopolitan dress they also in some cases sold components of regional dress and the materials necessary to make it. The homogenizing effects of mass production, mail order, and department stores were not necessarily as total as widely assumed. Ultimately, many styles of regional dress reached their zenith in the late nineteenth century along with the introduction of the very systems of production that brought about their replacement.

The pathbreaking work in the field of history which introduced a framework for examining traditions including regional dress was set forth in the series of essays in *The Invention of Tradition* edited by Eric Hobsbawm and Terence Ranger. In his introductory essay, Hobsbawm develops the concept of "invented traditions" as "responses to novel situations which take the form of reference to old situations, or which establish their own past by quasi-obligatory repetition. It is the contrast between the constant change and the innovation of the modern world and the attempt to structure at least some part of social life within it as unchanging and invariant, that makes the 'invention of tradition' so interesting for historians of the past two centuries."[10] This idea that modernity and its rapid pace of change is the impetus for cultures to seek continuity with the past is closely aligned with the argument of this book. However, it is in Hobsbawm's emphasis on "invention" that his argument differs from mine. There is a sense throughout the essays, in particular in the essay by Hugh Trevor-Roper on the history of Scottish dress, that traditions are simply made up and then falsely associated with practices in the past.[11] Trevor-Roper traces the origin of the kilt and related traditions as a means of exploring how the Scottish and English created and invoked history to reinforce their self-understanding. In particular, he claims an Englishman invented the kilt itself around 1730. By finding a starting point for the tradition he discounts its authenticity. The line of argument in his essay as well as the book as a whole suggests that there is an artifice to traditions. The approach to studying folk costume that developed out of this literature emphasized a rupture between authentic past customs and later traditions that merely purported to maintain a link to the past.

In my book, the word "tradition" is used in a different way from that defined by Hobsbawm. Hobsbawm contrasts traditions, which he characterizes as strictly invariant, with customs, which involved established practice yet allowed for flexibility and variance.[12] By contrast, I use "traditional" as a counterpoint to modernization and it thus refers to those dress practices that existed in rural Europe in which the production, function, and style of the clothing were integral to the lives of villagers. Regional dress is generally defined in opposition to urban styles. Rather than referring to these urban styles as "fashionable" with its implication of rapid change, I will call them "cosmopolitan." This better serves as a counterpoint with regional dress which also changes over time but is specific to a particular locale. These two systems coexisted and influenced each other in a relatively fluid way through the early decades of the nineteenth century. Ultimately the traditional system of production disappeared and the occasions when these traditional styles were worn were instead marked with cosmopolitan styles. Rather than simply abandon the styles, Alsatians reappropriated them for use on different occasions. This moment when these costumes shifted in their function and meaning was not a moment of invention but rather one of adaptation and alteration.

In discussing the evolution of regional dress through the twentieth and into the twenty-first centuries, the usages change so profoundly from its origins as religious dress that it is appropriate to distinguish these later presentations through the choice of terminology. While I will use "regional dress" to refer to both its early and late manifestations, "folk dress" will denote the costumes worn by folk groups and for participants in political events. The designation as folk dress is not meant to dismiss the cultural significance of these later performances and does not indicate a lack of authenticity.

Scholars in folklore studies, anthropology, and other disciplines have long debated this question of authenticity. Regina Bendix in fact characterizes it as a plastic word—"words that mean so much they really mean very little."[13] While ostensibly a straightforward attribute meaning original, genuine, or unaltered, authenticity is generally assessed by scholars or connoisseurs based on a variety of criteria. Siân Jones identifies two different approaches to assessing authenticity: the materialist and the constructivist. The former is concerned with determining whether the origins of the object are what they are said to be—that it is not a replica. This is the approach of museum professionals and collectors. This concern with the material properties of the object contrasts with the constructivist perspective which focuses on the cultural construction of the object and thus assesses authenticity based on audience and context.[14] This latter approach is more widespread among academics such as anthropologists and historians and would lead to the privileging of original or traditional use of object as more authentic—in this case religious function within village favored over urban performances for tourists. In tracing changes in both the context in which costumes are worn and the means by which they are produced, I do not attribute greater authenticity or value to the earlier forms. In taking a material culture approach to exploring modernization in the countryside, the physical attributes of the costumes themselves are central, but the question of whether the objects are genuine is rarely pivotal to this study.

While modernization has been the subject of a significant amount of historical study, the material culture of regional dress provides important new avenues for considering the place of regional identity in this process. In particular, an approach focused on costume provides perspective into the experience of rural society. This segment of the population left little written record, so the study of material culture, allowing for a direct look at their possessions, may lead to the most direct insights into their lived experience. The intricacies of regional dress reveal the complexity of rural society: the religious divisions, the differences between rich and poor, and the tension between the dueling desires to protect traditions and to adopt modern technologies and lifestyles.

People's engagement with their clothing is more complicated than that of other goods. As something that is worn directly on the body and thus an extension of the self, clothing is a component of a complicated system of communication and self-expression. The system of dress within a certain culture includes innumerable markers that may identify a range of information including the wearer's age, gender, marital status, political affiliation, and religion. Every individual by necessity participates in this system and the sense in which they are making unique personal choices when they get dressed is sharply limited by the available acceptable alternatives. Within a culture, the different aspects of a person's identity that are demarcated by dress vary. In almost all cultures men and women are immediately distinguishable by dress, but fewer distinguish between single, married, and widowed adults. Furthermore, even within a certain geographic and temporal boundary, different cultural systems of dress coexisted. For instance, in nineteenth-century rural Alsace, Jews, Catholics, and Protestants each dressed according to distinct rules and had their own means of differentiating men and women, children and adults, married and single. The extent to which these coded communications are understood depends on how familiar the viewer is with the levels of meaning. For people inside the system—of the same community or religion—clothing choices have different meanings than they do for outsiders. If all of these layers of meaning are not complicated enough, the entire system undergoes continual change. On the one hand, the task of defining and describing a system of dress may seem nearly hopeless because of the layers of subtle nuance and the inadequacy of language to communicate a sartorial act.[15] On the other hand, a broad examination of the fundamental shifts in the system can provide valuable insight into the culture and society. Along with the transformation of how clothing was made and sold, modernity transformed important aspects of the way people interact that were reflected in how people dressed.

The complexity of the relationship between people and their clothing arises out from the multifaceted levels of the engagement. All of the engagements people have with clothing, whether as maker, purchaser, wearer, observer, or collector, have always been deeply gendered. Certainly clothing plays a prominent role in the social construction of gender as arguably the most obvious visual signal of the difference between men and women, but such distinctions went far deeper than simple binaries such as men wear pants, women wear skirts. Men in rural areas, including but by no means only in Alsace, generally adopted cosmopolitan dress before women did, and the distinctive styles that did exist for men were more likely to signify their occupations rather than their marital status or religion as in the case of women. There was little distinction between the clothing of Catholic and Protestant men in the way there was between that of Catholic and Protestant women. In effect, men's and women's clothing in rural Alsace can be viewed as two distinct systems of practices. The separation between the systems extended to production, as women's clothes were made by women and men's clothes by men. In fact, sewing, repairing, and washing clothes provided a host of employment opportunities for women. In examining clothing, this book sheds light on many aspects of life for rural women and explores the distinctions in lived experience of men and women.

Overview of Alsatian History

As an indicator of how people wish to present themselves, dress is a useful vehicle for examining their experience of social change. The period between 1870 and 1945 was a period of exceptional change throughout France and Germany, but particularly in Alsace. During this period, the region switched from French control to German and back. Following the French defeat in the Franco-Prussian War, the terms of the Treaty of Frankfurt included the transfer of both departments of Alsace and a portion of neighboring Lorraine to the newly unified Germany. Alsace would remain part of the new German Kaiserreich until the end of the First World War, when it returned to France. Alsace-Lorraine did not become a full state or *Land* within the German Reich but rather was granted the status of a *Reichsland*, or Imperial territory. As a *Reichsland*, Alsace-Lorraine was governed by a representative of the Kaiser, first by an *Oberpräsident*, and then after 1879 by a *Statthalter*.[16] An assembly or *Landesausschuss* was formed in 1875, but served only as a consultative body until the constitution of 1911 granted Alsace a greater level of autonomy and it gained a true, albeit limited, legislative role. Upon their return to France, the three departments that had comprised the annexed territory were reintegrated into the French nation, but they retained exemptions to certain French laws that had been passed between 1870 and 1919. Both Germany and France faced political challenges incorporating the region into their political system and, more broadly, into their nation.

The political contest over Alsace was not the only reason for its distinctiveness. Even before the Franco-Prussian War, Alsace stood apart from the rest of France as one of the most affluent and best-educated regions. Alsatians also maintained their own distinct dialect, which was a variant of Alemannic, one of the families of German dialects. Perhaps more significantly, its religious diversity marked a sharp contrast with the religious homogeneity that prevailed throughout the rest of France. Protestants made up almost a fifth of the population of Alsace with particularly strong representation in the northern areas of Outre-Forêt and the Pays de Hanau as well as in the southern city of Mulhouse.[17] Alsace also boasted a significant minority Jewish population. I argue that it is the religious diversity of Alsace that led to the development of elaborate costumes worn for services and holidays. The religious tensions between the Catholics and Protestants were a powerful force complicating the development of the German nation following unification and were also a significant point of friction in the reincorporation of Alsace into France.

In many ways these aspects of Alsatian culture that set it apart as a region were divisive even within the region. Rather than one cohesive dialect, there are in fact significant variations in pronunciation and vocabulary between Upper and Lower Alsace. For example, the dialect of the Outre-Forêt along the northern edge of Alsace is a variant of Franconian, not Alemannic. The distribution of religious groups also created subregional differences in Alsace. While Upper Alsace was 90 percent Catholic, Catholics represented only 70 percent of the population of Lower Alsace.[18] Furthermore the Protestants of Lower Alsace were divided into Calvinists in the Outre-Forêt and Lutherans elsewhere, particularly in the Pays de Hanau. The development of distinctive dress styles served to distinguish adherents of different confessions from each other as well as reinforce coherence within the group. Upper and Lower Alsace each had distinctive economic development with greater industrialization in Upper Alsace, particularly around Mulhouse, while the northern and western expanse of Lower Alsace remained heavily agricultural. This study concentrates primarily on dress practices throughout Lower Alsace, which because of its greater religious heterogeneity was the area where traditional dress practices persisted into the twentieth century.

The population of Alsace underwent a period of great flux during the period of German control. According to the terms of the Treaty of Frankfurt, Alsatians wishing to remain French were given the *option* of leaving the region by October 1872.[19] Ultimately 50,000 Alsatians took the *option* by that deadline and an additional 50,000 left during the period of the Reichsland.[20] The loss of roughly 10 percent of the population led to a significant reordering of the social order, particularly because the émigrés drew largely from the bourgeoisie, especially industrialists from Upper Alsace. The population loss from this emigration, however, was more than offset by the 120,000 Germans who moved into the region. These Germans established a community that was generally isolated from the native-born Alsatians and was largely made up of people associated with the university, military, and civil service.[21] These substantial waves of immigration and emigration created simmering tensions between the native-born Alsatians who remained and the new class of German bureaucrats.[22]

Although the rural population by and large lacked the resources or incentive to leave through the *option*, a separate migration occurred within the region as people moved from the countryside to the cities. In 1851, the rural population in Alsace was 662,400 or 63.4 percent of the total population. By 1900 the number had dropped to 574,700 or 49.8 percent of the total, while the urban population had grown from 382,000 in 1851 to 580,000 in 1900.[23] Despite the overall growth in the population of Alsace, the number of people in rural areas declined and those who remained were older than the Alsatian population as a whole. Rather than remaining in villages, young men and women were leaving to find employment in cities. This exodus from rural Alsace contributed significantly to the sense that the encroachment of modernity threatened traditional culture.

The linguistic, religious, and economic divisions across the region made the development of a coherent Alsatian culture a complicated construct. The emergence of a single style of folk dress to represent the entire region out of a multiplicity of local styles of regional dress served a variety of political aims. While for rural Alsatians, the traditional dress styles communicated a range of nuanced information about the wearer including religious affiliation and even their village of origin, for outsiders, be they French or Germans or even urban

Alsatians, these subtleties of meaning were lost in favor of more simplistic readings. The ability of clothing to convey various levels of meaning depending on the audience allowed regional dress styles to accommodate competing notions of the local, the region, and the nation.

This book traces the process by which distinctive rural clothing practices gave way to cosmopolitan dress and the simultaneous transformation of these regional styles into folk dress worn for primarily political purposes. Each chapter considers a different facet of this transformative arc—or, rather, parallel arcs. These five different perspectives allow for an exploration of complicated ways that Alsace's situation at the crossroads of France and Germany affected the meaning, function, and appearance of clothing while also illuminating how modernity was experienced in rural Europe more generally. The chapters each consider costume in a different way: as a performance, as an image, as a consumer good, as a museum object, and, last, as a form of living history.

By situating dress within the context of performance, Chapter 1 traces the various contexts in which regional dress was worn. The elaborate dress styles evolved as an integral part of religious observance. The religious distinctions within and among the various regions in Lower Alsace were clearly reflected by the elaborate clothing that was worn for Sundays and special occasions such as weddings and communion. Gradually the association between the styles of dress and religious observance broke down. This chapter looks at the changing audience for the rural festivals and parades as well as the changing attitudes of the Protestant and Catholic leadership as contributors to the dissociation between religious practice and regional dress. The ultimate disassociation between regional dress styles and religious performance that occurred by the early twentieth century marked the transformation of the costumes from integral aspect of the lived experience to folk performance.

Chapter 2 focuses on the changing depictions of regional dress by artists and how such representations alternately reflected and introduced symbolism and meaning. During the early nineteenth century, a widespread movement took place where artists documented distinctive dress practices across Europe, including in Alsace. These sorts of ethnographic studies of costumes continued through the turn of the century and served to establish the image of Alsatian dress that became known throughout France and Germany. When the Franco-Prussian War resulted in France's loss of Alsace and Lorraine, artists such as Jean-Jacques Henner and Gustave Doré made use of the young Alsatian woman in a large headbow as a symbol for the region, which gained political charge. Images of regional dress became central to the work of artists involved the

"Alsatian Awakening" that occurred in the years leading up to the First World War. One of the artists at the center of this movement, Charles Spindler, was particularly interested in both documenting and preserving rural dress. While Spindler maintained a position of neutrality in the mounting political contest between France and Germany, the Awakening movement, which sought to cultivate distinctive Alsatian culture, included both native Germans and fervent French nationalists. Once war broke out in 1914, the image of the woman in the traditional headbow became widely used by French propagandists to signal Alsatian loyalty to France. Beyond shaping an image of regional culture for outsiders, the work of these men altered how Alsatians themselves used and understood the dress.

The decline of regional dress practices and the introduction of cosmopolitan dress into rural areas were driven by the adoption of modern systems of production and retailing. The third chapter situates the changes in the appearance of clothing with these fundamental changes in clothing production across Europe. Dressmakers and tailors throughout rural Alsace had created distinctive clothing particular to different villages and areas. These small artisans faced competition first in the 1870s and 1880s from department stores in France and Germany that offered mail-order and then from the arrival of large specialty retailers in Strasbourg and other towns by 1900. This chapter looks at the effects of regime change on how people dressed. Despite the symbolic charge of images of regional dress, the economic implications of clothing production and sales reflected significant integration of Alsatians into the German or French nation. The transformation of the system of clothing production occurred in tandem with changes in material aspects of the clothing, including not just its appearance, but also its value and craftsmanship. Chapter 3 also examines the process of switching from regional dress styles to cosmopolitan ones, which occurred not as sharp rupture but rather as a slow merging of the former into the latter. In addition to making use of photographs to follow the evolution of clothing styles worn for special occasions, this chapter makes use of estate inventories taken posthumously to contribute to an understanding of how rural Alsatians actually dressed, including their entire range of clothing. Rather than a nostalgic idealization of rural life, these inventories reflect the harsh reality that was confirmed by photographs of the same time. The introduction of cosmopolitan dress was widely received by rural Alsatians as an improvement, although there was unevenness in its adoption.

Chapter 4 focuses on how museums have influenced the meaning and function of regional dress through their practices of collecting and exhibiting.

The role of intellectuals in shaping the image of regional dress expanded beyond artistic production and into the realm of collecting, through the establishment of the Musée Alsacien. The founders of the museum were committed to promoting French interests in Alsace, and their project was in league with comparable projects elsewhere in France, such as the Museon Arlaten in Provence. The establishment of the museum in Strasbourg depended on the contributions of collectors whose political agendas diverged from those of the founders. In fact, the museum's origins can be traced to similar projects in Berlin and elsewhere in Germany as well as in France. The techniques for presenting people, clothing, and artifacts developed out of the series of World's Fairs such as those held in Paris in 1867, 1889, and 1900. While the focus of the Musée Alsacien was largely centered on how rural culture was threatened by modernity, it was this very modernity that transformed rural life into this form of spectacle. In fact, the founders of the Musée Alsacien sought to promote not just the preservation of regional dress but also its continued production as part of their agenda. The process of preserving objects within the museum context fundamentally changed the nature and meaning of the objects themselves.

The final chapter of the book looks at how people continue to wear regional dress in the twentieth and twenty-first centuries as a form of remembering the past and holding on to elements of traditional rural life. Regional dress is not simply an artifact from history, but an integral part of the efforts of twenty-first-century Europeans to both preserve and promote their regional culture. The folk groups who perform in Strasbourg's Place Gutenberg each summer and present their costumes to tourists engage in a form of living history. Many performances by folk groups take place in international festivals which bring together participants from villages across Europe and beyond. The transnational movement which led to the formation of folk groups largely emerged in the 1930s. The forms of performance that have continued into the present day differ in striking ways from the earlier forms that I examine in the first chapter. The religious and political agendas of Alsatians from the nineteenth and twentieth centuries may seem to have given way to entertainment and tourist purposes. Nonetheless, the folk groups who wear these costumes also engage in educational activities and play a central role in the social life of rural villages. This final chapter juxtaposes the narrative that these performers present as the meaning and history of these dress styles against the ways the costumes have actually evolved into an important part of the region's present-day reality.

1

Religious Performance

In understanding how regional dress evolved in response to modernization, it is first essential to understand its traditional origins that are intrinsically bound to the religious customs of the local areas in which it emerged. From its use at special occasions that are generally centered around the church, regional dress can even be viewed as a form of religious dress. The distinctive dress styles were generally worn for religious occasions such as Sunday services, weddings, and confirmations or communion. In general, the regions that developed the most elaborate sartorial practices were those where there was some form of friction affecting the practice of religion. In the case of Alsace, the friction was a result of the polarity between Catholics and Protestants. At the same time, Alsace was also home to other minority religious groups, notably Jews and Anabaptists. Distinctive dress practices served to distinguish these different religious communities. Living in close proximity, sometimes even within the same villages, adherents of different religions established boundaries through their clothing. In the early nineteenth century, regional dress differed significantly between different areas and even villages across Alsace. Rather than unifying the region, dress practices delineated difference.

While the clothing choices of Jews and Anabaptists have generally been viewed as "religious dress," Catholic or Protestant dress is regarded differently. Rather than reflecting a specific set of religious beliefs, dress practices of mainstream Christian denominations have been deemed the normative way of dressing. When rural, regional dress is distinguished from urban, cosmopolitan dress it is categorized as regional or ethnic rather than religious. Lynne Hume's book *The Religious Life of Dress* reflects this general trend. While she devotes a chapter each to the ways Jews and Anabaptists dress, her chapter on Catholics focuses nearly exclusively on clerical dress: vestments and habits.[1] The dress that Catholics wear for religious events such as communion or weddings is not discussed in this context.

Because Jews and Anabaptists were set apart from the majority population by religion, their dress practices have been analyzed within the context of their religion. In contrast, rural Catholics and Protestants were distinguishable from their contemporaries less by their religion than by their rural context, so their distinctive dress was viewed as a function of geography. However, through the mid- to late nineteenth century, religious practice was central to traditional village life in rural communities where regional dress was worn and shaped how people dressed. The ultimate transformation of mainstream Christian styles of dress into folk dress contrasted with the near complete disappearance of distinctive Jewish and Anabaptist styles. This disparity speaks to the normative status of Christianity and the exclusion of minority groups from the prevailing sense of regional identity.

It was only toward the end of the nineteenth and into the early twentieth century that rural Alsace saw a fundamental transformation in styles and usages of dress whereby distinctive, regional styles lost their association with religious observance. This disassociation of regional dress styles from religious practice has largely obscured the critical link between the two throughout their development in the nineteenth century. Once this link had been ruptured, regional dress styles came to function as folk dress. The quintessential Alsatian costume with the red wool skirt and enormous headbow, which at its beginning was worn only by members of certain religious groups in certain villages, could not become a unifying symbol of the region until it lost its religious significance. While the contexts for the wearing of folk dress into the twentieth and twenty-first centuries were generally secular, this transformation was not a reflection of the secularization of Alsatian society.

Relationship between Religion and Dress

The particular costumes that have become known as "regional" or "folk" dress were those worn for special occasions, which, during the nineteenth century, were generally centered around the Church. Across most of France the rural population was almost entirely Catholic. This homogeneity meant that religious events brought the population together. By contrast, in Alsace, the coexistence of several different religious communities meant that religious occasions drew attention to people's religious affiliation. Religious events became moments of differentiation.

Rather than being isolated into separate areas of Alsace, communities of Catholics and Protestants often lived side by side, even within the same villages. The lines of division between Catholics and Protestants in Alsace date back to the Reformation in the sixteenth century. At the time, the region was divided among various German duchies and principalities in the Holy Roman Empire. According to the Peace of Augsburg in 1555, the religion of the ruler determined the religion of the subjects. Rather than unifying the people of Alsace, this agreement compounded the lack of political unity by coupling political boundaries with religious cleavages. As a result, neighboring villages would adhere to different confessions.

While the settlement in Augsburg was premised on a polarity between Catholics and Lutherans, the Protestants split along additional lines, including Anabaptists and Calvinists. In Alsace Calvinism, known as the reformed church, was concentrated in urban areas, while rural Protestants were almost all Lutheran.[2] Calvinism was the dominant denomination in only a few villages, which were concentrated in the Outre-Forêt, the northern part of Alsace. While far less significant than the other Protestant denominations, Anabaptists also maintained a presence in Alsace.[3] During the critical formative period of the Reformation, Alsace was part of Germany. As a result, the religious culture of the region with the coexistence of different groups resembles that of Germany.

The process by which Alsace became French reinforced and even exacerbated the existing religious conflicts. Between the Thirty Years War and the wars of Louis XIV, the territories of Alsace fell into French hands. By 1681 all but a small portion of Alsace was French. Alsace became French just as Louis XIV took one of his most decisive steps to reestablish Catholicism as the religion of the country. While Alsatian Protestants continued to enjoy relative religious freedom, the French actively favored Catholicism in the region. Any community with more than seven Catholic families had to provide space for Catholic worship in the church, so in those villages that had both Protestants and Catholics, the church had to accommodate services for two different confessions. Known as the *simultaneum*, this policy heightened religious tensions in Alsace, particularly in those villages that were mixed. The *simultaneum* demanded that the two confessions establish schedules for their services and other uses of church in order to accommodate two completely separate groups of worshippers.[4]

Despite the influence of the *simultaneum* on religious tensions in Alsace, most villages had a large majority of one confession with a small minority of the other. In most cases of "mixed" villages, there was a significant Protestant majority with a relatively small number of Catholics resulting from the settlement of Catholic families under the encouragement of the royal decree.[5] While they only represented between 20 percent and 25 percent of the region's population,[6] Protestants had a profound impact on Alsatian culture in large part because they were concentrated in villages where they were the majority and they lived in close proximity with Catholics.

The regional dress worn in Alsace is closely linked to geography. Different areas and villages are associated with particular styles, an association that is in fact mediated by religious differences. In general there were three main areas with strong concentrations of Protestantism in rural Alsace: the Kochersberg, the Pays de Hanau, and the Outre-Forêt. These are also the areas with the most distinctive and persistent regional dress practices.[7] The cultural distinctions of these areas derive in large part from their division into separate principalities before and during the Reformation and the patchwork of religious communities that resulted from these divisions.

Alsatian regional dress carefully distinguished Catholics from Protestants, but not in a single, fixed way. The specific details of dress that serve to distinguish the two groups varied from village to village, but the basic components of the costumes were universal. Men wore hats, a coat, a vest, pants or breeches, shoes or boots, and a shirt that also served as underwear. Women wore a bonnet or cap, a shawl, a bodice and or jacket, a skirt and a chemise or underdress. The women's bonnet or headdress was the element of the costume that saw the greatest variation. In fact, a bonnet with an oversized bow of black or brightly colored ribbon has become widely associated with the region of Alsace as a whole, yet this style originated as part of the special occasion dress in the countryside around Strasbourg particularly in the Kochersberg and the Pays de Hanau.

The Kochersberg is the fertile region that lies between Strasbourg, Brumath, and Saverne. The exceptional fertility of the area encouraged the continued persistence of agriculture and made the area the most productive in Alsace.[8] At the same time, the proximity of this area to Strasbourg made this the most visible and accessible rural land, and the dress styles that developed in this area came to be representative of Alsace more generally. The earliest documentation of Alsatian regional dress focused specifically on Kochersberg, including two sets of colored lithographs from 1834, including Charles Emrich's *Collection de six costumes nationaux alsaciens et badois*.[9] Emrich included two different examples of women from Kochersberg, who both appear to be the same age (Plates 3 and 4). The dress of the two women is quite similar. They each wear brightly colored skirts paired with corselets and sleeveless bodices that lace up the front. The corselets were worn over long-sleeved white blouses and secured in the front over a stiffened triangular piece of fabric known as a stomacher (*plastron* in French). Both women wear their hair parted down the center then tucked in the backs into caps secured onto their heads with ribbon tied in the center front.

The outfits of the two young women differ principally in the color of the head bow and the length of the skirt. Although both plates bear identical captions indicating that they depict peasant women from Kochersberg, conventional wisdom maintains that the young woman with the red bow and full-length skirt is Catholic while the young woman with black headbow and mid-calf length skirt is Protestant.[10] Black bows were worn by Protestant women, young and old. In contrast, brilliantly colored bows were worn only by unmarried Catholic women. Upon marriage, Catholic women would adopt black bows. Over the course of the nineteenth century, the distinction in bow colors between unmarried Catholic and Protestant women continued although the appearance of the bow evolved. The bow gradually increased in size from the narrow ribbon depicted by Emrich into the remarkably wide ribbons worn by 1900.

This difference in bow color for Catholic and Protestant women occurred in regional dress not only across the Kochersberg and the area around Strasbourg, but also the Pays de Hanau. The Pays de Hanau was so called because it was historically part of the County of Hanau-Lichtenberg, one of the territories of the Holy Roman Empire and the largest feudal possession in Alsace.[11] During the Reformation, this area converted to Protestantism, becoming "the veritable bastion of rural Alsatian Lutheranism."[12] The dress styles and culture of this part of Alsace were generally similar to those in the Kochersberg and thus aligned with the common perception of Alsatian dress.

In the Outre-Forêt, on the other hand, the styles differed markedly from the stereotypical Alsatian dress. While the Kochersberg and the Pays de Hanau saw the development of the emblematic Alsatian dress, the Outre-Forêt was the home to less familiar clothing styles. Along the northern edge of Alsace surrounding Wissembourg, the Outre-Forêt is bounded on the north by the Lauter River that marks the border with Germany and on the south by the Forest of Haguenau from which it derives its name. The dialect in the region differs from that of the rest of Alsace; it is Franconian rather than Alemannic. As the northern extreme of Alsace, parcels of the Outre-Forêt became part of France later than the rest of the region.

Linguistically and historically set apart from the rest of the Alsace, the Outre-Forêt also differs religiously. It is the only rural area of Alsace with substantial populations of Reformed Protestants. Beyond simply facing tensions between Catholics and Protestants, some villages also suffered conflict between Protestant denominations. The villages in this area were tightly knit and developed very distinctive traditions, particularly regarding their costumes. These costumes continued to be faithfully worn throughout the Outre-Forêt long after such traditions had been abandoned elsewhere in Alsace. The geographic isolation and heightened religious and political tensions along Alsace's northern border favored both the development and the persistence of distinctive dress practices.

There were a variety of distinctive dress styles for women in the Outre-Forêt. A costume study drawn by Théophile Schuler in 1858 highlights the difference between the dress of Schleithal and Oberseebach (Figure 1.1). The dress of the Schleithaloise on the left was black or dark blue with a high waist and moderately full sleeves. The shoulders were wrapped in layers of shawls and collars that created the characteristic ruff or *fraise*. The head was topped with a bonnet of sheer white tulle secured under the chin with a wide white silk ribbon. This costume differed markedly from what a woman of Oberseebach would wear to church. While also dark blue or black, the bodice was more closely fitted through the sleeves. The elaborate ruff was not covered with a fringed shawl and the

Figure 1.1 Théophile Schuler, Costume studies of Schleithal and Oberseebach, 1858. Cabinet des Estampes et des Dessins de Strasbourg. Photo Musées de Strasbourg, M. Bertola.

bonnet was different in color and shape. Rather than a sheer white bonnet, the Oberseebach bonnet was of a dark silk. Young unmarried women adorned their bonnets with red ribbons that were tied in a small bow at the front above the forehead, while married women wore dark ribbons that hung loose and untied down their backs.

An examination of the Sunday best worn by the women of Hunspach reveals that the differences in costumes were not determined by village so much as religious affiliation (Figure 1.2). Catholic women of Oberseebach wore white tulle bonnets and heavy shawls in much the same way as the women of the Catholic village of Schleithal. The Protestant women of Oberseebach dressed in a manner that closely resembled the styles in Hunspach. The distinguishing markers of dress from the Outre-Forêt did not differentiate one village from another so much as they differentiated between the different religions.

Comparing the costumes of Kochersberg with those of the Outre-Forêt reinforces the idea that they signified religious difference, but also that the link between specific clothing details and religious doctrine was incidental. People may speculate that the black bow worn by young Protestants in the most familiar

Figure 1.2 Théophile Schuler, Costume studies of Hunspach, 1858. Cabinet des Estampes et des Dessins de Strasbourg. Photo Musées de Strasbourg, M. Bertola.

version of Alsatian dress was evidence of the greater sobriety of their teachings. However, unmarried Protestant women in Hunspach or Oberseebach wore red bows on their bonnets. In fact, there was little direct connection between religious teaching and bow color. The ways that costume marked religious difference varied based on local practice rather than doctrine.

While the details of Alsace's development of regional dress are distinct, the function of regional dress to distinguish between Catholics and Protestants is typical across central Europe. The proximity of different religious groups can be seen across Baden-Württemberg which, like neighboring Alsace, is sharply divided between Catholic and Protestant communities. The quintessential hat with red pompoms which has come to represent the Black Forest region originated in three small Protestant villages in the largely Catholic region.[13] The hat originally served as a marker of the Protestant faith. Alsace's religious demographics are similar to Germany's and the relationship between religion and dress is representative of the German speaking area.

The significance of religion in shaping regional dress is not unique to central Europe. Most areas of France, including Brittany, which has also developed distinctive regional dress, are noteworthy for their religious homogeneity. Through the nineteenth century France was almost entirely Catholic (only 2 percent of the population was Protestant and less than 1 percent was Jewish).[14] However, religious institutions were far from supported by the French state. The French Revolution, which began a systematic attempt to limit the power of the Catholic Church, had a lasting legacy on religiosity in the nation. The actual level of religious observance varied significantly among different regions of France. Brittany stood apart from much of France because of its high faith and church attendance. While in Paris only 17 percent of the adult population took part in Easter communion in 1854, in Rennes, Brittany the rate was 94 percent in 1883.[15] In fact the strength of the Catholic Church in Brittany put the region at odds with the French state and enforced regional culture at the expense of a greater sense of national belonging.[16] The attachment to regional dress was closely linked to the strength of religious faith in the region. The dress was an integral part of the distinctly Breton religious festivals known as "pardons," which occurred in villages across the region.[17] Along with weddings and Sunday services, these religious observances were important sites for the display of regional dress. Religion played a critical role in the emergence of distinctive dress styles in Brittany, just as it did in Alsace. Alsace was another region in France with extremely high percentage of religious observance through the nineteenth century.

Although the performance of religious affiliation had different implications in Alsace owing to its religious diversity, the fact that two of the most religiously devout regions in France have the most elaborate and celebrated regional dress practices is not a coincidence.

Processions and the Performance of Catholicism

The association between clothing styles and religious affiliation depended on the use of the clothing for religious services. Religious processions were the most obvious occasion for the integration of clothing into the performance and act of worship. In general, formal religious processions are fundamental to Catholicism. In fact, the proliferation of processions was one of the sharp points of contention between the confessions, particularly in mixed communities. At various points in history, processions were expressly prohibited in Alsatian communities that had a Protestant community, although by the late nineteenth century these restrictions mainly applied to the larger urban areas.[18]

Perhaps the most important of these processions is the *Fête-Dieu* or the Feast of Corpus Christi, which is commemorated on the second Sunday after Pentecost.[19] The procession enacts the transubstantiation, a doctrine that holds that the bread and wine consecrated in the Eucharist become the body and blood of Christ. This doctrine, in fact, has been a key point of conflict between Catholics and Protestants since the Reformation. As a commemoration of the Eucharist, the Fête-Dieu is essentially a celebration of Catholicism itself. While commonly observed throughout Alsace during the nineteenth century, by the early twentieth century, the observance of the Fête-Dieu was limited to only a few villages. Two Catholic towns in Alsace continued to celebrate Corpus Christi with solemn processions well into the twentieth century: Geispolsheim and Schleithal.

These two villages have long had a substantial Catholic majority with only a relatively small number of Protestants but both are nestled among neighboring Protestant villages. Geispolsheim is located seven miles south of Strasbourg. The rector Jean-Georges Laminit, who was the priest in the parish from 1686 to 1721, made the first recorded observation of the Fête-Dieu in Geispolsheim.[20] In 1847, a station on the rail line running from Saint-Louis to Strasbourg was built on the outskirts of the village. While it was at first isolated, the station became the nucleus of a satellite village—Geispolsheim Gare. Although this auxiliary settlement did not see a significant population surge until the 1920s when it attracted workers who could easily commute to Strasbourg or to factories in other towns linked by rail, it provided a number of conditions that reinforced the character of the original village.[21] In speaking with residents of Geispolsheim, the point is frequently made that the village is very insular and closed to outsiders.[22] The presence of the train station presented both a means for visitors to travel to Geispolsheim and an upstart settlement that contrasted with the long history and tight-knit community of the village.

Schleithal, in the Outre-Forêt, is even more insular and tightly knit than Geispolsheim. At the turn of the century, Geispolsheim had approximately 2200 residents.[23] In 1900, Schleithal had just over 1900 residents, over 95 percent of whom were Catholic.[24] The entire village is built along one long main road, earning for it the designation of the longest village in Alsace.[25] Rail service did not arrive in Schleithal until 1900—more than fifty years after it reached Geispolsheim.[26] In Geispolsheim, the maintenance of tradition occurred in reaction against the intrusion of urban life, whereas in Schleithal, the traditions persevered through greater isolation.

The Corpus Christi procession in each of these villages wound its way through the main artery of the village and transformed the public space into a religious space. The streets were converted into a Church as a representative of the Church carried the consecrated Host, which is to say the body of Christ, through the streets.[27] The rituals performed in each of the villages were very similar, as each participant acted out a part that was clearly identifiable through his or her costume. The representatives of the Church were dressed in their ceremonial religious dress. Altar boys carrying banners led the processions. Nuns in habits and wimples led the lines of school children. The priests in their vestments accompanied the host and the canopy. However, these religious figures were not the only uniformed participants. The mayor wearing a distinctive uniform with epaulettes, braid, and sash headed the processions. In Geispolsheim, firemen and brass bands also added to the parade. The representatives of both the church and the municipalities were dressed to signify their profession or official role in the community. The uniforms of the official representatives of the church and of the state did not vary between villages. With the exception of the nuns, the uniformed participants were all men.

The clothing of the laity who attended as worshippers differed markedly between the two villages. In the processions in both Geispolsheim and Schleithal, a group of adolescent girls in regional dress carried a statue of the Virgin Mary. The costumes worn by these girls were distinctive not only to the occasion but also to each village. In Geispolsheim, they wore a large red headbow and red skirt with white lace apron (Plate 2). The headdress has become the defining feature of the ceremony but more generally has become emblematic of Alsace. In Schleithal, on the other hand, the girls wore simple wreaths of white roses on their heads.

The association between red bows and Catholicism that appeared as early as the 1830s in Emrich's plates is heavily reinforced through the visual power of the red bows worn for this ceremony in Geispolsheim. The striking headdresses became strongly associated with the quintessentially Catholic ceremony and by extension Alsatian Catholics. Although the headdresses were the most prominent feature of the girl's costumes, they were not exclusive to the Fête-Dieu. While the red bows were worn by unmarried girls for every event demanding special occasion dress, the gloves and apron were only worn for this procession.

While the Geispolsheim costume has come to be seen as the quintessential Alsatian regional costume, the Schleithal costume is virtually unknown. As in Geispolsheim, the young women who carried the figure of the Virgin Mary wore a variation of their special occasion dress (Figure 1.3). One of the hallmarks of

Figure 1.3 Fête-Dieu procession in Schleithal, ca. 1930s. Photograph by Lucien Blumer. Archives de Strasbourg, 1 Fi 189.

women's costume from Schleithal was its distinctive bonnet of white tulle. The girls in the procession, however, did not wear these bonnets or for that matter any bonnet.

The range of costumes worn for the Fête-Dieu processions underscores the complicated relationship between the costume's function as signifying faith and village of origin. The costumes from Geispolsheim and Schleithal differed significantly in aesthetics, but the overall presentation of the procession revealed commonalities in significance and symbolism. The transformation of the public space into a site of worship served to unify the population and imbue the participants with a sense of belonging and community. The costumes worn by the participants were integral to the event.

While the outfit worn by the adolescent girls has come to be seen as representative of the whole ceremony, particularly in Geispolsheim, it was only one of many different costumes. The earliest photographs of these ceremonies date to the 1900s. Based on these images it is clear that girls dressed as shepherdesses accompanied statues of saints. Dressed in green with wide brimmed hats, these girls carried staffs or small lambs. To aid in the enactment of spiritually symbolic characters in the procession, these outfits merely reflected the girls' religious formation and not the town or region. There were also boys and girls who participated in the ceremony dressed in white formal clothing. Over the course of the twentieth century, these outfits have adjusted to conform to contemporary fashion.

At the turn of the century, the women of the town who accompanied the procession through the streets also wore distinctive dress. They wore the regional Sunday dress for women of Geispolsheim. Over their long skirts they wore an ornamental apron and around their shoulders they draped a fringed shawl. Topping it all off, they wore ornate caps topped with enormous bows. The women who were part of the congregation were the ones who took part in the procession, for which they dressed as they would for church services. Attendance at church services warranted a distinctive costume.

The differences in the costumes between Schleithal and Geispolsheim appeared primarily among the women. The male dress received so little attention from photographers that it is difficult to find photographs of Fête-Dieu processions that even document the male dress. By the beginning of the twentieth century, the male villagers in Geispolsheim attended the procession dressed in their regular dress, which did not differ in any meaningful way from cosmopolitan, urban dress. In Schleithal, some of the male villagers continued to wear regional dress. This male regional dress was not distinctive to Schleithal, but rather adopted by men across all Lower Alsace. The outfit included a short jacket or a long redingote as well as a vest with two rows of brass buttons and broad-brimmed, flat-crowned hat. Unlike women's regional dress that differed between Catholics and Protestants, the men's regional dress was distinctive to Christians from the region, but not linked to a particular denomination.

The prominence of Catholic processions as the occasion for the development of regional dress can also be clearly seen in the case of Brittany. While the region also saw commemoration of the Fête-Dieu with elaborate parades through villages, Brittany was well known for its distinctive ceremonies known as pardons. These forms of devotion were peculiar to the region and combined a solemn, penitential ritual the first day with a festive procession the following day.[28] The strength of religious observance in the region, which extended into the development of a distinct regional form of devotion, found direct expression in the elaborate costumes. As in Alsace, Breton costume varied from one locality to another. For instance, the costumes from the area of Cornouaille near the Western end of Brittany were well known in part because of the fame of the pardon held at the chapel at Sainte-Anne-la-Palud. The pardons were a draw for the region and people attended from across lower Brittany. Different villages or parishes in the area had distinctive costumes, which included elaborate lace caps for the women.[29] The different parishes were represented in the pardons by parishioners who participated together as a group in the procession, carrying their own banners and distinguished by their distinctive costumes.[30]

Performance of Protestantism

While processions are generally believed to be rituals integral to Catholicism but not Protestantism, there are in fact occasions when rural Alsatian Protestants would process *en masse* through the streets of their villages. In fact, Sunday services created an occasion for all members of a congregation to walk together through the village dressed in their Sunday best. As an example, two photographs from either side of the turn of the century captured Protestants on their routes to and from church (Figures 1.4 and 1.5). Both represent very similar scenes of women in Oberseebach, in the Outre-Forêt, walking home from church. The earlier photograph, by Charles Spindler, probably dates to the 1890s while the later, by Lucien Blumer, dates to the 1930s. These two photographers were acquainted with each other, and Blumer may have been familiar with the photographs that Spindler had taken. The scenes are so similar that Blumer may

Figure 1.4 Charles Spindler, Exiting the church, Oberseebach, ca. 1890s. Spindler Archives.

Figure 1.5 Exiting the church, Oberseebach, ca. 1930s. Photograph by Lucien Blumer. Archives de Strasbourg, 1 Fi 189.

have deliberately recaptured the earlier image, although nothing appears staged about either image.

In a comparison between the two photographs, the street appears virtually unchanged in forty years except for the addition of poles for electrical wires. While the women's costumes have changed, they are all dressed uniformly. In the later image the women are wearing plain dark skirts and bodices without the elaborate ruffs and *coiffes*. Despite the evolution of these costumes, they remain distinct from cosmopolitan dress of the 1930s. Instead, they conform to a particular outfit for church. The ritual attached to church attendance extended to the adoption of appropriate attire and the act of walking to and from services as a group.

These "processions" took on an even more formal character on occasions such as weddings. Spindler captured scenes from a wedding in Hunspach, which most likely occurred in the 1890s, in which the women and the men paraded through the village separately.[31] The wedding procession formed as the party traveled to the church for the wedding ceremony and reformed following the ceremony as the group moved on for the next stage of the festivities.[32] In the first photograph, the women walked double file with the bride and a young man leading the line (Figure 1.6). There were about two dozen women followed by

Figure 1.6 Charles Spindler, Wedding procession, Hunspach, ca. 1890s. Spindler Archives.

about a half a dozen girls walking along the center of a street lined with half-timbered houses. A similar line of men can be seen just behind the line of women.

A second photograph of this wedding shows just the line of men, who were walking two or three abreast along the exact stretch of street that the women passed in the first photo (Figure 1.7). All but one of the women in the procession wore complete regional dress. Similarly, and more remarkably, all of the men wore regional dress except for one. In fact, many of the men, including those in the first row, were dressed in long, knee-length redingotes and three-corner hats. The uniformity of dress with the obvious adherence to strict rules mirrored the formality of the formation. The fact that the men and women walked separately reinforced this conformity. The women presented an uninterrupted line of identical skirts, aprons, shawls, and headdresses. This line was followed by a similarly uniform group of men in dark hats and long dark coats with small triangles of white at the throat. The costume was a piece that only became whole when the residents assembled. The arrangement of the people in the procession further enforced this cohesion. The girls followed the women, and while their dress was the same, the arrangement by size added to the harmonious effect.

Whereas Spindler's photographs recorded the tradition of men and women processing separately, later photographers recorded weddings in which

Figure 1.7 Charles Spindler, Wedding procession, Hunspach, ca. 1890s. Spindler Archives.

couples processed together. The wedding that Lucien Blumer photographed in Oberseebach in the 1930s was of the latter tradition[33] (Figure 1.8). As late as the 1930s, the residents of Oberseebach continued to outfit themselves completely in regional dress and to parade through the village according to wedding traditions. Whereas his photograph of women leaving church in the village suggested that the dress practices had changed, with the women no longer wearing the elaborate *coiffes* and shawls, his pictures of weddings, also from the 1930s, provide a more nuanced picture. While weekly Sunday costume may have abandoned the full costumes, the dress for festivals and the most formal occasions still called for full regional dress.

While the gathering of villagers on their way to and from church presented a picturesque scene that appealed to artists and photographers, the true function of the ritual was not to please spectators but to foster community. As Anthony Steinhoff writes, "The act of congregating at a particular time and place explicitly created and made visible the religious community."[34] The coherence of the dress contributed to the solidarity and sense of belonging among the members of the congregation.

While a similar purpose applied to dress practices in both Catholic and Protestant worship practices, one difference in particular is worth noting. In the

Figure 1.8 Wedding procession in Oberseebach, ca. 1930s. Photograph by Lucien Blumer. Archives de Strasbourg, 1 Fi 189.

formal Catholic processions, the identities of different participants were clearly distinguished through their dress; the priests, acolytes, and nuns dressed for their respective roles. The laity, in turn, also distinguished themselves through their clothing. For example, in the Fête-Dieu processions, the youngest girls as shepherdesses dressed differently from the girls who carried the statues. In contrast, among the Protestants, the dress practices served to unify rather than divide. There were not sharp divisions among the participants and different roles. The pomp and ceremony of the Catholic rituals were cast aside in favor of a more equitable coming together of neighbors.

Other Minority Religious Groups

The fact that such special occasion dress was worn for religious observance is largely overlooked by those who study rural culture. The fundamental link between religion and dress that underlies Alsatian regional dress is partly obscured by the extent to which the rural population is assumed to be Christian, more specifically Calvinist, Lutheran, or Catholic. This underlying assumption is exposed more clearly in analyzing the distinctive dress practices of Anabaptists and Jews.

Anabaptists followed one of the most radical strains of Protestantism introduced during the Reformation. The sect was originally concentrated in Switzerland, but as a result of persecution in the seventeenth century, many Anabaptists from the canton of Berne relocated to Alsace, particularly around Sainte-Marie-aux-Mines, in the Haut-Rhin. The number of Anabaptists in the region always remained quite low, but their preservation of the Bernese dialect and their distinctive dress practices distinguished them from their neighbors.

For Anabaptists, the specific details of their dress practices derived directly from their religious dictates. An obligation to preserve simplicity generally extended to restrictions on clothing. Anabaptists rejected vanity and pride, and they saw the ornamentation of clothing as contrary to their conception of Christian humility. The restrictions that Anabaptists observed regarding their dress were largely established by the elders in the community. The rules were in accordance with their principles, but not necessarily explicit biblical dictates. Men wore beards but no mustaches, simple hats, and dark colors. Women also wore dark colors, concealed their hair in bonnets and wore no jewelry or ornament.[35] These restrictions also limited the types of fasteners. While lacing and hooks were permitted, buttons and buckles were not.[36]

Religious Performance 33

An examination of early nineteenth-century plates documenting Alsatian regional dress reveals how Anabaptists dressed.[37] In Jan Lewicki's series from 1834, *Costumes d'Alsace et de Bade*, a plate that pictures an Anabaptist couple is the only one that identifies the subjects' religion.[38] To truly appreciate the simplification and restraint of the Anabaptist dress, it helps to compare the illustration against other plates in the series (Plate 5) (Figures 1.9 and 1.10). The Anabaptist couple was distinguishable from the couples in the other plates largely because of the plainness of the clothes. By comparison, Lewicki included two plates to show the regional dress of Kochersberg: one of an older couple and one younger. While these two plates show the older couple to be more conservative than the younger couple, the level of ornamentation for even the older couple far outpaced that of the Anabaptists.

The Anabaptist woman was dressed all in a dull blue except for her white apron. Her bonnet was plain and lacked the prominent bow that adorns the bonnet of each of the other women who appeared in Lewicki's plates. Her bodice fastened in front with two bows, which was the permitted form of fastening.

Figure 1.9 Jan Lewicki, "Paysans du Kochersberg, âge avancé" from *Costumes d'Alsace et de Bade*, 1834. Coll. et photogr. Bibliothèque nationale et universitaire, Strasbourg.

Figure 1.10 Jan Lewicki, "Anabaptistes" from *Costumes d'Alsace et de Bade*, 1834. Coll. et photogr. BNU, Strasbourg.

While generally similar to the bodices seen in the other plates, the Anabaptist's lacked the decorative front insertion or stomacher that was worn by the young women from Kochersberg or the pleated edging that adorned the bodice of the older woman from Kochersberg. Her skirt was longer than those of the other women, and overall her costume was more severe. Nonetheless, all of the women's costumes basically included the same elements: bonnet, apron, skirt, and bodice. Whereas Protestant and Catholic women distinguished themselves from each other in their selection of ornaments—particularly ribbons, the Anabaptists were distinguishable by their rejection of ornamentation altogether.

While the distinctions between the dress of Catholics and Protestants in Alsace appeared almost exclusively in women's dress, the clearest distinctions between mainstream Christians and Anabaptists appeared in the men's clothing. The Anabaptist man depicted by Lewicki was also more severe than the other men included, and the cut of his clothes differed markedly. The most distinctive aspect of the man was his beard. While all of the other men were clean-shaven, the Anabaptist had a very full beard and no mustache. The broad-brimmed hat was relatively unremarkable, but his suit of unrelieved gray also set him apart. Although his dark hair and beard suggested he is young, the length of his coat was more similar to those of the older men. In contrast the only other figure who wore long pants as opposed to knee breeches was the young man from Kochersberg. The other men all wore vests that contrast in color with their coats, while the Anabaptist's was the same grey. His coat, pants, and vest were completely unadorned; he had no buttons, pockets, tie, or even lapels.

The buttons in particular were a noticeable absence, since they were an obvious ornament on the other men's coats, vests, and even pants. The coats were not intended to fasten and the row of buttons down the pants of the young man from Kochersberg was obviously purely ornamental. Although on its face it sounds extreme to reject buttons, the actual use of buttons in the early nineteenth century favored ornament over function. The resulting ensemble worn by the Anabaptist man clearly set him apart from his contemporaries. In fact, this juxtaposition between the Anabaptist and his neighbors is fundamental to understanding his dress practices. More than simply serving as a marker for identifying Anabaptists as distinct from Catholics and Protestants, these sartorial choices represented a rejection of their worldliness and materialism. The dress practices paralleled and encapsulated the ideological differences between Anabaptists and mainstream Catholics and Protestants. Dress was not simply a signifier to represent religious faith but rather an integral part of living out their faith. Because the dictates governing Anabaptists' dress were part of their religious observance, their general styles of dress were not unique to those living in Alsace.

Like Anabaptists, Alsatian Jews were distinguishable from Catholics and Protestants by particular dress practices. The way they dressed made up only one of the factors that set them apart. In contrast to the geographically isolated Anabaptists, the Jews of Alsace often lived right in the villages alongside their Christian neighbors. Before the French Revolution, when Jews were given full rights of French citizenship, they were not permitted to live in the largest cities in Alsace including Strasbourg, Colmar, and Mulhouse. Instead, they formed communities in rural villages across Upper and Lower Alsace. In 1784 Jews lived in 183 of the towns and villages in Alsace, which was fewer than 20 percent of all localities.[39] Within these communities they remained apart from Christians. In part their isolation derived from the use of a distinctive dialect, which was a variation of Yiddish.[40] Another factor that further distinguished Alsatian Jews from Christians was the legacy of earlier restrictions against owning land and running public shops.[41] The lasting result of these restrictions was that a large number of Jews found employment as peddlers, livestock dealers, and moneylenders even after earlier restrictions were abolished with emancipation.

While the rules that governed Anabaptist dress practices were in accordance with their principles, they were not necessarily explicitly drawn from biblical dictates. Jewish dress practices, in contrast, often derived directly from scripture. For instance the requirement that men wear side locks, or *peoth*, derives from Leviticus 19:27: "ye shall not round the corners (*peoth*) of your heads neither shall thou mar the corners of thy beard."[42] This passage also has been interpreted to require men to wear beards, particularly when taken along with the restrictions on shaving with a razor. In Alsace, Jewish men did not customarily grow out their side locks in the manner that is customary among orthodox Jewish men from Eastern Europe, but beards were a distinguishing feature of Jews in the region. In an account of travels though Alsace in 1801, the writer Jean-Louis Fresquet explained to his French readers that Jews could be distinguished "by their long beard and by a costume that is particular to them."[43]

One aspect of Jewish dress practice that was common to both men and women is covering the head. In fact, this practice was common to men and women of all confessions in Alsace; men traditionally wore hats while women wore some form of cap or headdress. Ironically, while headgear was a common feature of all faiths, it was also one of the clearest marks of distinction among them. The lines between head covering as custom and as religious dictate are blurry. The Old Testament does not include any explicit text in which men are commanded to cover their heads. Nevertheless, the custom for Jewish men can be traced back to the Talmud. In contrast, the practice for married Jewish women to cover their heads has more complicated roots in biblical text where it derives from a reference in the Torah (Numbers 5:18) regarding humiliating an adulterous woman by uncovering her hair. The requirements for head coverings were laid out in the Mishnah. According to the Ketuboth (7:6), married women were required by Jewish practice to cover their heads. This text specifically distinguishes this requirement from those derived from Biblical law.

In contrast, Christians can trace the rules regarding head coverings back to an explicit passage in the New Testament: "Every man praying or prophesying, having his head covered, dishonoreth his head. But every woman praying or prophesying with her head unveiled dishonoreth her head; for it is one and the same thing as if she were shaven."[44] This Biblical passage establishes a clear distinction between Christian and Jewish practices regarding hats: Christian men remove their hats during religious services while Jewish men wear them during prayer and services. Although this clear distinction is made for men's practices, Jewish and Christian women are both required to cover their hair or head. All of these dictates demanding that women cover their heads are focused on modesty and honor. Shame, humiliation, and dishonor are each invoked as results of women appearing bareheaded. The covering of the hair for Jewish women in particular was associated less with religious observance than with public display. Appearing in public bareheaded was deemed shameful.

While these doctrinal differences governing the use of head coverings for Christians and Jews played a minor role in distinguishing the two groups, it was the shape and style of hats and caps that played a key role. As covering the head is a matter of custom rather than direct biblical injunction, the style of headgear has varied widely over time and by region. Historically in Europe, Jews wore distinctive hats as a marker to set them apart. The wearing of such hats has long involved a complicated tension between a desire among Jews to distinguish themselves and pressure from Christians to mark them as separate.

Throughout medieval Europe, Jews were required by law to wear a *Judenhut*, a pointed, conical hat often yellow in color.[45] Through the sixteenth century, the distinguishing hat worn by German Jewish men was a sort of flat wide felt beret. By the eighteenth century, however, German Jews had adopted the fashionable three-cornered hat.[46] Several of the images in the book *La Vie juive*, by David-Léon Cahun, illustrated by the Alsatian artist Alphonse Lévy, show men wearing such hats (Figures 1.11 and 1.12). These illustrations suggest that Jewish men in rural Alsace continued to wear three-corner hats into the nineteenth century well after they ceased to be fashionable, which paralleled the persistence of such hats worn by Christian Alsatians. The accompanying stories by David-Léon Cahun in which these tricorns are mentioned indicate that these hats were "antique" and worn by the elderly characters.[47] One of Lévy's illustrations of a Seder showed the eldest man wearing a tricorn while the rest of the men wore other more fashionable hats, including variations of top hats and a bowler (Figure 1.13).

While Alsatian Jewish men did not have to distinguish themselves through their headgear and could wear similar styles of hats as Alsatian Christians, there were styles of headgear that were uniquely Jewish. Lévy also depicted men wearing skull caps or *kippot*, such as the man seated and contemplating the world outside his window (Figure 1.14). These distinctive hats, however,

Figure 1.11 Alphonse Lévy, *Schulé klopfer* from David-Léon Cahun, *La vie juive*, 1886, p. 10. Hanna Holborn Gray Special Collections Research Center, University of Chicago Library.

appear only in images of men in their homes and not outdoors. These hats were not worn out of pressure from Christians but rather were a signal of observance.

While many of the headwear choices of Alsatian Jews were quite similar to those of their Christian neighbors, they were markedly different from those of Jews from different areas. In particular, Jews from Eastern Europe were culturally quite distinct from Alsatian Jews and were readily distinguishably by their dress. The former wore fur hats known as *streimel* and grew out their *peoth* in long curls. During the eighteenth century, many rabbis who served in Alsace immigrated from the east. The fur hats worn by these immigrants became a distinctive mark of the rabbinate. However, by the late nineteenth century, Jewish immigrants from Eastern Europe who came to Germany,

Figure 1.12 Alphonse Lévy, Couple walking outside from David-Léon Cahun, *La vie juive*, 1886, p. 82. Hanna Holborn Gray Special Collections Research Center, University of Chicago Library.

including Alsace, to escape persecution became an increasing presence. The distinctive dress practices of these Russian or Polish Jews were conspicuous and contributed to the animosity they faced not only from Christians but also from the more assimilated Alsatian Jews.[48] These Eastern European Jews appear in the works of Lévy, particularly in the scenes of the Passover Seder[49] (Figure 1.13). As it is customary to welcome a stranger to the Seder, artists have depicted the stranger as a Polish Jew. In these works, the heavy beard, *peoth*, and fur hat of the Polish Jew served to indicate that he is foreign, not that he is Jewish. While distinctive dress practices identified the wearer's religion, just like the regional dress worn by Christians, the markers were undeniably linked to place of origin. Just as Catholics from Schleithal dressed differently from Catholics from Geispolsheim, Jews from Galicia dressed differently from those from Alsace.

Figure 1.13 Alphonse Lévy, Seder from David-Léon Cahun, *La vie juive*, 1886, p. 30. Hanna Holborn Gray Special Collections Research Center, University of Chicago Library.

Alsatian Jewish women also wore head coverings that differed both from those worn by Christians and from those worn by Jews outside of Germany. The older women in Lévy's illustrations wore a particular white cap with a ruffle that framed the face. There were some variations in the caps: some had a bow at the center front, some had lappets, or ribbons hanging loose at either side below the ears, while some had ribbons tied under the chin. The caps seem to be derived from the boudoir caps commonly worn in the home by older women, regardless of religious affiliation. The Jewish caps, however, had a more distinct ruff framing the face and were clearly distinct from the *coiffes* worn by Catholics and Protestants.

In his account of the mid-nineteenth-century Jewish customs that he observed in Alsace, Daniel Stauben wrote, "Women wear ... a bonnet of tulle trimmed with red ribbons. A band of velvet takes the place of the hair, which has been, since the wedding day, carefully held back."[50] One illustration by Lévy showing the interior of a booth built for Sukkot includes a Christian woman who is clearly identifiable by her large headbow tending to the child[51] (Figure 1.15). The other young women in the scene were bareheaded while the older, married woman was wearing a white cap. These white caps could

Religious Performance 41

Figure 1.14 Alphonse Lévy, Man wearing a kippah from David-Léon Cahun, *La vie juive*, 1886, p. 59. Hanna Holborn Gray Special Collections Research Center, University of Chicago Library.

also be seen in the works of Moritz Oppenheim, who depicted German Jews from a moderately affluent bourgeois background, which suggests that the custom was common throughout Germany (Figure 1.16). The Eastern European custom of wearing a wig known as a *scheitel* to cover the head was not practiced in Alsace in the mid-nineteenth century.[52] Because of the caps, Alsatian Jewish women were easily distinguishable from Alsatian Christians and from non-Alsatian Jews.

Exclusion of Minority Religions from Public Spaces

Catholics and Protestants wore their special occasion dress in very public ways. In contrast, the other minority religious groups engaged in much fewer public religious rituals. Both Anabaptists and Jews faced conflicting pressures between following religious dictates and conforming to practices of their rural villages.

Figure 1.15 Alphonse Lévy, Sukkot from David-Léon Cahun, *La vie juive*, 1886, p. 104. Hanna Holborn Gray Special Collections Research Center, University of Chicago Library.

Figure 1.16 Moritz Oppenheim, Seder, ca. 1867. Hanna Holborn Gray Special Collections Research Center, University of Chicago Library.

While certain sects of these faiths are strongly linked in the popular imagination to distinctive dress practices, namely the Amish and Hasidic Jews, those Anabaptists and Jews who lived in Alsatian villages in the nineteenth century were not so identifiable. The Anabaptists remained largely out of the public view, partly because of their small numbers and partly because of their isolation. The Anabaptists did not live in villages alongside Catholics and Protestants. Rather they cultivated farmland that was isolated—either on the outskirts of the villages or in the mountains.[53] The area around Sainte-Marie-aux-Mines was in the Vosges and presented a generally inhospitable landscape that assured the Anabaptists the isolation they sought. This withdrawal from society corresponded with their religious dictates.

Furthermore, Anabaptists deliberately forswore any ostentation or display. Public processions would have been completely antithetical to the Anabaptist philosophy. In fact, the adherents did not worship in a church or any sort of building specifically built for the purpose. Instead, their services were held in the home of one of the members of the community.[54] The Protestant critiques of the pomp of Catholic processions were shared by the Anabaptists who completely avoided such performances. The lack of public performances of religion corresponded with a lack of special occasion dress. Nevertheless, the clothing worn by Anabaptists was scrutinized by members of the community. In fact, the Anabaptists enforced adherence to their rules by shunning and banishing those who transgressed.[55]

While the Anabaptists may have been critical of members of their own congregation, they were not hostile in the way that Christians could be. In response to an 1850 administrative inquest, the prefect of the Bas-Rhin wrote:

> An Anabaptist is as easy to recognize as an Israelite: he wears a long beard, a hat that resembles the form of those recently adopted by communists, his suit of a stiff, bizarre cut is secured with hooks; his shoes without buckles are large and heavy. The women and girls of the sect are always dressed in black, of an irreproachable decency, and coiffed with a disgraceful bonnet that leaves no place to coquetry.[56]

The dress practices that served to distinguish Anabaptists and Jews made them susceptible to prejudice and hate.

Pressure to not stand out encouraged the Jews to practice their religion discretely. The sorts of parades that characterized Christian practice in rural Alsace were not performed by Jews. However, the walk to the synagogue on Saturday would have been an occasion for Jews to walk together through the streets. In his book *Scènes de la vie Juive en Alsace*, published in 1860, Daniel Stauben describes the Sabbath customs in the Jewish village of Bollwiller. Rather than being called to worship by bells, the Jewish are summoned by knocking by the *Schulé-Klopfer* ("synagogue knocker") (Figure 1.11). At this signal, the men and women process to synagogue in their "Saturday dress," which Stauben describes as "particular to Jewish villages."[57] He fills a complete page with descriptions of both the men's and women's costumes:

> Those of the men consist of wide pants of black wool cloth that are covered almost entirely by large oiled boots, an enormous blue redingote with a very short waist and collar and lapels that are disproportionately developed, a hat that is narrow at the base widening towards the top, and a chemise of a coarse but white linen, this shirt ends in a collar so formidable that it completely hides the face, so starched that in order to look from one side to the other, these brave men must make a half turn to the right or the left. The women wear a dark colored dress, a large red shawl decorated with green palms and a tulle bonnet trimmed with red ribbons.[58]

Stauben approached the scene as a local who had left Alsace and been formally educated in Paris.[59] Thus, as an outsider, he was able to identify the distinguishing features of the suits with a clear focus on scale and proportion. In an implicit comparison to some sort of normative style, Stauben selects a series of adjectives that convey the exaggerated dimensions of the pieces. These alterations to the "normal" cut were not intrinsically linked to Judaism; rather they deviate from prevailing fashion in theologically arbitrary ways. The mental image that this description evokes is slightly ridiculous, particularly with respect to the stiffness of the collar. The response to unfamiliar clothing styles will almost invariably be one of humor. In the case of the rural Jews, this reaction to the foreignness is heightened by the resemblance to outmoded fashions. The tall collar and redingote would have been legacies of the fashions of the first quarter of the nineteenth century. The development of these styles among rural Jews would have been more closely linked to rural Alsatian styles worn by Catholics and Protestants than to those of Parisian Jews.

Regardless of the discretion of their religious practices and dress, Alsatian Jews could not remain inconspicuous because of their exclusion from the forms of regional dress reserved for Catholics and Protestants. The association between the regional dress and church attendance directly excluded Jews from adopting these styles. Through the mid-nineteenth century, Jews' ability to assimilate the dress practices of their Christian neighbors was limited. There were no non-religiously charged sartorial choices available to them. They appeared distinctly provincial to the Parisian Jew and distinctly Jewish to the rural Christian.

Dress as Ritual

While the Christian processions seem antithetical to the privacy of Jewish devotion, there were aspects of the Christian dress practices that are private. A series of photographs of the 1937 wedding of Georges Corneille and Marguerite Niess in Oberseebach documents some of these moments. Included in a book on the village's history, these photographs remained in the hands of the couple's son.[60] The couple was Protestant; in fact, they were members of the Reformed Church.[61] The photographs capture the minutia and complexity of the preparations and ritual, including one as the bride had her hair done by her mother into the distinctive style that coordinated with the *coiffe*. The hair was parted in the center and then drawn straight to the nape of the neck and looped back up into a bun under the bonnet. While the bonnets were the obvious regional element on the head, the hairstyle was just as distinctive and critical to the overall appearance. Unlike an item of dress that could be stored and then donned for the appropriate occasion, the specific hairstyle highlights how critical the process of dressing to the ceremonial importance of dress. The act of getting dressed was as ritualized as any stage in wearing the regional dress. The costume was not simply an inanimate object that was put on by the wearer. It was a complicated interaction between the wearer and the clothes. It was the layering of the shawl and the fastening of the apron. The process of getting dressed was part of the ceremony of the wedding. The centrality of dress to the ritual occasions in these village of Outre-Forêt helps explain why these villages preserved their distinctive dress long after the rest of Alsace had abandoned it.

Many elements of women's regional dress required knowledge of how to properly assemble and wear them. The most obvious of these elements is the *coiffe*, particularly the styles from Kochersberg or the Pays de Hanau which consisted of a cap with the large headbow. The bows were actually tied from very wide ribbons and affixed to the cap. There were a few different methods and styles of tying them. The ribbon was pleated lengthwise then the center of the ribbon was attached to the center back of the cap. The bow was formed by further elaborate pleating.[62] The bows might be stored tied rather than being retied at each wearing, but the entire process needed to be performed occasionally in order to ensure the proper form (Figures 1.17 and 1.18). The elements of the headdress—the cap and ribbon—were not enough to make the distinctive styles, they also demanded knowledge of the proper techniques. The variations in headdresses from village to village must have grown out of differences in the styles of wearing these same items.

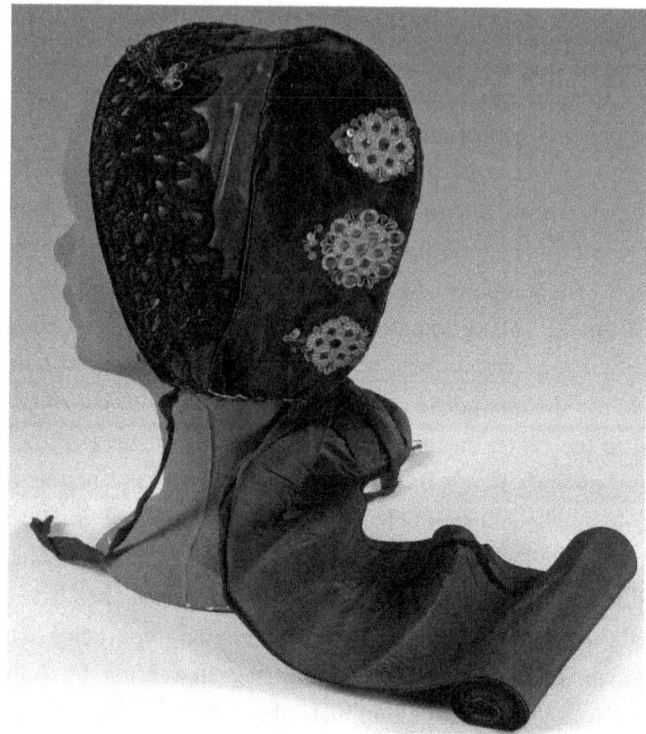

Figure 1.17 Embroidered bonnet with untied ribbon. Second half of the nineteenth century. Collection of the Musée du Pays de Hanau de Bouxwiller, Photo A. Mertz.

While the regional dress served a public purpose that created community through visible conformity, the act of wearing the dress served additional purposes both religiously and socially. The complicated interaction between wearer and clothing seen in regional Christian dress practices had important parallels in Jewish custom. In fact the religious purpose of some Jewish garments was linked to ritual use rather than appearance. The prayer shawl for instance served as a reminder of the wearer's religious obligations.[63] Although it was an identifying mark of Judaism, it was not worn prominently in public. Its purpose was to assist personal contemplation rather than to be seen. The *kippah* was another clear hallmark of the religion, and it was also not seen in any of Lévy's work showing Jews in the public sphere. The custom was to wear fashionable hats, such as top hats or bowlers, in public and reserving the *kippot* for the home and synagogue. The skullcaps may, in fact, have been worn concealed beneath the fashionable hat. Rather than serving as identification, several religious garments worn by Jews were concealed, thus serving private ritual rather than public ceremony.

Figure 1.18 Bonnet with wide ribbon tied into a bow, nineteenth century. Collection of the Musée du Pays de Hanau de Bouxwiller, Photo A. Mertz.

Declining Link between Regional Dress and Religious Observance

By the early twentieth century, the use of regional dress for religious occasions declined sharply. A clear illustration of the gradual replacement of the regional forms of dress by more fashionable ones comes from looking at specific religious ceremonies. Both Catholics and Protestants marked the transition from childhood to young adulthood with a special ceremony. Catholics celebrated their first communion while Protestants underwent confirmation. Each of these ceremonies necessitated special outfits. The use of regional dress for these occasions underscored the fundamental link between these clothing styles and religious observance.

Photographs of classes of communicants from Geispolsheim dating to the turn of the century demonstrate how first communion dresses evolved.[64] In the years around 1900, young women attending their first communion either wore their regional dress with the large headbows, shawls, and aprons or dressed in the fashionable style of wearing all white with white veils and gloves. Within a decade the number of girls wearing fashionable styles grew to eclipse the ones wearing the distinctive Alsatian styles. The outfit these Alsatian girls began to adopt for the occasion followed the broader tradition of Western dress. The white dress and veil were worn by communicants throughout France and Germany. European fashion plates since the mid-nineteenth century regularly featured fashions for first communion.[65] The girls were invariably dressed in the fashionable silhouette but completely in white with a white veil.

Among the rural population, the clothing worn for special occasions during the late nineteenth century would have differed markedly from cosmopolitan dress. The everyday dress styles may have varied from cosmopolitan dress because of differences in means and availability rather than a deliberate choice. However, the clothes selected for special occasions, such as first communion, were deliberately distinctive both from everyday clothing and from cosmopolitan dress. Both rural and urban Alsatians marked special occasions such as first communion with distinctive dress. The particular details of the cosmopolitan and regional dress differed but the underlying custom of marking important life events with special clothing was not particular to regional dress.

Within the Protestant church, confirmation was the rite of passage for adolescent boys and girls. Photographs of confirmands from Bouxwiller over the years also demonstrated the gradual disappearance of regional dress like that seen in Geispolsheim although there were notable differences. One of the most evident differences was the timing. Whereas in Geispolsheim, the regional dress had significantly waned by 1905, the majority of girls in Bouxwiller 1923 were still wearing regional dress.[66] Unlike the Catholic communicants who replaced the regional dress with a new form of distinctive dress, the Protestant confirmands who had not adopted the regional style were dressed simply and sternly in somber colors. They were dressed in conservative styles for the early 1920s including dark gloves. This conservative style continued into the 1930s by which time it had completely replaced distinctive Alsatian regional styles. Interestingly, the abandonment of regional dress styles did not completely eliminate confessional distinctions in dress. The "modern" dress worn by Catholic girls for communion differed markedly from that worn by Protestant girls for confirmation.

Considering the strong association between regional dress and religious practice, it would be tempting to correlate the disappearance of the former with a diminution of the latter. This conclusion would be consistent with a theory of modernization that viewed secularization as an essential component. Such an analysis, however, would misattribute the reasons for the changes in dress patterns. But more importantly, it underestimates the continued centrality of religious faith to Alsatian village life through the twentieth century. While the dress worn by girls who were taking first communion or undergoing confirmation may have changed in the early twentieth century, this change did not prove a loss of religious fervor. The number of children undergoing these rites of passage fluctuated but did not show a consistent decrease throughout the early twentieth century.[67] Religious institutions remained relevant in Alsace but did not serve to support the regional dress practices. In fact, if anything, they may ultimately have encouraged conformity to more cosmopolitan rather than local styles. Both religious practice and regional dress continued to be important to village life, but the association between the two diminished. A shift occurred whereby the clothing lost its integral part in the shared religious experience and was increasingly worn for secular activities. This change was not in the diminution of religious experience, but rather in different occasions for wearing the clothes.

While religious conflicts in Alsace were largely responsible for the development of elaborate costumes and the performances in which they appeared, the religious establishment was not inherently supportive of the regional distinctions. The performance of Fête-Dieu processions should rightly be viewed as a manifestation of the deep religious devotion among rural Alsatians, but the persistence of regional dress practices in these performances was remarkable. These examples in which the Catholic Church has accommodated popular religious practices were the exception rather than the rule. In fact, the very grand Catholic processions that occurred in Alsace during the early twentieth century did not reflect regional particularities.

For example, Geispolsheim hosted a Eucharistic Congress in 1927.[68] These international congresses were organized by the Catholic Church in order to combat secularization. As a celebration of the Eucharist, these events were similar in spirit to the Fête-Dieu, but more closely linked to the international Church rather than the local parish. Photographs of the processions in Geispolsheim indicate that the official participants were appropriately dressed in their liturgical vestments. However, these grand events did not involve the villagers in their regional attire. To host the grandeur of Rome in their modest village, the residents erected triumphant arches that they adorned with garlands. Then the villagers became spectators rather than participants in the ceremony. One surviving picture does show villagers in their regional dress, but they are relegated to the position of observers and disappear into the sea of spectators. As the Catholic Church fought the perception of waning enthusiasm, they created spectacles that lacked the local flavor of regional practice. These congresses emphasized the universal, international character of the Church.

Figure 1.19 Grand'messe pontificale held in Strasbourg July 21, 1935, auteur non mentionné. Archives de Strasbourg, 1 Fi 2 / 7.

A similar grand mass was held in Strasbourg in 1935.[69] This *grand'messe pontificale* saw the ritual of Catholic Mass performed through the streets of Strasbourg. As in Geispolsheim, the participants were dressed in spectacular Catholic vestments while the Alsatian faithful lined the streets to watch. Those in attendance were dressed in fashionable suits and dresses (Figure 1.19). These photographs also document the difference between the weekly village worship that was dominated by women and the official performance of the Catholic Church that was exclusively male. Absolutely no regional dress appears in the photographs. While such regional dress would not have been worn as a matter of course in Strasbourg, the fact that the ceremonies in Strasbourg and Geispolsheim involved identical clothing speaks to the larger trend within the Catholic Church for universal visual vocabulary of ritual. By the early twentieth century, the Catholic Mass had become virtually identical throughout Europe. The local distinctions in dress and ritual had largely been eliminated. Even in its official efforts to promote faith, the Church disregarded the local particularities in favor of the universal. Margaret Anderson aptly described the universalizing force of the Catholic clergy in terms of clothing choices:

> When the protestant pastor was discarding the sartorial marks of his calling for the dark suit of the bourgeois professional, that same garment was being replaced

on his catholic counterpart by the distinctive long black soutane. The French name, like the style itself, cropped up in County Cork as in the Rhineland. It marked its wearer as a uniformed soldier in a disciplined cosmopolitan army: "the black international," as it was called, of ultramontanism.[70]

In Alsace the clergy played no role in supporting regional dress, although a different story was seen in neighboring Baden. One of the most significant players in the effort to preserve Badische regional dress was a Catholic priest, Heinrich Hansjakob. In 1892, Hansjakob published a short work which stimulated interest in protecting regional dress.[71] In the book he points to a particular incident which inspired his decision to write the book. After Sunday services in the Black Forest, he was speaking with a peasant who was with his two daughters. One daughter was dressed traditionally and the other fashionably. The fashionable daughter had taken a job in town and had spent all her money on clothing. Hansjakob praised the other daughter for her decision to continue to dress traditionally, claiming that the clothing was more flattering and appropriate.[72] The involvement of clergy such as Hansjakob in the movement to preserve regional dress added a moral judgment. He even equated cosmopolitan dress with the devil. Underlying his efforts to encourage the continuation of regional dress was his belief in its inherent virtue that stood in contrast to the sin of urban dress and presumably urban life more generally. Ultimately Hansjakob made the argument that preserving the costume was essential to maintain the church.

The publication by Hansjakob inspired many across Baden to form organizations for the preservation of regional dress, but it also found objection from Richard Nuzinger, a Protestant pastor from Gutach (the town where the hat with the red pompoms originated). Nuzinger also regretted the loss of regional dress but did not agree with the Catholic priest's argument that the costume was key to religious faith or practice. He went on to argue that the folk festivals designed to preserve regional dress promoted vanity among the young girls and were thus actually not promoting Christian values at all.[73] The dispute between Hansjakob and Nuzinger demonstrates that support from the clergy for regional dress was far from universal in Baden. It is difficult to know how representative each man's opinion was of clerical attitudes more generally, but the dispute exposed tensions between Catholics and Protestants that erupted surrounding questions of dress. Nuzinger's point of view found approval not only in the press in Baden but also in neighboring Alsace.[74] Perhaps this is unsurprising given that the attitude of Nuzinger echoes the lack of support among the clergy in Alsace for regional dress.

While Protestantism largely lacked the powerful, centralizing authority of the Catholic Church, the Protestant clergy also served to undermine popular religious practices, including the wearing of regional dress. In his study of Alsatian folk dress, August Kassel, a doctor and folklorist, cites one pastor who in 1893 preached that it would be better if the headbows were smaller and faith were stronger.[75] One example in which the conflict between popular religious practice and the Protestant church played itself out was in the case of the *messti*, a traditional Alsatian festival. Kassel wrote a book, *Messti und Kirwe im Elsass*, about these festivals. The word itself developed from *Messtag* and came to signify the festival held in Alsatian villages to celebrate the feast day of its patron saint.[76] The first recorded description of a *Messtag* in Alsace was from the thirteenth century. Following the Reformation, these celebrations remained popular in Protestant villages.

While associated with ostensibly religious celebrations, the messti became an occasion for activities and behavior that the clergy ultimately sought to eradicate. Kassel cites efforts by clergy throughout the early nineteenth century to suppress messti activities. One clergyman's characterization of the festivities articulates the objections:

> Not only is there dancing for three days and even three nights in a village where such a festival is celebrated, money is squandered and intemperance and bawdry is often prevalent, but also for the duration of eight weeks or more, during which one village after another is celebrating "*Kirchweihe*," the young and even the elderly are drawn to these locations, Sunday after Sunday, where they find the opportunity for such misbehavior again and again.[77]

The concerns of church representatives on the issue of peasant festivities were consistent with the general conflict that arose between popular religious celebration and the clergy throughout France and Germany.[78] In fact, in describing the relationship between the Catholic Church and popular religion, Ralph Gibson goes so far as to declare: "Tridentine religion and popular religion were not only quite different entities, but even polar opposites."[79] The messtis demonstrate that this opposition held true for Protestants as well as Catholics. The drinking, dancing, and other expressions of celebration were deemed objectionable by the clergy. The example of the messtis illustrates a general trend of divorcing popular culture and religion. Through the early nineteenth century, the village festivals, which were a central point in the origins of many elements of popular culture that would be adopted into folklore, lost the sanction of the Church. The special occasion dress which was originally associated with religious activities came to be associated with festivities which lost their religious association.

By the end of the nineteenth century, rural Alsatians were increasingly conforming to cosmopolitan dress in place of regional dress practices. As clothing in the countryside became closer to cosmopolitan dress, this homogenization facilitated greater integration for groups that had previously been outsiders. The declining association between distinctive dress and Catholic and Protestant worship enabled members of minority religions to assimilate in their dress practices. For the Anabaptists, although the dictates to forego the vanity and ostentation of society were directly in conflict with the pressures to conform, during the course of the nineteenth century, the distinctions that marked them as separate from other Alsatians diminished. Jews also lost many of the rustic characteristics of rural life both through the adoption of fashionable dress and through emigration to cities. Alphonse Lévy and Daniel Stauben sought to capture a disappearing rural Jewish culture, and even by the time their work was published, these rural distinctions were losing ground. Increasingly, rural Jews, including Lévy and Stauben, were moving away, both to larger cities in Alsace, including Strasbourg and Mulhouse, and to Paris and other French cities. The rural Jewish communities in small villages were largely disappearing.[80] The loss of rural culture marked progress for Jews in their efforts toward assimilation, but at the same time meant the erosion of a distinctive way of life. While Christian forms of traditional culture were transformed into folk culture, many of the Jewish traditional practices just disappeared.

Conclusion

The ways in which the religious situation of Alsace shaped the development of regional costume are at once particular and yet instructive into the broader phenomenon of regional dress across Europe more generally. The styles of dress that developed into folk dress by the beginning of the twentieth century generally began as special occasion dress in the early nineteenth century. These special occasions in most cases centered around the Christian calendar, whether dress for Sunday services, feast days, first communion, confirmation, or weddings. The distinctive dress worn for these occasions was therefore religious dress although this association is not considered in the same way that dress worn by Jews or Anabaptists is seen as religious. The notion of "folk" is aligned with mainstream Christian confessions to such an extent that the religious foundation is obscured. Juxtaposing conventional notions of regional dress against dress for rural Jews helps to illuminate the religious aspects. Regional dress is generally thought of as distinguishing by place with differing villages having distinctive styles. In Alsace, as neighboring villages or even neighbors within villages adhered to different religions, the differences in dress signaled differences in religious allegiance. These religious distinctions are central to the elaborate dress that developed not only in Alsace but in villages across neighboring Germany and Switzerland as well.

The domination of the public space by Protestants and Catholics in the form of processions served to normalize their religious observance as part of the rural culture. Catholicism is most closely associated with processions and other very public performances of religious devotion. The development of elaborate dress for these rituals occurs in many Catholic regions including notably Brittany. While less obvious than Catholic processions, Protestants in Alsace also publicly displayed their distinctive dress—when going to church or during weddings. On the other hand, Jews and Anabaptists were less public in their display of their religions. While Anabaptists lived apart from mainstream Christians making their distinctive dress less visible, Jews often concealed the identifying symbols of their religion such as their skull caps and prayer shawls. However, because rural dress was strictly coded for Protestants or Catholics, Jews could not remain neutral in their dress until the homogenizing effects of cosmopolitan dress became widespread. The development of a unifying single style of regional dress, which we will examine in the next chapter, could only occur once the costume lost its association with religious practice. The link between dress and religious observance was not reserved for those performances that were public. There were acts of devotion related to dress that were private. The process of getting dress was critical to the final look of the outfit and was performed as one of the most intimate acts that a person engaged in. It would only be observed by members of the household, if that. Dress was at once a public performance and a private devotion.

While the link between religion and regional dress was strong through the nineteenth century, it ultimately broke down by the turn of the century and saw a decline in the years before and just after the First World War. One of the contributing factors of this disassociation was the lack of support or even antagonism that regional dress received from the clergy. When confronted with the threat of secularization, the religious establishment did not embrace popular religious expression in the form of dress. This lack of institutional support is reflected in the shift of how people dressed for special occasions. Girls who underwent first communion or confirmation gradually abandoned regional dress in favor of fashionable urban styles. It is easy to see the decline in wearing regional dress as a decline in religious observance but in fact the documentation of communion and confirmation shows as many people undergoing the rituals but merely substituting one style of dress for another. The dress lost its association with special occasions related to the church as they gained association with other secular functions.

2

Visual Representation

The characterization of regional dress as a fundamentally modern development depends first on its separation from its religious origins but just as importantly on its ability to represent regional and national identity. Artists and their depictions of rural dress played a central role in regional dress' shift from being a part of religious observation to becoming a symbol of political propaganda. Ultimately the collective message that the work of these artists communicated was that rural dress practices remained frozen in time. Seemingly unchanged over decades, such dress became a way of visualizing geographic regions. While some artists focused on the diversity of dress within regions, the duplication and reproduction of a few select images led to the emergence of a single style of folk dress out of a multiplicity of local styles. This reduction in the inherent complexity of regional dress facilitated its development into a symbol of an entire region. Representative of the region as a whole, the dress became a perfect vessel to communicate political meaning in a society increasingly shaped by competing forces of regionalism and nationalism.

In researching the history of regional dress, it is necessary to rely on representations of dress that have been produced by artists. These images now found in libraries, archives, and museums provide needed evidence to understand how rural residents dressed. However, it is important to keep in mind when looking at these images that they are not neutral windows into the past. Each one was produced by an artist who had a purpose and message to communicate. These examples of visual culture—the lithographs, oil paintings, book illustrations, or photographs—were not interchangeable with the material articles of clothing. They were themselves artifacts that had their own circulation and influence. In his work *The Fashion System*, Roland Barthes calls attention to the fundamental difference between "image clothing," the garment that appears in a photograph or painting, and "written clothing," the way the garment is described in text.[1] In many cases historians of dress work primarily on spinning out "written clothing" but depend on sources that are "image clothing." This particular chapter will focus on how "image clothing" was designed and circulated and how it in turn affected real or "technological clothing."

This chapter will look in turn at several different types of representations: the prints and photographs which documented various different folk costumes from around Europe including particularly France and Germany, genre painting that depicted scenes of rural life, book illustrations that accompanied literature focused on rural life, and ultimately the emergence of art depicting Alsatian women intended to serve as political propaganda. The audience for the images was far larger than those who would ever see people actually wearing the costumes. Many of the images were intended for an audience far from Alsace and became the means for developing an understanding of the region.

Artists such as Théophile Schuler and Charles Spindler paid great attention to the variations across different areas of Alsace and different religious groups. However, despite their attention to diversity in dress practices, artistic depictions of Alsatian regional dress collectively led to the consolidation of the style with the large headbow that was popular in the areas around Strasbourg as the quintessential Alsatian costume. The work of successive generations of artists resulted in the development of a visual vocabulary to signify Alsatianness that was available to communicate a political message once Alsace came to the forefront of French politics in 1870. By the conclusion of the Franco-Prussian War, the Alsatian woman in regional dress and large headbow became a powerful and resonant symbol for the region.

Field Guide to the Folk

Many of the early depictions of European regional dress were compiled in collections of illustrations that included rural people from different regions. Frédéric Maguet analyzes this type of serial collection of plates and argues that they were instrumental in constructing the idea of the region. Because of the visual aspect of dress, it had the power to immediately and tangibly signal that a person belonged to a particular region. Through their production and dissemination, these collections not only created a visual vocabulary which linked specific elements of dress with a geographic area, they enforced the very idea that such a link existed—that there was a recognizable Breton or Alsatian.[2]

While Maguet confines his analysis to examples from across France from the early to mid-nineteenth century, such collections were produced for regions all over Europe and their origins were established much earlier. In fact, there are examples that date back to the sixteenth century which show how Alsatians dressed.³ However, such books made important gains in popularity during the eighteenth century. Notable examples of this genre include Jacques Grasset de Saint-Sauveur's various encyclopedic compilations that illustrated people from around the world. His illustrations are some of the earliest to depict clothing that shows characteristic elements consistent with styles that continued through the nineteenth century. Grasset was a world traveler who was born in New France in 1757 and served in consular posts across the Levant and central Europe.⁴ He was also an artist who drew people from diverse lands. His drawings were transformed into illustrations that were published and republished in a series of different compilations between 1782 and 1810. For republications the illustrations of Parisians were updated to reflect changes in fashion, but those featuring provincial women were left unchanged. The implication was that while fashion changed in Paris, the dress remained frozen in provincial areas including Alsace.

Grasset included five plates illustrating Alsatians of various occupations. These illustrations were among the earliest to show the beginnings of the Alsatian cap with its bow. The text accompanying the plates in the *Encyclopédie des voyages* reinforces the implicit idea that people in different localities have different inherent sensibilities when it comes to wearing clothes. Grasset makes it clear that he is not discussing fashionable Alsatians; instead,

> this scene only considers the Alsatian woman for whom taste has not spoiled in imitating foolishly our fashions, our Parisian fantasies. It belongs to those who, always wise, faithful without coquetry to the climatic customs of the country, not looking to follow the principles of this nature always simple always natural.⁵

Grasset presents the humble dress of Alsatians as a virtue that stands in contrast to the frivolity of Parisians. This sense of provincial residents as being pure and lacking vanity characterized the urban view of the provinces. In part this simplification of Alsatians depended on an understanding of their styles as fixed in contrast to a view of Parisians as seeking novelty by abandoning styles. Furthermore, the fixed styles of dress were tied to place. This concept of an essential link between geography and dress practices underlay not only Grasset's project but connected his work to the publications that followed.

Just at the same time as Grasset's illustrations were published showing the dress of rural residents and the working class, the earliest fashion magazines were also being published. The 1780s marked the appearance of the earliest fashion magazines in Paris. These early publications only enjoyed brief runs interrupted by the French Revolution and succeeding turmoil.⁶ The first successful fashion magazine was *Journal des dames et des modes*, which ran from 1797 until 1839. The publication of this journal followed the publication of Grasset's *Encyclopédie des voyages ...* by a year. Like the *Encyclopédie*, the fashion magazines with their focus on clothing were intended for and read primarily by women.

The two genres had important points of divergence. Dress in provincial areas was presented as fixed and not changing over time in contrast to the changeability of fashionable, Parisian dress. The fashion magazines appeared every week. Each new issue reinforced the idea that the last week's fashions had outlived their fashionableness. Grasset's book of costumes was republished but at several year intervals. The message in republishing them was not to communicate that the dress had changed in the meantime; rather, the republication of identical plates decades later implied that there was no change. Unlike later examples of documentation which often had at its heart the desire to capture rural styles facing disappearance, in the eighteenth century, the text of the books did not suggest the idea of rapid change. Instead, the goal was to document variety and characterize distant places. The documentation of the dress was a form of gaining knowledge of a place, much the same as documenting newly discovered species of birds or butterflies on field explorations.

Although the underlying message differed between Grasset's encyclopedias and contemporary fashion magazines, the format of their illustrations was remarkably similar. Both made use of engravings surrounded by a framing rectangle, which enclosed one or two figures. Any color added to the images was done by hand after it was printed. Grasset's illustrations include some conventions then common among fashion plates such as an additional figure shown from a different angle, for instance, the back so that the details of the entire garment could be seen (Figure 2.1). Because both ethnographic plates and fashion plates had the shared goal of illustrating clothing, these common conventions are unsurprising. While publishers in Paris were developing techniques for showing off the latest styles, illustrators who were trying to document peculiarities of dress in faraway places adopted these same methods. They both combined a text that discussed appropriate behavior with plates illustrating clothing.

The parallels between early fashion magazines and these collections of plates depicting regional dress truly converged in the work of Louis-Marie Lanté and Georges-Jacques Gatine. Lanté, an illustrator, and Gatine, an engraver, frequently collaborated to create fashion plates for the *Journal des dames et des modes*. In 1819, the publisher of the magazine commissioned the pair to create a series of plates depicting regional dress from Normandy.⁷ The resulting

Figure 2.1 Jacques Grasset de Saint-Sauveur and L. F. Labrousse, "Homme et Femme de Housberg, près Strasbourg" from *Costumes de Différent Pays*, ca. 1797. Collection of the Los Angeles County Museum of Art.

series of 105 plates was ultimately published in 1827. Unlike travelogues such as Grasset's encyclopedias, this series of plates was not accompanied by text beyond the captions. The plates follow the same conventions as their fashion plates, but rather than presenting a style for the viewer to emulate, they identify the subject as distinct—set apart by her village of origin. While Lanté created the illustrations based on observation from life, the nature of the collection of plates generalizes from specific examples of individual dress choices to presenting the outfits as representative of a geographic region. Because the entire series is constrained to Normandy, the series breaks down the geographical area into villages, each of which has a distinctive style associated with it. What is more, the illustrations only present women, thus presaging the near exclusive focus on women in regional dress as the symbolic bearer of identity.

While the series of Norman dress explored the variety within a region, other series appeared which were dedicated to entire countries. Lanté and Gatine created another series, *Costume de divers pays*, which was published in 1827.[8] This work combined illustrations of women from across Europe including Germany, Spain, and Italy. Included among the plates were a few which depict women from Alsace. This series was just one of a multitude produced during the 1820s and 1830s when the depiction of regional dress was a project that was widely popular across Europe. The organization of these series reflected competing conceptions of geography. Some were confined to a country with different images showing various regions, while others were confined to a smaller region with each image showing a different village. This period of widespread popularity of these series coincided with a formative period of nationalism across Europe as well as the development of regional identity.

Alsatian dress appeared not just in series such as Lanté's and Gatine's that spanned various countries but also in those dedicated to just that immediate region, most notably Jan Lewicki's *Costumes d'Alsace et de Bade* and Charles Emrich's *Collections de six costumes nationaux Alsaciens et Badois*, both of which appeared in 1834.[9] The inclusion of both Alsace and Baden within the same collection of prints reflected cultural similarities while disregarding national borders. While the shared culture across the Rhine included speaking closely related variations of the Alemannic dialect of German, such linkages were difficult to capture for distant readers. The visual aspect of their distinctive dress was easily digestible information communicated through the prints. Although Emrich's work refers to regional dress as "national," the use of the designation does not refer to the political nation-state. At this time Baden was a Grand Duchy within the German Confederation and the people's consciousness as being from Baden would likely have superseded any concept of Germanness.[10] Alsace at the time was part of France, but the grouping of the region with its German neighbors suggests an understanding of regional identity that did not yet map neatly onto French nationalism.

The organization of these series of regional costume plates into geographic areas that spanned national boundaries occurred along the French–Spanish border as well. The popular illustrator Paul Gavarni created a series of studies of people in the Pyrenees which he published as *Les Montagnards des Pyrénées françaises et espangoles*. Again the distinctive culture around the Pyrenees defied the well-established political border between France and Spain. Peter Sahlins analyzes the emergence of national identity along the French–Spanish border and finds that a self-understanding as French or Spanish occurred as early as the eighteenth century but the formal delineation of the boundary itself was not complete until 1868.[11] He distinguishes between the awareness among the residents of the border lands who were particularly concerned with which nation they lived in, with such awareness among political powers from the center of the nation whether Paris or Madrid who showed less interest in defining the boundaries. Through the early nineteenth century when collections of regional dress became popular, the logic of the geographic divisions remained fluid. The variations in how the collections were grouped whether by region or by nation reflected this fluidity. It is largely during this period when the salience of Alsace as a region with coherent cultural features emerges. The documentation of a characteristic regional dress which corresponded to the geographic region served to reinforce the idea of regional distinction.

The emergence of recognizable regional dress depended not just on the documentation in these collections but on the coherence of the images across different collections. Lanté and Gatine's series *Costumes de divers pays*, published in 1827, includes several women from Alsace. The most influential one, however, was the illustration entitled "Alsatian peasant from Kochersberg" (Plate 6). The plate shows a woman at a three-quarters angle to the viewer wearing a red and green skirt and coordinated bodice and stomacher. She wears a white apron over the skirt, a black scarf around her neck, and has both a cap on her head and a wide straw hat in her hands. The background is completely empty. There is a second illustration in the same series which bears the same caption and shows a woman in roughly the same outfit except from the back. Instead of holding a hat in front of her, she holds a basket of vegetables on her head with her right hand while her left hand holds back her white apron. Like a fashion illustration, this image provides details on how the outfit looks from the back—for instance, it looks like the bodice tucks into the skirt and the blouse has a square collar which extends over the bodice. While Lanté captured his illustrations of women from life, he records no details about them beyond their dress.

The power of Lanté and Gatine's depictions came not only from their circulation as a series of prints but through their reuse as they were copied in later prints. The image of the woman shown from the front appeared again seven years later in one of the six plates in Emrich's series (Plate 4). Both women have the same pose where they are leaning slightly forward and glancing toward the viewer. They hold their straw hats in front of their apron. The only significant difference between the two works is that skirt in Lanté and Gatine's falls slightly longer. In fact, three of Emrich's six plates appear to be based on Lanté's earlier illustrations, including in addition to the peasant from Kochersberg, the peasant from Kehl in Baden, and the gardener from Strasbourg. However, while Lanté and Gatine included only women in their series, Emrich adds two men: one peasant from Kehl and one from Strasbourg.

The inspiration for these additional figures in Emrich's series may have come from Jan Lewicki's illustrations that were also published in 1834. Jan Lewicki (1795–1872) was a Polish illustrator who moved to Strasbourg in 1832 after the November uprising.[12] Unlike Lanté and Emrich's plates, each of Lewicki's images shows a couple (Plate 5) (Figures 1.9 and 1.10). While Lewicki introduces men to the series, the categories of people otherwise repeat Lanté's: peasants from Kochersberg, gardeners from Strasbourg, and Anabaptists. Lewicki didn't simply copy Lanté's system of classifying people, he also copied the illustrations themselves. While Lewicki's copy of the peasant from Kochersberg changes her position slightly, it clearly duplicates the outfit from the earlier drawing. However, Lewicki not only adds men to the images, he also adds backgrounds including architectural features, horses, and greenery. The contextualization situates the figures in their place of origin, thus reinforcing the designations in the captions that they were representatives of these places. The repetition of not only the categories but the nearly identical clothing reinforces these linkages.

The practice of copying plates from collections of regional dress echoes similar copying of fashion plates which was customary. Through the 1830s, following the death of the original publishers of *Le journal des dames et des modes*, copying illustrations became rampant.[13] Illustrations were reused in other magazines put out by the same publishers but were also taken without permission. Copies were particularly prevalent abroad, for example, in Germany. Magazines, such as *Journal des Luxus und der Moden*, which ran from 1813 to 1814 or *Pariser Moden-Zeitung für deutsche Frauen* published in 1827, copied plates from the Paris original.[14] Clearly this practice of copying further tied practices of fashion magazines to these plates showing regional dress.

The copying of the image of the peasant from Kochersberg did not end in the 1830s, and it occurred both in French and German publications. An interpretation of the image appears in the eighth volume of the book *Les français peints par eux-mêmes* published in 1842.[15] This particular volume of the work looks at the people of the different French provinces. The diversity of the population and of their clothing styles is reduced into single image that precedes the chapter entitled "L'Alsacien." This image shows a man and a woman with arms interlocked and bears the caption "Alsacien et Alsacienne" (Figure 2.2). The woman holds the broad-brimmed straw hat and has a bow on her head. Although her pose is new, and her apron is tucked into her bodice, the elements of her dress closely follow the model first introduced by Lanté and Gatine. Now rather than being a peasant from Kochersberg, she represents the entire region of Alsace. The book's project was to classify the French people. The illustrations

Figure 2.2 "Alsacien et Alsacienne" from *Les français peints par eux-mêmes: Encyclopédie morale du dix-neuvième siècle. Province. Tome Troisième*, 1842. Bibliothèque nationale de France.

accompanied text to create both visual and textual "paintings" that sorted the French people into types. While the earlier volumes sorted primarily Parisians into types based largely on class and occupation, the later volumes turned to the provinces and painted with an even broader brush as all of the residents of a province fell into sweeping categories such as the Breton and the Alsatian.

The image was also copied in a series of costume illustrations published in the German magazine *Münchener Bilderbogen*. This series was entitled *Zur Geschichte der Kostüme* and appeared in 125 issues between 1861 and 1905.[16] The series included both historical costumes and folk costumes from around the world. The costumes from various parts of Europe including Germany were first published in the 1880s. Ultimately Braun & Schneider, the publisher of the magazine, republished the series as a single book. The book, also titled *Zur Geschichte der Kostüme*, was first published in 1898, but underwent several subsequent publications.[17]

The issue dedicated to Alsace included four pictures, which took up a single page of the book. Each of the pictures was made of a vignette combining costumes from three or four different villages in Alsace. In one of these vignettes, the girl from Kochersberg shared her space with young women from Krautgersheim, Colmar, and Oberseebach. These four villages or cities are spread all over the region. The illustrations juxtaposed then current regional dress with historic costumes. By the 1880s regional dress was no longer worn in Colmar but was still common in Oberseebach. The Kochersberg costume depicted was historic as it was copied closely from the one that first appeared in illustrations in the 1820s, sixty years earlier. Regional dress was still worn in Kochersberg in the 1880s but it had changed significantly. In fact another of the illustrations on the page shows the contemporary regional dress of the surroundings of Strasbourg, which included Kochersberg. The illustrations of regional dress in Braun & Schneider's publications mixed contemporary and historic garments in a way that confused the difference between the two. The costumes were identified purely by location and not by time period. The copying of sixty-year-old sources reinforced the idea that regional dress was ahistorical and did not change over time.

The republication of Lanté's illustration meant the continued circulation of this particular image, which became the quintessential image of Alsatian dress out of all proportion to its actual representativeness. Had it been properly identified in Braun & Schneider as being from the 1820s it could have revealed how much regional dress had changed. Instead it communicated a message of timeless and unchanging rural dress.

Photography of Regional Dress

Just as improvements in technology had enabled the creation of series of lithographic prints in the early nineteenth century, technology in the mid-century had enabled the reproduction of photographic images. Among the early collections of photographs to depict Alsatian regional dress was a series of stereoscopic photographs by Charles Lallemand and Ludovic Hart. One of these series was entitled *Galérie Universelle des Peuples*, which included a volume dedicated to showing costumes from Alsace, and also included volumes on Baden, Württemberg, and Syria.[18] Another iteration of this collection of photographs was published by A Varady & Co. of Basel. These images were from a series labeled *Deutsche Volkstrachten*.[19] Based on the date when the series were published, the photographs were taken around 1864 or 1865 and capture images of women and children posed in regional dress in outdoor settings.

The images have similarities with the earlier collections of plates. Several of the images capture women wearing the costume from the area around Strasbourg which included a large, but floppy bow on the top of the cap[20] (Figure 2.3). Other images show costumes from other villages, particularly in the Outre-Forêt (Figure 2.4). Rather than reinforcing existing stereotype, these images suggested the diversity of Alsatian dress and also showcased the dress as it was worn in the 1860s. The limitations of photography at that time demanded a long exposure time and thus the subjects had to remain still for at

Figure 2.3 Charles Lallemand and Ludovic Hart, Stereoscopic image of women from Blaesheim, Alsace, 1860s. Private Collection.

Figure 2.4 Charles Lallemand and Ludovic Hart, Stereoscopic image of family from the Outre-Forêt, 1860s. Private Collection.

least fifteen to twenty seconds. These technical factors demanded staged poses by the subjects. The villagers in their costumes were not captured in candid moments but instead were posed in their best clothes. Despite the wealth of information communicated through these photographs, the photographs are slightly less clear than lithographic prints such as Lewicki's images. The contrast against the background provides less definition and the areas of white lose detail. On the other hand, while the clarity of information may be slightly diminished based on the state of photography in its early days, faith in its accuracy is strong. Photography directly captured the image that was presented before the camera and was therefore believable in a way that illustration was not.

Photographs could be reproduced and republished. This is very obvious from the series of Lallemand and Hart images which were published at least four or five times. The images could reach a wide audience. This very series was published in multiple languages in multiple cities, including in Paris, Strasbourg, and Basel. The widespread diffusion of these prints and photographs led to widespread familiarity with the appearance of folk costumes. The technological improvements that facilitated the reproduction of these lithographs and then the development of photography proved essential in giving people across Europe an idea of what people in Alsace wore, however imperfect the impressions were.

In contrast to Lallemand and Hart who captured some of the variety in Alsatian regional dress, the photographer Adolphe Braun (1812–77) reinforced the growing stereotype. Braun was from Mulhouse; Alsace and his career represented a link between manufacturers in southern Alsace and the artistic community in Paris. He received an education in industrial design in Mulhouse before striking out for Paris where he founded a business that produced designs that could be used for textiles, wallpapers, and ceramics. While originally he worked with lithography, he became an early experimenter with photography. He published several series of photographs including a book of flowers that was intended to serve as inspiration for industrial designers. His studio also photographed artwork from institutions including the Louvre. He explored the possibilities of photography as a medium of reproduction as well as art.

In the late 1860s Braun published a series of photographs of women in Swiss regional dress. He staged the photographs in his garden and studio in Dornach, near Mulhouse.[21] He assembled related props and even grass and branches to set the stage for the photographs. One of the novelties his series of photographs offered was that they were presented in color; watercolor paint was applied by hand directly to the albumen prints.[22]

Figure 2.5 Adolphe Braun, *Alsace*, ca. 1871. Boston Athenaeum.

Soon after he offered the series featuring Swiss regional dress, the Franco-Prussian War occurred, and the Alsatian photographer was drawn to represent Alsace with a young woman in regional dress (Figure 2.5). Unlike his photographs of the young Swiss women, he completely rejected props and sets. The image of Alsace in particular became widely known, thanks in large part to its reproduction as an engraving. It was even copied onto ceramic plates and dishes. Prussian authorities discouraged the circulation of the image and tried to spread the rumor that the model was the fiancée of a Prussian officer, but the image nevertheless took on significance as a symbol of French pride.[23]

Realism and Regional Dress

While collections of images of folk costume such as Grasset's and Lallemand's shed some light on rural life, French academic art from the early nineteenth century rarely had any use for rural people other than to add local color in pastoral scenes. As Raymond Grew put it, "their visual function remained the same: a decorative evocation of pastoral calm and rural simplicity …"[24] However, the generation of artists born in the 1820s began to change the way rural scenes were depicted. These artists, led by Gustave Courbet, focused on common people including both urban working-class and rural agricultural laborers and depicted the reality of their lived experience.

The painting, *Burial at Ornans* completed by Courbet in 1850, was a turning point in the development of the Realist movement (Plate 7). The village of Ornans in Bourgogne-France-Comté was just south of Alsace. The painting depicts the moments before the funeral ceremony is set to start.[25] Members of the clergy dominate the left third of the painting while the remaining area is filled with the villagers. All the figures fill the space as they stand close together in a shallow depth of field. Except for a couple of the men who wear breeches which were decidedly unfashionable for urban dress by 1850, the men's dress is not distinctive to the area. In contrast, several of the women wear distinctive bonnets with deep brims that continue around to the back and high puffy crowns. The range of costumes distinguish the social groups that made up Ornans society. Courbet was clearly an insider to the community and able to depict the nuanced relationships among the people.[26] Rather than simply depicting farm workers in the field, Courbet showed the diversity of country life. In choosing to depict the character of rural life it is significant that he has shown a religious scene.

Courbet presented his work at the Salon of 1850–1 where it stood out for flouting the conventions of its day. The Academy had established a clear hierarchy of artistic subjects in which history painting stood as the top of all the arts with genre painting holding a clearly inferior position.[27] By painting the genre scene of a village funeral on a monumental scale, Courbet turned conventions on their head. This hierarchy was again disrupted with the awarding of the grand medal of honor at the 1868 Salon to Gustave Brion's *Bible Reading. Protestant Interior in Alsace.* The success of this particular genre painting reflected a shift in the art establishment which showed a greater interest in the depiction of everyday life more generally.[28]

Gustave Brion, who was born in Rothau, Alsace in 1824, was influenced by the work of Gustave Courbet as well as other realist artists including Jean-François Millet. Brion took a religious scene as the subject of his celebrated work, *Bible Reading. Protestant Interior in Alsace.* The whereabouts of the painting itself are not known but it can be analyzed based on a reproduction of it printed in the press at the time (Figure 2.6). The focus of the room, which is sparsely furnished, is the man at the left. He is seated with the book across his lap. The other people

Figure 2.6 Print that appeared in *L'univers illustré* based on the original painting by Gustave Brion, *Bible Reading. Protestant Interior in Alsace*, 1868. Louis Bertrand/Alamy Stock Photo.

are all listening to him. There are five women sitting and children and servants standing amidst the seated figures. The seated women dominate the picture, and they are dressed in regional dress with wide but floppy bows on their heads. They have shawls wrapped around their shoulders except for the woman the farthest to the left who wears a wide white collar. Brion showed a variety of different options including with and without shawls rather than simply creating a fixed style. He did showcase the most familiar style of regional dress as it was worn in the late 1860s and exercised care to accurately represent it. While he was not illustrating the costumes in the way that Grasset or Lanté did, he situated them in the original circumstances in a way that the other illustrators had not. The religious focus of village life is clearly presented in Brion's work just as it had been in Courbet's.

Brion began painting in Alsace but, in 1850 when he was twenty-six, he moved to Paris. He shared his first apartment in the capital with other Realist artists including Jules Breton.[29] Even after his move to Paris he continued to paint Alsatian scenes. The first of his paintings to receive a medal at the Salon was a painting of a man driving a sled filled with logs (a *schlitteur*) in the Vosges. While other realist painters had a sharper edge of political activism in their paintings of working class in labor and the difficult conditions of their life, Brion took a different direction in romanticizing traditional life in his native Alsace.

Brion was one of a number of painters in France who took as their subject rural scenes. His one-time roommate, Jules Breton, also became widely known for his paintings of rural people. Breton is best known for his paintings of men and women working in the fields; for instance, he painted his own versions of the gleaners, a subject made famous by Millet. He also devoted much of his work to capturing scenes of religious observance. He painted scenes such as *Young Communicants at Courrieres*, which took place in the village in Artois where he was born and lived most of his life.[30] He also painted *The Blessing of the Wheat in Artois* in 1857.[31] This large-scale painting shows a religious procession including young women in white carrying a religious figure followed by clergy in their robes and the priest under a canopy carried by four men. Along the route of the procession there are villagers kneeling in respect and prayer. Breton's depictions of rural life clearly express the piety of the people.

While Breton certainly captured scenes in his native Artois, he devoted much of his work to painting scenes of Brittany, which was the setting for as much as a third of his paintings.[32] Brittany, even more so than Alsace, was a subject for artists drawn to charming regional costumes. Breton was drawn to both the rugged beauty of the landscape and the beauty of the women. He recognized that the costumes were an integral part of religious ceremonies and carefully recorded them in those circumstances. He rejected an understanding of folklore that failed to recognize the integral part the costumes performed in solemn rituals. Breton was charmed by the pardons, a form of processional pilgrimage performed in Brittany.[33] For instance, his *A Great Pilgrimage in Brittany* depicts a central group of men dressed in their *bragou-bras* or full breeches (Figure 2.7). The ceremony took place in the evening so the men and the gathering of women who surrounded them on all sides were carrying long candles. The resulting shape of the men who were dressed all in dark colors surrounded by the white coiffes of the women creates a dramatic and stirring image. The costumes contribute to the visual effectiveness of the image but also set the scene apart as a distinctive display. Breton's painting clearly captures the integral relationship between the performance of religious ceremonies and the distinctive regional dress. This relationship was as true in Brittany as it was in Alsace. Both Breton and Brion painted scenes which clearly connected regional dress with religious observation. However, the religious piety which was the true subject of the work gained less attention than the quaintness of the costumes.

While Brion lived in the Parisian art scene and knew important participants in the Realism movement such as Courbet and Breton, he was also inspired by German artists such as Ludwig Knaus (1829–1910) and Benjamin Vautier

Figure 2.7 Photographic print of Jules Breton, *A Great Pilgrimage in Brittany*, 1862–5 published by Goupil & Cie. Digital image courtesy of the Getty's Open Content Program.

(1829–98).[34] Peasant scenes enjoyed great popularity in Germany. Attention to ethnographic detail in paintings has strong precedents in German art. In his early work Vautier painted the regional costume of his native Switzerland but ultimately switched to dedicate more of his attention to depicting people from the Black Forest. Vautier even painted scenes of Alsatian village life such as in his painting *Tanzpause auf einer elsässischen Bauernhochzeit* from 1878. Like many of Brion's paintings of Alsatians wearing their regional dress, the tone of Vautier's *Tanzpause* focused on social interactions and events of daily life.

This style of painting Alsatian country life was also followed by painters such as Camille Alfred Pabst, Frédéric Lix, and Charles-François Marchal. Paintings such as Marchal's 1864 *La Foire aux servantes* and Brion's 1873 *Cortège nuptial* attest to the enduring popularity of this genre (Figure 2.8; Plate 8). Both paintings take place in village streets. In Marchal's painting, a group of men stand in the middle while a line of young women stands along the side of a building to be scrutinized and chosen as servants. The men in the center are assessing the merits of the line of young women. One young man at the left of the picture is reaching out to hold the face of a young woman. All of the young women in the painting are dressed in similar costumes with small black bows on their caps, white aprons, and red and blue skirts. The men, while also dressed in regional dress, display a variety of different hats and coats. All of them wear red vests, breeches, and white gaiters on their legs. Two wear fur hats, one who is the central figure wears a bicorn and the man who is closest to the line of women wears a brimless, high crowned hat. The uniformity of the costumes serves to familiarize viewers with Alsatian regional dress. The tone of this and similar paintings which depicted regional dress in a festive atmosphere helped dissociate the dress from its original religious context.

Brion's *Cortège nuptial* similarly shows the domination of the street by the activities of people dressed in regional costumes. In Brion's painting a group of people processing in front of a decorated wagon led by two horses arrives at the front door of a house where they are met by a couple. The young woman in red who is carrying a distaff loaded with hemp and has an ornament in the center of her headbow appears to be the bride while the young man holding his hat aloft to her left appears to be her groom. He wears ribbons along the front of his jacket. Traditionally the groom picks up his bride in a wagon into which she piles all of her belongings including a spinning wheel and a distaff wrapped with flax or hemp. Her maids of honor accompany her in the wagon while the friends of the groom ride alongside.[35] While the wedding itself was a religious ceremony, the celebration and customs depicted in the painting emphasized the festive over the pious.

Figure 2.8 Photographic print of Charles-François Marchal, *La foire aux servantes à Bouxwiller*, 1864 published by Goupil & Cie. Collection of the author.

Book Illustrations

Similar wedding customs to those that appeared in Brion's painting were also described and illustrated as early as 1855 in the book *Strasbourg illustré* by Frédéric Piton. The scene illustrated by Alfred Touchemolin of the interior of a farm in Kochersberg shows a wagon filled with young women dressed in regional dress with headbows and shawls[36] (Figure 2.9). Books, such as Piton's *Strasbourg illustrée* or the slightly later *Dictionnaire topographique, historique et statistique du Haut et du Bas-Rhin* published in 1865, provided images of Alsace for curious readers.[37] These books include illustrations adapted from paintings. The imagery which captured scenes of Alsace accompanied text documenting the cultural and geographic features of the region. These books attested to the developing awareness of a culturally distinct region in which the scenes of life with regional costumes were an integral part.

Illustrations for all sorts of books were a common way for artist's works to be disseminated. Vautier translated the narrative style of his paintings into

Figure 2.9 Alfred Touchemolin, Detail of "Intérieur d'une ferme du Kochersberg," from Frédéric Piton, *Strasbourg illustré en panorama pittoresque historique et statistique de Strasbourg et de ses environs*, 1855. Coll. et photogr. BNU, Strasbourg.

illustrations. He drew genre scenes for magazines, calendars, and published collections of his drawings as well as illustrating a number of novels.[38] Brion illustrated editions of Victor Hugo's *Les Misérables* and *Notre Dame de Paris*. His paintings also were translated into engravings so they could be reproduced in magazines. His painting *Mariage Protestante en Alsace* was made into a print by Paul Rajon. Examples of this print also have the title translated into English indicating that the image circulated in the English-speaking world as well as in France. While the bride and groom in this painting were dressed fashionably, several of the guests are dressed in Alsatian regional costumes.

Théophile Schuler (1821–78) was another Alsatian artist whose greatest renown came from his illustrations. While he created a number of important paintings including the creepy *Le char de la mort* in 1848, he was best known as an illustrator. Schuler studied art and painting in Paris from 1838–48. Unlike most artists of his level of accomplishment, Schuler left Paris after a brief period of study to live the remainder of his life in his native Alsace. His departure was partly spurred by the Revolution of 1848, but also by the health of his father. In returning to Alsace he became familiar with and influenced by German artists. The work of Benjamin Vautier was among the influences on his work.[39] His study focused not just on oil painting but also on engraving, lithography, and other media. Between 1854 and 1865 he worked with a variety of publications including *L'Illustration* and *Magasin Pittoresque*. From 1865 on Schuler worked almost exclusively for the publishing house edition Hetzel in Paris. He drew illustrations for the books by the writing duo Erckmann-Chatrian. These two men from Lorraine wrote stories that took place in the area around Alsace and Lorraine, allowing Schuler the opportunity to draw Alsatian regional costumes in these illustrations. Schuler also created illustrations for works by Jules Verne and Victor Hugo.[40]

As an illustrator of novels and short stories, Schuler focused on creating a narrative in his drawings. His work told stories. These stories and images made an impression on their viewers—and they were widely viewed. Schuler was known by people from the arts and letters ranging from Victor Hugo to Delacroix to Vincent Van Gogh.[41] The familiarity of his work went hand in hand with familiarity of Alsatian regional dress. The illustrations of rural life that Schuler did to accompany *L'Ami Fritz* and other stories by Erckmann-Chatrian familiarized the French with Alsatian costumes including the oversized headbows.

Schuler took genuine interest in Alsatian traditions. This led him to immerse himself in the culture rather than simply add headbows onto female figures. His illustrations often focused on the costumes of the Outre-Forêt including his studies of the costumes from Schleithal and Oberseebach done in 1858

(Figure 1.1). He not only drew the two figures in identical poses, he also added a little sketch of a neckline showing how the stomacher fit into the dress, indicating his attention to small details. Schuler focused on the diversity and complexity of Alsatian regional dress rather than simply falling back on the shortcut of depicting the headbow. Schuler did not simply use regional dress to evoke the concept of Alsace, he deeply plumbed many aspects of Alsatian traditions and included the costumes as one harmonious part.

While Schuler chose to live in Alsace rather than in Paris where he had studied, other Alsatians including Gustave Doré (1832–83) remained in Paris. Doré was an artist and illustrator who achieved even greater fame than Schuler. His illustrations circulated widely, appearing in a French edition of *Don Quixote*, works of Lord Bryon, Milton, Dante, Rabelais, and Balzac. He also displayed paintings at the Salon in 1867.[42] Doré produced a few illustrations featuring Alsatian regional dress including his illustration for La Fontaine's fable *The Ant and the Grasshopper* published by Hachette in 1868 (Figure 2.10). Doré

Figure 2.10 Gustave Doré and Adolphe François Pannemaker, *La cigale et la fourmi* (*The Ant and the Grasshopper*) from Jean de la Fontaine *Fables*, 1868. Bibliothèque nationale de France.

interpreted the figure of the ant, who is dutiful and industrious, as a woman dressed in Alsatian regional dress. She wears the bow on her head as well as a shawl and apron. In addition, she holds knitting needles and has a pair of scissors suspended from her waist. The older of the two children who stand between the Ant and the Grasshopper wears a fur hat and a vest with a double row of buttons. This outfit is a male version of Alsatian regional dress. The use of regional dress signals that the Alsatian family forms an association with being hardworking and ungenerous.

Unlike Schuler who attentively explored the details of how regional dress was worn, Doré was imprecise. The bow on Ant's head sits upright at a strange angle and her hair underneath is loose and curled. Customarily the bows were worn straighter and the hair below worn smoother. The shawl is wrapped haphazardly in disregard of the precise style of layering. Doré uses the costumes to evoke Alsatianness through the inclusion of recognizable symbols: the headbow, the fur hat, the shawl, and the apron. He does not pay attention to the details in how the bow is tied, the shawl draped. He also provides few architectural details to signify that the house is in Alsace. The headbow and costume become symbols to refer to Alsace instead of careful evocations of regional traditions.

Doré continued to use this vocabulary to refer to Alsace in a pair of larger-scale paintings that he produced in 1869 that he titled *Soir en Alsace* and *Lorraine*.[43] The former painting depicts four young women in regional dress lined up against the corner of a wall (Plate 9). They are surrounded by a flock of geese being driven by a distant figure in the background and above the girls is a window with four young men leaning out. The young women dominate the scene particularly the central girl who gazes directly at the viewer. She is dressed in the same sort of regional dress as the Ant in the earlier drawing although in color her skirt is a deep, rich red and her apron is a pale blue. As in the earlier illustration, the bows sit at an upright angle and the shawls are wrapped carelessly. Doré adds to the link between the region of Alsace and these regional costumes with this painting. His painting *Lorraine* also appears to show a woman in Alsatian regional dress, but it has a more haunting and wistful mood. These two paintings together represent the introduction of personifying Alsace and Lorraine as young women, and they were completed the year before the Franco-Prussian War.

The visual language that Doré built up in these works were put to use in his painting *L'Alsace Meutrie* in 1872 (Figure 2.11). Painted a year after the conclusion of the Franco-Prussian War, the image features a woman in Alsatian dress in deep mourning. Just behind her stands a French flag which hangs down

Figure 2.11 Gustave Doré, *L'Alsace meurtrie*, 1872. Copyright: Collectivé européenne d'Alsace – Sébastien Sutter.

and she holds close to her chest. Her expression and posture clearly indicate deep sadness. She is not simply a woman from Alsace, but she is the personification of the region itself, sad to part with France. This persona of the *Alsacienne*, as representative of the region, has a clear legacy in the many depictions of women in Alsatian costume. When national events placed Alsace in the center of attention, this representation was readily available to be adapted into political charged use. As in *The Ant and the Grasshopper* and *Alsace, 1869*, Doré paints a bow that sits upright as well as the casually draped shawl and the stomacher. Doré was far from alone to make use of this regional symbol.

An earlier artistic response to the Franco-Prussian War and one of the defining images was Jean-Jacques Henner's 1871 work *L'Alsace. Elle Attend* which shows a woman dressed all in black with a black headbow which has a small cockade affixed to it[44] (Plate 10). The figure symbolizes the mourning that Alsace felt at the break with France and the vigil she would keep until being returned to France. The painting was commissioned by Mme. Kestner who sought to offer it to Léon Gambetta, a leading opponent of the Franco-Prussian

War.[45] Like Doré, Henner (1829–1905) was a native of Alsace who studied art in Paris where he remained after 1871 when he opted to remain French. In general, Henner's work placed little importance on narrative elements including costumes or decoration. Rather it was often marked by a strong contrast between dark backgrounds and luminous skin tones. *L'Alsace. Elle Attend* typifies this approach. Although the Alsatian woman in the painting wears the coiffe and a black shawl, the dress she wears is actually closely in line with cosmopolitan dress of the period. The image of the *Alsacienne* focused largely on the headbow as the defining aspect along with a shawl, which was sufficient to communicate Alsatianness.

The notable innovation in Henner's painting was the addition of the cockade. The inclusion of this element of pro-French political symbolism created an enduring link to the developing iconography of Alsace. These cockades became a typical component in the pro-French appropriation of Alsatian imagery, for instance, in Adolphe Braun's photographs. Cockades were even adopted by Alsatian women when they wore the costume. The work of artists in depicting the regional dress not only took on a political valence that was not inherent in the dress itself, but it in fact also influenced the way that Alsatians styled their own clothing.

Art Nouveau and the Alsatian Awakening

By the 1890s, the generation that was born in the years immediately before and after the establishment of Alsace-Lorraine as a German Reichsland was maturing into the artists and intellectuals shaping Alsatian culture. Given their upbringing in the region during a period of strongly competing national interests, these artists responded to the duality of their culture with their art. In seeking subjects that were distinctly Alsatian, many of them became enraptured of the beauty of rural dress and festivals. The most influential of these artists included Charles Spindler and the intellectual community who gathered around the estate of Anselme Laugel at St. Léonard. These men (and they were only men) took an interest in folk dress and other aspects of popular culture as a means of furthering their agenda of constructing a distinctive Alsatian culture.

Born in Boersch, Alsace on March 11, 1865, Charles Spindler was French at the time of his birth but became German by his sixth birthday.[46] Because of this heritage, he spoke and wrote equally comfortably in French and German in addition to speaking and understanding Alsatian. He was raised in a bourgeois family as one of nine children, but his father died when he was ten, leaving his mother to depend on a widow's pension and the generosity of an uncle, the painter Pierre-Louis Spindler.[47] Thanks to his artistic relative, he was allowed to study art in classes taught by the widow of Théophile Schuler.[48] When he was older he went on to study art in Berlin, Düsseldorf, and Munich with a scholarship from the German government.[49] After finishing his military service in 1890, Spindler joined his friend Anselme Laugel on his estate at Saint-Léonard, near Boersch. In his memoire Spindler describes how Laugel opened his home to welcome artists. Owing to its localization around the home of Laugel, this group of artists and intellectuals became known as the *Cercle St.-Léonard*.

Anselme Laugel was born in 1851 and received his early studies in Strasbourg and Metz.[50] After finishing his *baccalauréat* he left Alsace to pursue his studies and began a career in politics. This move to Paris coincided with the conclusion of the Franco-Prussian War and demonstrated Laugel's strong desire to maintain his French nationality. While he favored French national interests, his love of his native region and passion for art proved a stronger draw than his professional and political career in France; he returned to German-controlled Alsace in 1891. Laugel's commitment to politics did not end upon his return to Alsace; in 1891 he was elected to the Bezirkstag or district council of Bas-Rhin; then he went on to serve in the Landesausschuss from 1894 to 1911.[51] Laugel's story epitomizes the struggle that Alsatians loyal to France faced. As a politician, Laugel's professional opportunities were best if he remained to Paris; yet, the interests of Alsace would suffer with the loss of the best-educated and most cultured members of society. Despite Laugel's clear position in favor of French control of Alsace, he proved himself open to welcoming into his home artists and intellectuals with different loyalties and beliefs. He socialized frequently with Spindler's German friends and showed a willingness to learn more about their culture.[52]

The members of the Cercle St. Léonard belonged to the generation that was born in the years immediately before and after the conclusion of the Franco-Prussian War, meaning that they had either been very young when Alsace passed into German hands in 1871 or were born soon afterward. The first decade of the twentieth century, when the Cercle St.-Léonard was most active, represented a period of great artistic production in the region and coincided with a growing accommodation of German authority. In fact, the members of the Cercle included not only Alsatians, but also a few Germans including Josef Sattler and Werner Wittich. The group, however, did not include any members who were from elsewhere in France.

Charles Spindler not only participated in the social scene among local artists, but also displayed his works in the major exhibitions of his time, including as part of the German contribution to the Exposition Universelle of 1900 held in Paris. Spindler likened the German participation in that exposition to their victory over the French in the Franco-Prussian War, thus clearly expressing his strong preference for the innovation and originality of the decorative arts coming out of Germany at the time.[53] He considered the artistic production of France stagnant when compared with the more dynamic scene in Germany. Nevertheless, Spindler observed that the Alsatian public preferred French styles and resisted the modernity of art and design that was taking place across the Rhine.[54] Traditionally in Alsace, those with the closest ties to France had been the social elite. Those families such as the Laugels who represented the landed elite of the Alsatian population were the most likely to have "opted" to leave for France following 1870. The wealthy leaders of business and industry, particularly in southern Alsace, were also the most sympathetic to France. This association between elite culture and the French was not simply the perceived superiority of French taste, but rather the resonance between the interests of the upper classes in Alsace with those of France. This correspondence between class and national loyalty helps to explain the popularity for French architectural and decorative styles in Alsace at the turn of the century. It also highlights the significance of the turn that Spindler and the Cercle St.-Léonard took in drawing inspiration from local, rural culture.

The works of these artists and intellectuals have been a subject of interest to both historians and art historians. The latter have situated Spindler and his circle as the center of the *Art Nouveau* or *Jugendstil* movement in Alsace.[55] Spindler's participation in international expositions put him in close contact with the artistic scene in France, Germany, and across Europe. By the late nineteenth century in Europe, questions of nationalism and regionalism were so pervasive that the production of art and culture became subsumed into this broader political discourse. The struggles to celebrate the cultural expressions of regions with burgeoning political consciousness, including not just Alsace and Lorraine but also regions such as Catalonia, Scotland, Poland, and the Czech lands resulted in important centers of modern artistic production being located in peripheral cities such as Nancy, Glasgow, and Prague. The artistic production of Alsace around the turn of the century sheds light on the place of vernacular, regional culture in the development of modern, international style and provides insight into the relationship between the international artistic movement and contemporary politics.

Historians have also looked to the artistic production of this group involved in the Alsatian awakening (*reveil alsacien*) as instrumental in the articulation of a culturally coherent Alsatianness largely inspired from elements drawn from popular culture.[56] Detmar Klein argued that before the 1870s, the idea of Alsace as being a cultural reality rather than simply a political, geographic did not yet exist.[57] This claim seems to disregard the considerable literature on Alsatian history and culture that had already been written before the Franco-Prussian War including the works already discussed in this chapter for their illustrations.[58] The members of the Alsatian awakening drew from this existing oeuvre as they struggled to situate this Alsatian consciousness within the polarized political landscape. Rather than offering a single vision of the political aims of Alsatian elite, the members maintained competing ideas of their purpose as artists and intellectuals and their role and power in effecting political change. While Spindler aimed to create a cultural expression that epitomized the fusion of German and French culture, his harmonious vision was not able to gain traction. Ultimately the French victory in the First World War shaped the legacy of these artists' work as the pro-French aspect of their interpretation of Alsatian culture ultimately prevailed.

Spindler as Photographer and Ethnologue

When Spindler first returned from military service in Germany, he and Laugel planned to collaborate on an album of photographs celebrating "rustic life" in Alsace.[59] Although this project did not come to pass, it seems to have been the beginning of Spindler's ongoing efforts to take photographs of traditional practices in Alsace. He first took up photography around 1886. He described the state of the medium thus: "At that time, the discovery of dry plates had put photography within the reach of everyone and artists, in particular, saw in it a means of facilitating the study of drawing."[60] The silver-gelatin dry plate process that was used by Spindler was invented in 1871 and, as he suggests, made photography much more portable. By 1883 William Schmid began selling a hand-held camera, freeing the photographer from the tripod.[61] Spindler traveled around rural Alsace with his camera, visiting the areas where regional dress practices were still observed. Despite the general inaccessibility of many of these areas he made regular excursions. At that time, these villages were not widely visited by tourists, who would instead go to the Vosges or villages along the wine route where there were vineyards.[62] Spindler's exploration of northern Alsace began around 1889 and continued as late as the 1920s and 1930s.[63] He took advantage of his travels to document weddings, religious ceremonies, and festivals such as the Fête-Dieu. In making these excursions he claimed that he "had become the most knowledgeable man on the costumes and customs of our Bas-Rhin."[64]

The photographs that Spindler took remain an invaluable resource in documenting rural life at the turn of the century. A considerable portion of these photographs recorded people dressed up in their special occasion clothes, whether they were posed specifically for the photographer or in the course of their ceremonies. Spindler captured a number of ceremonies such as Fête-Dieu processions in Geispolsheim, in Schleithal, and in Boersch just outside of St. Léonard. He also took photographs of the processions to and from Sunday services as well as those for weddings. His camera allowed him to capture lively activities such as dancing associated with messtis (Figure 2.12). He was interested in the activities and the ritual as well as the clothing. Spindler documented festivals and processions in addition to static, posed figures. The pictures of people dressed up in their best clothes were only a sample of his work. His work also includes scenes of people laboring: fishing, plowing, weaving, spinning, and various other hard, manual work. While there is a pastoral beauty to many of these scenes, they show the brutal roughness of rural life. His images of

Figure 2.12 Charles Spindler, Messti, ca. 1890s. Spindler Archives.

shepherds with tattered, patched clothing and scenes of women washing their clothes in the river leave no illusion as to the difficulty of life in the countryside (Figures 2.13 and 2.14).

Clothing was obviously an important subject of his work, but the variety of his photographs suggests that he was interested in capturing real clothing rather than a preconceived idea of what it should look like. Many of his images were portraits of families, such as the image of a family in Steinselz in the Outre-Forêt. While the people have obviously posed for the camera there is a very genuine connection between the family members. The man who sits in the center of the image is the focus of attention of the two women on either side (Figure 2.15). Their gazes both meet on him and create a strong composition. This photo is actually one of a number of photographs he took of the same family (Figure 2.16). While he clearly arranged the people to create the composition he wanted, the clothes are neither elaborate nor even in good condition. The man's sweater or jacket is disheveled and his vest is very dirty. Spindler added a notation on

Figure 2.13 Charles Spindler, Shepherd and child in mended clothes. Spindler Archives.

Figure 2.14 Charles Spindler, Women at a river doing laundry. Spindler Archives.

Figure 2.15 Charles Spindler, Family in Steinselz. Spindler Archives.

the paper to which the photograph is mounted which indicated that girls in Steinselz never wear headdresses. The notation provided a valuable complement to the image. Rather than an exceptional case in which the women's heads are uncovered, he indicated that this was the rule. The notations supplement the visual information in the photograph which was itself a means of documenting the way people dressed.

The portraits he took of people posed in their best clothes present an interesting study of the firmly established conventions of ethnographic photography. Spindler was very much aware of this genre as he had a sizeable collection of plates and photographs that had been created by earlier aficionados of folk costume. Among the pieces in his collection were stereoscopic photographs from the series *Deutsche Volkstrachten* by Lallemand and Hart from 1865 that captured images of groups of women and children posed in regional dress in outdoor settings[65] (Figures 2.3 and 2.4). Spindler's collection includes photographs not only of Alsatian costume but also of costumes from other regions of Germany.

While Spindler did create many photographs that followed a similar composition to these earlier photographs, his work demonstrated a greater degree of variety in composition, which was made possible by improvements in photographic technology. Spindler's photographs vary significantly in

Figure 2.16 Charles Spindler, Family in Steinselz. Spindler Archives.

perspective: some such as the portraits of the women in Steinselz are taken very close to the subject emphasizing the expression on the face as well as the texture of the clothing, while others are taken at greater distance and show groups of people together. The earlier photographs by Lallemand and Hart are fixed at a certain distance from the subject. The cameras in the 1860s were much larger and less mobile than those two decades later and imposed certain restrictions on photography. Nevertheless, many of Spindler's photographs echo the composition as well as subject of the earlier works. For example, his photograph of a family of four in the Outre-Forêt is strikingly similar to one of the Lallemand and Hart photographs in his collection that also shows a group of young women and children (Figure 2.17). Spindler's photograph is zoomed in closer and the subjects are looking more directly at the camera. In fact, the earlier picture appears less staged and more candid. Spindler was clearly familiar with the genre of ethnographic portraiture and his work appears studied and deliberate rather than spontaneous. While Spindler captured the Alsatian people, the image he presented was fitted to his vision.

Figure 2.17 Charles Spindler, Family in Outre-Forêt. Spindler Archives.

A comparison of his original photographs to his artwork reveals that Spindler copied the photographs into his watercolors, illustrations, and marquetry. In fact, he took photographs for the purpose of interpreting them into further artworks. Rather than seeing photography as an art form in and of itself, he saw it as a replacement for making sketches. Some of the photographs have grid marks scratched into their surface in order to allow for enlargement and recopying into other media (Figures 2.18 and 2.19). During his lifetime, these photographs were not published as such. Ultimately, however, this use for these photographs determined their survival as a collection. They remained his property and subsequently the property of his descendants. Spindler's retention of these images enabled him to control their diffusion to the public—a diffusion that was first filtered through his own stylization into illustrations and other forms.

Spindler collaborated with Laugel on a book about Alsatian customs, *Costumes et coutumes d'Alsace*. The book combined watercolors, drawings, and photographs by Spindler with text by Laugel. The preface describes their goal: "To allow the reader to visit the villages of Alsace, to show him how our peasants

Figure 2.18 Charles Spindler, Photograph of young woman from Steinselz showing grid marks. Spindler Archives.

Figure 2.19 Charles Spindler, Illustration of girl from Steinselz copied from photograph. Coll. et photogr. BNU, Strasbourg.

live, how they dress, how they are housed, these valiant workers of the earth, to define their character, analyze their habits, find the picturesque note that so often dominates in Alsace and displays itself in such varied ways, that is our goal."⁶⁶ The book is designed to allow the reader to vicariously travel through the region. In keeping with the book's premise as a sort of travel guide, the five chapters each cover a geographic section of the region: the surroundings of Wissembourg, the former county of Hanau, the surroundings of Strasbourg, the Vosges and the Rhine. In organizing the book geographically, the authors reinforce the primacy of place in the significance of the costumes. The heavy concentration on the north of Alsace belies the author's objective as set forth in their preface: "Our general plan consists of traveling all over Alsace from the north to the south, from Wissembourg to Belfort, and to recount, quite simply, our impressions."⁶⁷ The portion of Alsace that is treated in the book is the rural north with almost no attention paid to the south. Owing to its early industrialization, southern Alsace did not maintain a distinctive dress. However, the preface by suggesting that all of Alsace was encompassed in the book sought to in fact bring Alsace together with a common cultural experience.

The very idea to produce a book documenting the rural costumes and culture suggests that it was intended for an audience unfamiliar with the subject. The costumes must have been sufficiently unusual that Spindler and Laugel saw fit to document them. In fact, the extent of formal research that the pair did for the book suggests that the customs were not their own and that they wrote for an audience like themselves, curious about, but not really of, rural Alsace. The readers were likely those either in urban Alsace, most notably Strasbourg, or those people from Alsace who had left the region. Spindler himself acknowledges that before beginning his projects on Alsatian culture he didn't know very much about his native region and that "among the many friends that I had in Strasbourg, there were not many who could boast of knowing [Alsace]."[68] Spindler felt that his work documenting and publishing information about regional culture was received by a readership that was otherwise ignorant of the region. Even though the image of the woman in oversized headbow had been widely circulated throughout France and Germany since 1870, Spindler believed that the range, variety, and complexity of regional dress and practices were unfamiliar even to those people who had lived their whole lives in Alsace. A curious disconnect arose between the implicit claims that traditional customs were a defining aspect of Alsace and the fact that urban Alsatians were ignorant of said customs. In celebrating rural culture, Spindler and Laugel were also introducing these aspects of popular culture into high culture.

During his travels, Spindler not only photographed people he encountered but he also began purchasing clothing from them. He became a collector of the regional clothing that so interested him.

> During the course of my reconnaissance trips, I bought specimens of all the costumes that I saw, which was at that time still relatively easy, and gradually I found myself in possession of the most complete collection of costumes, a collection that I managed to complete by purchasing the costumes from the ateliers of the painters Ensfelder and Lix.[69]

In discussing the sources of his collection, Spindler reveals a telling detail. His acquisition of costumes from other artists confirms the fact that the costumes that appeared in the paintings and illustrations by important Alsatian artists were not the costumes worn by people under natural circumstances but were props owned by the artists. While these costumes likely originally came from the wardrobes of ordinary people who would have worn them on special occasions, their inclusion in art was staged. More significantly, rather than artwork illustrating a representative sampling of regional costume, these individual garments would have appeared over and over again. The styles of these specific pieces would take on a disproportionately prominent place in depictions of regional dress. The influence of the artists in popularizing particular styles would have been even more pronounced if the costumes owned by one artist were passed on to another artist. It is quite likely that an ensemble owned by Frédéric-Théodore Lix would have appeared not only in his paintings but also in the illustrations and even the books of Charles Spindler.

A careful examination of Spindler's photographs reveals that the same exact garments did appear over and over. He clearly employed models who posed for him in his collection of costumes (Figures 2.20 and 2.21). Despite his explicit goal of documenting the great diversity of regional dress, Spindler repeatedly posed his models in the most familiar style of Alsatian costume, including the white blouse with wide ruffled collar, abbreviated corselet, patterned apron, all of which were inevitably topped with the quintessential headbow. While hundreds

Figure 2.20 Charles Spindler, Model dressed in costume from Spindler's collection. Spindler Archives.

Figure 2.21 Charles Spindler, Illustration from *Images alsaciennes* copied from photograph of model, 1893. Coll. et photogr. BNU, Strasbourg.

of his photographs and illustrations testify to the innumerable variations of regional dress, Spindler helped encourage the popular simplistic image of Alsatian regional dress by his repetition of the stereotypical image.

Development of *l'Alsacienne* as a Symbol of Alsace

Spindler adapted his illustrations of the quintessentially Alsatian young woman into a sort of allegorical figure of the *Alsacienne* that he used to represent Alsace in general. The flexibility of the potential political uses for this symbolic figure becomes apparent in its deployment in la *Revue Alsacienne Illustrée*, a magazine founded by Spindler in 1899. Inspired by the art magazines coming out of Germany, which were playing a critical role in disseminating the ideals of modern art, Spindler sought to create a bilingual *"revue de grand luxe"* drawing stylistically from both France and Germany.[70] Spindler added images of the *Alsacienne* throughout the *Revue* (Figure 2.21). She appears at the beginning of each issue in a sort of cartouche, generally just shown as a head with a bow that is flanked on one side by a quill and on the other by a paintbrush.

While Spindler contributed to the use of the *Alsacienne* to stand in for the region, in the early days of the magazine he did not strongly favor allegiance to France over Germany. However, the leadership of the *Revue Alsacienne Illustrée* ultimately passed to a fellow member of the Cercle St.-Léonard, Pierre Bucher who was strongly pro-French in his political leanings. As Bucher became more involved in directing the *Revue*, its perspective in turn increasingly favored the French. The visual representation of the girl in the headbow increasingly represented not just the region but the region's allegiance to France. The diverging political viewpoints between Spindler and Bucher are further explored in Chapter 4 as they are also involved in the establishment of the Musée Alsacien.

The image of the *Alsacienne* was also a key component in the work of Jean-Jacques Waltz, who was better known by his Alsatian nickname "Hansi." A native of Colmar and the son of the curator of the Musée Unterlinden, Hansi was an acquaintance of Charles Spindler although he was not affiliated with the Cercle St.-Léonard. In contrast to Spindler who maintained an admiration for the Germans and their culture, Hansi was deeply anti-German. His work focused on celebrating Alsace, but also on caricaturing Germans. In contrast to his treatment of Germans whom he depicted as unattractive, unfashionable, and humorless, he idealized the Alsatians who were portrayed as simple and pure (Plate 11). His work became popular in France following the publication of his satirical work such as *Professeur Knatschké* and *Mon village*, which also resulted in his arrest and imprisonment by German authorities.[71] Hansi's work was largely aimed at children, and he also featured children wearing regional dress as the central characters in his work. Unlike the earlier depiction of the *Alsacienne* by artists such as Henner and even Spindler which showed adults, albeit relatively young ones, Hansi adapted the imagery into a juvenile mold. This extremely youthful *Alsacienne* emphasized the innocence and sweetness of Alsace.

The use of regional dress as a symbolic representation of the region depended almost exclusively on the image of women. As Vlossak describes, the uses of the allegorical image played upon ideas of women's vulnerability and victimhood.[72] French propaganda posters from the First World War epitomized this characterization of Alsace as in need of protection and saving.[73] The choice of a woman as symbol is both consistent with the message of subjugation that the imagery was intended to convey and with the persistence of distinctive dress practices among women. Very few Alsatian men continued to wear regional dress by the late nineteenth century. The switch that Hansi made to reimagine the *Alsacienne* as a girl reflected a shift toward folkloric dress as being appropriate for children. Although the generation of children born after 1900 was increasingly unlikely to wear regional dress, folk dress during this period was adapted into play dress for children. The evolution of the imagery created by artists was reflected in the evolving usage of folk dress.

The focus on women as the wearers of regional dress was a counterpoint to the exclusively male domain of folklore studies. All of the artists and ethnographers involved in the project of studying and documenting were men. The picturesque aspect of regional dress clearly appealed to men such as Spindler, Laugel, and Hansi. The text of *Costumes et Coutumes* shows the complicated tensions between the prejudices against "peasants" and the admiration for the rustic beauty of *Alsaciennes*. Laugel writes:

> What is striking first about the peasant, it is the mistrust (*méfiance*) ... Tricked, exploited, obliged to flee, often without recourse of any sort against theft and bad faith, he has no trust in any but himself ... We are not surprised therefore if he demonstrates against any stranger a sort of hostility and hereditary repugnance. He is patient and a little clumsy (*lourd*), and he owes this to his continual contact with nature.[74]

This disdainful attitude contrasted with the admiration he expressed for the beauty of girls dressed up for ceremonial occasions:

> Nothing equals in color the Fête-Dieu in Geispolsheim when the long file of girls following the procession is stretched out: the scarlet skirts, the red bows, the white shirts, and the aprons and the multicolored shawls offer a glimpse of the marvelous intensity of tones, above all when the radiant sun spreads the glory of its rays over the village.[75]

The gendered depiction of Alsatian regional dress reflected the preference of members of the bourgeoisie for seeing the picturesque, idealized aspect of the pastoral culture rather than the complicated class tensions that were called to mind with the idea of rural and working-class men.

Conclusion

The availability of the *Alsacienne* in her regional costume to serve as the representative of Alsatianness depends on the proliferation of imagery that had been produced for a century. The genre paintings and collections of folk costumes developed a set of features that immediately served to identify Alsatian regional dress. Such visual representations date back to at least the late eighteenth century when early versions of the Alsatian headbow first appeared. Grasset's collection of prints captured Alsatians of different walks of life wearing bonnets with bows at the front. He continued to produce these images over a span of twenty years, thus communicating that provincial dress remained unchanged. The development of plates featuring regional dress proceeded in parallel to the development of fashion plates, although the two differed significantly in the approach to change. Fashion is defined through its continual change over time so in contrast the gradual development of regional dress was confused with resistance to change.

The growing familiarity that people across Europe, particularly France and Germany, developed with regional dress was fostered through genre painting. Artwork that captured scenes of daily life in villages across Alsace became increasingly popular in the quarter-century before the Franco-Prussian War. Artists from Alsace who had settled in Paris were important in depicting village scenes including Gustave Brion and Gustave Doré. Artists who settled in Alsace including Théophile Schuler and Adolphe Braun also created critical works that helped alternately attest to the diversity of regional dress and popularize the quintessential headbow as distinctly Alsatian. While oil paintings made an impact at Salons in Paris, book illustrations achieved a wider audience.

When the Franco-Prussian War ended with the transfer of Alsace to Germany, the disruption was strongly felt by all of these Alsatian artists. In expressing their despair, many naturally turned to the persona of the young Alsatian woman in regional dress that they had been developing in their artwork for years. Jean-Jacques Henner is recognized as having painted the defining version with the addition of the cockade on the bow. In signaling the French loyalty of the Alsatian woman, he created a lasting addition to the regional costume. In seeking to create a shorthand to refer to the region of Alsace as it gained an important place in the French imagination, the woman in her Alsatian regional dress was an ideal symbol. The development of the imagery paralleled the development of regional consciousness which reached its peak in the years leading up to and during the First World War. For over a century, artists had developed the increasingly familiar image which took on political meaning as the region became strategically critical.

3

Material Goods

While artists played an important role in documenting and even influencing the appearance of regional dress, their role was not as critical as that of the artisans who made the actual garments. The traditional means of clothing production depended on both the labor and the expertise of village dressmakers and tailors. Ultimately the style of regional dress grew out of the relationship between the producers and the consumers. By the end of the nineteenth century this relationship gradually changed as residents of isolated villages increasingly abandoned their distinctive, age-old clothing styles when faced with the temptations of modern consumerism: ready-to-wear clothing and department stores. The local nature of the early-nineteenth-century rural clothing system had delayed the impact of these changes; however, by the turn of the century, rural clothing was increasingly integrated into a fashion system that was closely linked to national and international markets. In understanding this process of modernization, regional dress must be viewed as a commodity in an economic exchange. The aesthetic changes in the product were a result of the profound shifts that occurred in how the clothing was made, sold, and purchased.

The case of Alsace is a particularly interesting choice for this examination first because the distinctive style of dress in its rural areas marked a strong contrast with the cosmopolitan dress that replaced it, and second because its position as a border region complicated its experience of this modernization as the residents were exposed to the distinctive developments of the fashion industries of France and Germany. By the end of the nineteenth century, Alsace was integrating into Germany both economically and legally; nevertheless, France continued to exert a powerful influence as the origin of fashionable styles. While we have looked at regional dress as a signifier of regional and national identity through how it is worn and depicted, the clothing industry more broadly served a role in the construction of national identity through people's engagement in the economy as workers and consumers. The modernization of the organization of the clothing industry through ready-to-wear and department stores ultimately favored nationalism but this process was gradual rather than an abrupt rupture. The disappearance of regional dress styles was only the most visible signal of the transformation in how clothing was bought and sold in rural Alsace.

An examination of a particular wedding dress highlights the changes in consumer practices. Odile Schmitt was married on February 9, 1903 to Isidore Hartmann in Bernolsheim, Alsace. Both the bride and groom were born in Bernolsheim, a village of roughly 500 people 15 miles due north of Strasbourg. For the occasion, Schmitt wore a dress of royal blue silk trimmed with jet beads at the wrists and along the bodice. The dress is now in the collection of the Musée Alsacien, albeit without the apron and headbow[1] (Plate 12). The museum also has copies of photographs taken of the Hartmanns in 1906 and 1914, in which Odile wears the same dress she wore as her wedding dress (Figures 3.1 and 3.2).

Figure 3.1 Odile Schmitt and Isidore Hartmann with their children, 1906. Musée Alsacien de Strasbourg.

Figure 3.2 Odile Schmitt and Isidore Hartmann, 1914. Musée Alsacien de Strasbourg.

She accessorized the dress with an apron and an enormous headbow. While the accessories lend a regional aspect to her entire outfit, her dress does not conform to the stereotypical idea of rural dress from the area around Strasbourg. The high neck and modestly puffed sleeves were hallmarks of cosmopolitan dress from the late 1890s to early 1900s. Her outfit complicates the black and white separation that is often drawn between rural and urban dress. Rather than a sharp division between the two, rural and urban styles operated side by side and evolved simultaneously. Rural Alsatians participated in the general transformation from nineteenth-century clothing practices to twentieth-century ones. The encroachment of modern systems of clothing production and sales was paralleled by a gradual evolution of the goods themselves. This chapter will connect the modernization of rural dress practices that occurred in Alsace with the changes in clothing production and distribution in order to explore the relationship between style and the underlying systems of production and consumption.

Examining rural dress as a commodity depends on its consideration as an example of material culture. This provides a different set of information than viewing its appearance in visual representations. It also demands different forms of source material. Understanding historical dress benefits enormously from examining surviving garments in museum and personal collections. Odile Schmitt's wedding dress, for example, provides a more nuanced picture of how regional dress actually looked than illustrative plates or genre painting. The pairing of the seemingly cosmopolitan bodice and skirt with the regional coiffe and apron complicates the sharp divisions between these categories of dress. It also is more instructive to see the garment itself than to see the photographs of it taken in the 1910s—the blue color becomes apparent as does the suppleness and shimmer of the ribbed silk and the dimensional quality of the contrasting black jet trim. Situating these nuances of stylistic choices within their historical context depends on supplementing surviving costumes with written documents. As clothing was an important commodity, its progress from production to consumption was recorded by a number of businesses and government bodies. Traces of the system of clothing production emerge from an examination of a range of written clues from department store records, mail order catalogues, newspaper advertisements, and the records of the Chamber of Artisans. Some of the most fruitful sources are notarial acts. The material circumstances of the wearer shaped urban and rural dress alike, and notarial acts serve as a unique means of examining this relationship between material circumstances and dress. These documents recorded the full range of financial and personal transactions across all socio-economic lines, including inventories taken after death, auction records, marriage contracts, and bankruptcy reports. The inventories after death are particularly useful because they contextualize a person's wardrobe among the complete record of their possessions. By listing the items in people's wardrobe and affixing prices to them, the inventories help answer three basic questions: what types of garments did nineteenth-century rural Alsatians wear; how many articles of clothing did they own; and how much were those pieces worth?

Basic Components of Rural Alsatian Wardrobes

The notary in Truchtersheim, which is situated about 10 miles northwest of Strasbourg, served the villages throughout the area known as the Kochersberg. The Truchtersheim inventories sampled from a broad swath of the population, including a range in occupations and wealth. Because the majority of the inventories were done for people who died leaving minor children, they recorded the possessions of people in the prime of life. This fact favors the representativeness of the inventories because they record the same stage of life. Nearly all the inventories refer to clothing, although the level of detail recorded by the notary ranged from a blanket valuation of all clothing to detailed accounting of each article of clothing.

The descriptions of items listed in the wardrobes reveal that rural clothing was composed of a number of basic pieces. Both men and women wore a shirt or *Hemd*, which would have served as the undergarment worn as the base layer against the skin. Men's shirts were long, roughly to the knee, and extended under the pants as well as the jacket. As a woman's garment, this element is often referred to in French or English as a chemise and would have been even longer than the man's shirt. These items would not only be worn during the day but also doubled as nightshirts. Shirts appeared in almost every inventory in which clothing was itemized confirming that this was an absolutely essential item and making them the most useful point of comparison among inventories. The shirts never appeared singly; every wardrobe included multiple shirts. As the undergarment, the shirt was the article of clothing that would become dirty and would need to be washed. It would also protect the more valuable outer garments. With very few exceptions the inventories did not mention the materials of these garments. In the late nineteenth century, they may have been linen, cotton, or a mixture.

The descriptions of the actual garments were very limited and rarely mentioned materials, color, or decoration. The absence of such details complicates efforts to draw concrete links between the inventory records and the appearance of the clothing in order to determine whether these skirts and dresses were in the distinctive styles associated with the region and how they might have changed over time. In some instances, the choice of words provides important insights into the clothing. In the inventories from 1875, the principal woman's garment was usually described as a "skirt" (*Rock*). The German word *Rock* replaces the French *jupe* that had appeared in the inventories from 1870 when the language was French. Whereas nearly all of the women's inventories in French also included a *casaquin*, which was the term for a sort of jacket or bodice, only a few of the inventories in German seem to indicate a bodice. The infrequency of any reference to the bodice suggests that the word *Rock* was being used to indicate not just the skirt but also the bodice. Examples of skirts from the collection of the Musée Alsacien demonstrate the incorporation of the bodice into the skirt. The corselet is attached to the skirt and would go over the shirt, but it functions more like suspenders than a true bodice (Figure 3.3).

An examination of extant garments in the collections of the Musée Alsacien and the Musée d'Art et d'Histoire de Saverne provides more insights into the distinctive features of women's bodices. Both of the collections include a number of bodices that are catalogued as *casaquin* or *Kaseweck*, the German or Alsatian equivalent. Each collection has bodices of a type that closely resembled fashionable bodices of the 1860s. A patterned purple silk taffeta bodice from the village of Geispolsheim that is now in the collection of the Musée Alsacien showcases many of the distinguishing features of these bodices which represent a blend of urban and regional elements[2] (Plate 13). The neckline is round, fitted close to the neck, and edged with piping. The bodice opens at center front and fastens with a row of hooks and eyes. The sleeves are long, and the relative fullness is drawn in at both the shoulder and wrist with shirring. These

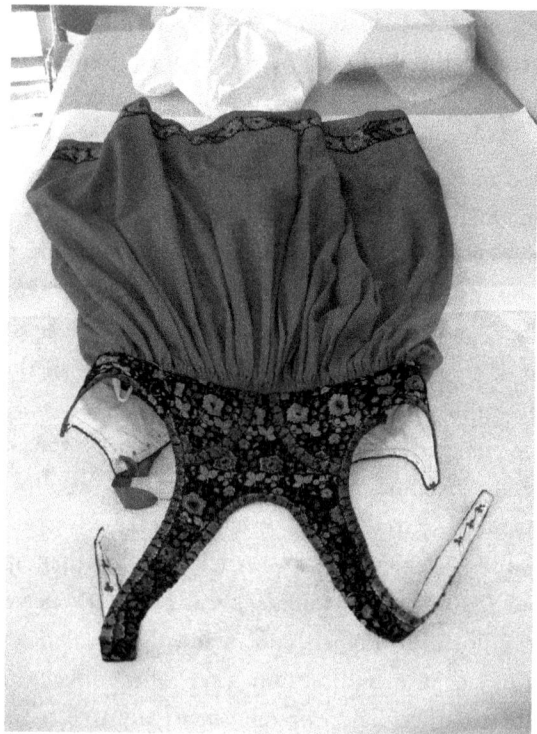

Figure 3.3 Attached skirt and corselet. Collection of the Musée Alsacien de Strasbourg.

parallel rows of gathering stitches are the most distinctive decorative feature on the piece. While the basic cut of these bodices, all of which are made of silk, closely corresponds to the cut of urban bodices from the 1860s, particularly the round neck, waistline, and placement of the boning, the shirring at the shoulders and wrists would not have been fashionable since the 1840s. The persistence of shirred sleeves on these bodices clearly distinguished them from urban dress. While the luxurious material, boning, and piping were all typical of urban dress of the mid-nineteenth century, the wearing of such bodices seems to have continued in rural Alsace for decades after the urban prototypes lost favor. Similar fitted bodices with shirred sleeves appear in a number of photographs by the Alsatian artist Charles Spindler. Spindler's photograph of a pair of girls in Geispolsheim dressed for a festival shows the sleeves of the seated girl, which were shirred at the wrists (Figure 3.4). The continued appearance of similar bodices in photographs by Spindler who worked in the 1880s and 1890s attests to the slow evolution of rural clothing. This

Figure 3.4 Charles Spindler, Girls in Geispolsheim wearing shirred sleeves, ca. 1890s. Spindler Archives.

retention of "outdated" features did not mean that regional dress remained fixed over time. Furthermore the elements that seemed to lag behind the more rapidly changing urban dress were not necessarily those associated with the stereotypical image of dress from the region. Examining pieces from museum collections complicate the picture of what regional dress actually looked like and how it evolved over time.

Shift to Coordinating Outfits

A shift in terminology begins to appear by the 1880s that suggested that there was a transition in what women were wearing. Gradually women's clothing was being described as dresses and outfits rather than skirts and tops. Rather than a simple substitution of one word for another there was an overlap of the terms, suggesting that what were described as skirts before were not simply being considered as part of an outfit later. All of the women's inventories from 1895–7 use "dress" or "ensemble" (*Kleider*) rather than "skirt" (*Rock* or *Kutte*). This shift from describing skirts to dresses paralleled the changes seen in the jackets. The *casaquin* began as a separate piece that could be worn as a jacket over the skirt and corselet. By the 1880s, the *Kaseweck* had become a coordinated bodice and no longer needed to be listed as a separate item on the inventory since it was subsumed into the ensemble.

The idea of coordinating garments did not characterize mid-nineteenth-century Alsatian clothing. An examination of surviving examples of regional dress reinforces the idea that the garments were not preserved as entire ensembles. Furthermore, the lack of matching even within single items speaks to this consideration of individual components rather than the ensemble. The elements of trimming on skirts and corselets were rarely coordinated. The trim around the edges of the shoulder straps rarely matched the material of the corselet or the skirt, nor did it match the trim around the hem of the skirt. In a similar manner, the apron, shawl, bonnet, and stomacher were not made from the same material or trimmings. This lack of coordination stood in contrast to urban women's clothing styles in which trimmings were carefully matched to dress fabrics. At the middle of the nineteenth century, women's fashions favored one-piece dresses in which skirts and bodices were attached. By the 1860s, women's cosmopolitan outfits increasingly consisted of matching but separate skirts and bodices. The shift in descriptions in the inventories to entire outfits by the end of the nineteenth century suggests a similar but slightly delayed adoption of coordinated outfits. Just as the inventories reveal a change from women's wardrobes being composed of skirts and bodices to being complete outfits, the photographic record also reveals that the fundamental garments that make up special occasion dress became a coordinated skirt and a bodice. The wedding costume of Odile Hartmann, described above, further demonstrated this evolution. The bodice that Odile Hartmann wore matched the material of the skirt. Even if the rural outfits were not exactly fashionable, the way the pieces were coordinated reflects the influence of urban clothing practices on rural dress practices.

A parallel shift toward grouping clothing into outfits occurred in men's inventories as well. Through the 1870s the inventories simply listed pants, vests, and jackets. This formula continued across the change in language in 1873. As in the case of women's inventories, the inventories from 1880 included both those which enumerated each article of clothing and those which presented complete suits, using the terms *Kleid* or *Anzug*. Of the twelve men's inventories analyzed from 1880–1, six listed complete suits and five listed component parts while one listed both a suit and a pair of pants. The inventories from 1895–7 showed much less variation in terminology.

The addition of an indication about the clothing's use accompanied the shift to listing complete outfits. Among the inventories analyzed, the designation of occasion did not appear in women's inventories until the 1890s. In those analyzed from 1895–7, each woman's inventory listed at least two complete outfits, which were designated for workday, Sunday, or feast day. For the men, such designations appeared earlier. In the inventories from 1880–1, the variations in whether to list clothing in outfits or as individual garments occurred alongside variations in designations. In addition to the two words for suit, one inventory described the suit as a "church suit" (*Kirchenanzug*) while most used the term "Sunday suit" (*Sonntagskleid*). Similarly the less formal suit appeared alternately as a "workday suit" (*Werktagsanzug* or *Werktagskleid*) or an "everyday suit" (*Alltagskleid*.) These variations almost certainly did not denote material differences between the items. By the mid-1890s, these variations had disappeared. Every man's inventory from this period, with the one exception mentioned above, listed either one Sunday suit and one workday suit or just one Sunday suit. The shift in terminology reflected a conceptual shift from considering clothing as individual pieces to conceiving of them as outfits and connecting those outfits to specific uses.

The practice of describing clothing by occasion was characteristic of urban dress practices, but in these inventories the outfits described were likely regional dress. Although the descriptions are limited, it is reasonable to assume that for the women's inventories "Sunday dress" (*Sonntagskleid*) and "feast day dress" (*Festtagskleid*) described outfits that corresponded to the quintessential Alsatian regional dress. The appearance of such designations in the inventories coincided with the use of other distinctive vocabulary, particularly in relation to women's caps. The inventories from the 1870s simply listed caps (*Kappe*) without any modification or elaboration. By 1880, references to the bow begin to appear. For instance, the inventory for the wife of Kilian Triebel, a carpenter in Dingsheim, includes four caps with bows (*Kappen mit Schleife*).[3] The inventories from 1895–7 frequently list *Bendel or Bendelskappen* meaning "ribbon" or "ribbon caps." These entries obviously referred to the quintessential Alsatian headdress with the large bow. The inventory of Maria-Magdalena-Leonie Kieffer, the wife of a farmer in Dossenheim, made the link between the bow caps and special occasion dress explicit by specifying that her outfits for feast days and Sundays included bows.[4] The inventories thus include vocabulary that distinguished the items as distinctly Alsatian.

This transition to evaluating rural clothing according to the occasion for which it was worn coincided with the period of increasing interest among intellectuals in regional dress. Through the 1870s, such elements as caps and aprons were likely viewed as humble peasant dress that did not warrant special mention. The shift in terminology that emerged in the inventories through the 1880s occurred at the same time as the emergence of the movement among folklorists to study regional customs and costumes.[5] This regional and national movement to document regional dress led to a greater awareness of the distinctiveness of these forms of dress. Furthermore the proliferation of images of *l'Alsacienne* in propaganda heightened popular consciousness of Alsatian regional dress. The shift in how rural dress was described in the inventories through the 1880s occurred at the same time that folklorists and anthropologists were beginning to frame their own systematic approach to documenting these styles. The movement that sought to document rural dress practices may well have shaped how rural Alsatians viewed their own clothing styles.

Just as there were descriptions of quintessentially Alsatian regional dress among the wardrobes listed in the inventories, there were inventories that clearly listed urban dress. Margaretha Lapp, the wife of Michael Reyss, a farmer in Quatzenheim (Truchtersheim), owned one silk dress as well as "two other dresses and a skirt."[6] The reference to the material, silk, clearly distinguishes this dress not just from her two others but the dresses in the other inventories. The inclusion of the adjective in this case suggests that the dresses listed elsewhere were not silk. This inventory is remarkable for its relative size and value. However, despite the likelihood that at least some of the dresses were consistent with urban styles, evidence also suggests that she did have regional dress as well. Among the items listed were shawls, kerchiefs, aprons, and caps. This wardrobe in fact points out the complexity of rural clothing at this time. Rather than a simple dichotomy between urban, cosmopolitan dress and regional dress, there was very likely a range of options. It is possible that she wore a silk dress as her best dress for Sundays or feast days, but she may have worn a headdress and a silk apron with it.

Quantity and Value of Clothing

The inventories do not simply provide insights into what people wore, but also into how much clothing people owned. The inventory of Margaretha Lapp is remarkable not only for the descriptions of clothing but for the sheer quantity of garments listed. Her total wardrobe, which was valued at 143.20 Marks stood in sharp contrast to the inventories at the low end of the economic spectrum, such as that of Ludwig Hammacher, a day laborer in the village of Pfettisheim. His wardrobe listed in an 1875 inventory included one jacket, one pair of pants, two shirts, one pair of shoes, and a blouse worth a total of 6 M. His wife, Catharina Kaiser, had owned one overskirt, two underskirts, two shirts, one pair of shoes, and one cap worth a total of 8 M.[7] This couple's clothing represented close to the bare minimum. Such inventories attest to the wide range of material wealth in Alsace. Furthermore, they provide context for the wardrobe by outlining a person's occupation and range of possessions.

It is valuable to analyze the differences between the inventories of people of modest means with those of greater affluence. Such a comparison provides insights into patterns of consumption across the economic spectrum. While differences in the overall value of the wardrobes stemmed from both differences in the number of items and in the value of each item, the variations in the number of items most clearly correlate to differences in overall value. There is a direct relationship between the number of items (specifically shirts) and the overall value of the wardrobe: those people with greater means had more items of clothing. The value of individual shirts in the wardrobes was not as clearly correlated with the overall value of the wardrobe. Made of either cotton or linen, the shirt or chemise did vary in quality as indicated by variations in their valuation. The true range of values for shirts within each inventory cannot be fully evaluated because they are added together in most cases. A few of the inventories divide the shirts into categories, generally white and colored. In these instances, the white shirts were worth more than the colored shirts.

The overall average cost per shirt for the Truchtersheim inventories was roughly 1 M. Half of the wardrobes had an average value per shirt of less than 1 M. In nearly a third of the inventories the average value per shirt was exactly 1 M and in the remaining inventories (roughly 20 percent) the values were between 1.20 M and 2 M. The reality for most Alsatians then was that their shirts were most likely quite plain and coarse, because the variation in value of shirts was remarkably small. The small range in values also suggests that there was little relationship between the person's wealth and the value of their shirts. The numbers bear this supposition out. The inventories with shirts valued at more than 1 M each were mostly among the people whose overall wardrobe was at the high end. However, several people with extensive wardrobes also had shirts worth less than 1 M. Those who could afford it would buy more shirts but not necessarily better shirts. The pattern that emerges from the inventories is one where clothing was a necessity and rarely an extravagance. The benefits of having more shirts outweighed the luxury of having very fine shirts.

While men and women certainly dressed differently, the average size and value of women's wardrobes did not differ significantly from those of men, although because these inventories were performed for those people who chose to have a prenuptial marriage contract, the sample may have favored the inclusion of women who had relatively high means. The median number of shirts did not vary significantly between men and women. Likewise, the median total value of the wardrobes was comparable. There was, however, much more variability in the value of women's wardrobes. Men's wardrobes mostly fell in a fairly narrow range between 10 and 30 M. In fact 70 percent of the men's wardrobes fell within this range, while 15 percent were above and 15 percent were below.[8] In sharp contrast, only 38 percent of women's wardrobes were within this range, while 27 percent were below and 35 percent were above.[9] The most modest wardrobes belonged to women, including Anna Brucker, a widow who only had 1.5 M worth of clothing,[10] and Margaretha Berst, the wife of a farmer, who only had 3 M worth of clothing.[11] At the other extreme, the most extensive and expensive wardrobes also belonged to women. The most valuable wardrobe belonged to Margaretha Lapp.[12] The total value of her clothing was 143.20 M, including a dozen shirts worth 24 M, but she only had three complete dresses and one skirt. Comparing the inventories of women to those of men reveals broader insights about their relative economic circumstances. Among the wealthy, women's wardrobes attest to the emergence a consumerism in which women were the primary target.

Among the inventories analyzed, there were four in which the wardrobes of both husband and wife were accounted for in the same inventory. Of these four cases, three had the total value of the two wardrobes differing by no more than 2 M. In the fourth case, the wife, Maria Josephina Heydmann, had a total wardrobe valued at 52 M while her surviving husband declared his own wardrobe to be worth 22 M.[13] The three couples with evenly matched wardrobes owned at most 20 M each of clothing. Working with limited means, both the men and women ended up with similarly valued wardrobes. In contrast, the more affluent couple showed the greater divergence of clothing. With greater means at their disposal, clothing could be more variable and individual. At the more affluent end of the spectrum gendered differences in consumer practices began to appear.

While the shirt was a basic piece that varied little in quality or cost, the same was not true for the suits or dresses. The variability and inconsistencies among inventories in how these garments were described make the sort of statistical analysis performed for the shirts impossible. However, it is very clear that there was a significant range in how much a suit or dress was worth. In the inventories from the 1870s, when the individual pieces were entered separately rather than grouped, the pants could range from less than a Mark to as much as 5 M. The jackets had a similar range between a few pennies (*pfennige*) to up to 6 M. Women's dresses tended to be in the 3–8 M range. By the 1880s, as the inventories began to list outfits by occasion, the differences between Sunday best and everyday clothes are easier to quantify. The values of outfits not only varied person to person, but individuals had clothing that varied significantly in value. For most inventories, the value of the Sunday outfit could be twice that of the workday outfit.

Some of the inventories include not only Sunday and workday clothes but also a separate entry for "feast day dress." Invariably this latter category is valued more highly than the other two. While the conventional wisdom about regional dress maintains that villagers wore distinct outfits according to the liturgical calendar, an analysis of people's wardrobes suggests that such distinctions were unlikely. The possession of a special occasion dress beyond that for Sunday was the exception rather than the rule.

Not only do the inventories permit comparison among wardrobes, but they also enable the wardrobe to be situated among the totality of a person's possessions. Most inventories, particularly those in which there has been a marriage contract, indicate the total amount of moveable goods owned by the couple. This communal property often consisted largely of livestock and crops. In general the most valuable item was a cow or calf, and very few of the inventories surveyed did not list at least one. The value of the cows ranged from 100 M to 250 M. In rural Alsace, not only farmers owned livestock. Masons, shoemakers, and farriers are among the many artisans whose property included cows and calves. The prevalence of livestock and crops throughout the inventories is a testament to the significant portion of the region's wealth that was in agriculture. The amount of these rural Alsatians' resources that were invested in livestock and in furnishings, such as beds, supports the assumption that, although many rural Alsatians were well off, theirs was not a consumer culture in which wealth was easily liquid and disposable. The conventional rural pattern of clothing ownership entailed few garments but ones that were relatively valuable. The investment in a relatively limited number of ensembles for Sunday or festivals demonstrated the priority that participation in local observances held for rural Alsatians.

In tracing the changes in wardrobes over time, one might expect to see an increase in the number of garments people owned and a decrease in the value. Such a change would be consistent with changes in urban consumption patterns in which access to goods such as clothing improved and prices dropped. A comparison of the number of shirts in wardrobes in 1875, 1880–1, and 1895–6 reveals that the number of shirts did indeed increase. In 1875 the wardrobes had an average of 4.8 shirts per wardrobe. In 1880–1 the average was 7.6 shirts per wardrobe; by 1895–6 the average had increased to 9.2 shirts per wardrobe. Similarly, the average price per shirt also declined slightly over time: from 1.20 M in 1875 to 1.00 M in 1880–1 and 0.84 M in 1895. Yet these statistics are based on a small number of inventories, and the variation among individual inventories makes it possible for a few data points to sway the averages significantly. While such considerations do limit the reliability of these statistics, the general overall trend does correspond with the expected pattern. These findings suggest that rural Alsatians gradually followed urban patterns in changing their consumption patterns toward the end of nineteenth century.

Evolution of Special Occasion Wear

The quantifiable changes in clothing that the inventories document are subtle, but they support the idea that regional dress practices were changing. Surviving photographs of rural clothing further bolster the argument that rural clothing underwent a transformation. While few photographs documented rural clothing before the 1880s, such photography became much more widespread through the 1890s and the first decades of the twentieth century.[14] The events that would have warranted special clothing were those very events that were most likely to be photographed. Weddings were well-documented events, and they were one of the occasions where regional dress persisted the longest.

A photograph from the 1904 wedding of André Muller and Eve Irrmann in Berstett is representative[15] (Figure 3.5). The bride and groom sat in the center of the front row, and more than forty guests flanked the couple. The bride wore regional dress. Her head was covered with an enormous headbow, her shoulders were draped in a shawl, and an apron concealed her skirt. These accessories obscured her dress itself. Of the twenty or so women included in the photo, only two were not wearing regional dress. The other women, young and old, were dressed in the same manner as the bride: with caps, shawls, and aprons. While the overwhelming majority of the women were dressed in regional dress, the inclusion of the women dressed in urban styles attests to the lack of isolation of these rural communities. This pattern is clear through all of the photographs studied.[16] The wedding guests included a mix of women in regional dress with others who are dressed in cosmopolitan styles. The photographic record testifies to the fact that the preservation of regional dress occurred alongside clear alternatives.

Figure 3.5 Wedding of André Muller and Eve Irrmann in Berstett, 1904. From *Berstett: Un village pittoresque du Kochersberg* (Strasbourg: Editions Coprur, 1993), p. 161.

One of the foreshadowing elements of the Muller wedding photograph was the children's dress. All four of the girls positioned in the front of the picture were dressed in urban styles. None of them wore the regional coiffe. They even forsake the regional hairstyle with the center part; instead, they have their hair pulled directly back from their forehead. Although most of the women continued to dress themselves in the regional manner, none of them dressed their children in that way. This pattern was present in every wedding photograph examined from this period from the area where the large headbow was worn. Although young women faithfully wore the regional dress, the generation born after 1900 dressed in urban styles.

The men of this region also dressed in a way that was nearly indistinguishable from urban dress. This photograph, like all of the wedding photos studied, shows that while women continued to dress in regional styles, men in Kochersberg no longer did so by the turn of the century. The pattern by which men abandoned regional styles before they disappeared among women was not exclusive to Alsace. In fact, this general trend could be seen across Europe and beyond. This pattern likely related to men's participation in work outside of the home. Men's occupations dictated their clothing, and when men dressed in their finest clothes such as for Sunday services or a wedding, they conformed to urban conventions. Like most if not all systems of dress, regional dress was a strongly gendered system. Men and women did not simply dress differently but according to an entirely different set of rules. Men dressed according to their occupation while women dressed according to their religion and village. Although folk dress for Alsace preserved a characteristic man's style for the Kochersberg, these styles seem to have disappeared altogether by the 1880s. Women's styles continued to evolve for a few more decades before being largely abandoned.

Development of Retail in Alsace

The replacement of regional styles of dress by urban styles coincided with changes in retail in which the case of Alsace was typical. By the 1880s and 1890s, a number of retailers throughout Alsace offered a selection of dress fabrics and ready-to-wear garments. These operations were consistent with the business model for department stores that predominated throughout Germany at the time. The development of department stores and the clothing industry in Germany followed a slightly different course than those in France. While in France, the development of department stores began in Paris and radiated outwards to large provincial cities, in Germany many of the early department stores were located in smaller cities with populations under 100,000.[17] These early stores between the 1870s and 1890s were basically large *Spezialgeschäft*, or specialty stores. Although they maintained greater specialization and did not have multiple departments like early French department stores, these early German retailers included many retailing innovations such as fixed prices, low profit margins, and abundant advertisements.[18] The shift in retail development whereby department stores opened in large cities began in the 1890s but truly took hold after 1900.[19]

The Alsatian specialty stores of the 1880s and 1890s clearly shared such ideas as fixed prices and low profit margins with larger department stores and also made generous use of advertising. Rather than department stores in which there were several different departments, these stores, which were characteristic of early German department stores of the period, were essentially large specialty stores.[20] Strasbourg saw the largest concentration of these specialty stores in Alsace, but in accordance with the trend across Germany, smaller towns such as Saverne and Wissembourg had stores which adopted many of the new commercial principles. Despite the clear link in the public imagination between fashion and France, the development of clothing stores in Alsace followed the German model rather than the French one.

The principal strategy for department stores was to sell a large volume of goods with a low markup. This system satisfied demand for lower priced goods that were within the means of a broader swath of the population. The department stores provided goods that were not high in price but were also not high in quality. Within the urban context, the market for high-quality, luxury goods continued to be met by smaller-scale boutiques. While Paris saw the early introduction of department stores, it remained renowned for the production and sales of high-end, luxury goods.

The differences between French and German retail strategies developed alongside differences in the clothing production as well. While the clothing industry in Paris included a concentration of high-end production including haute couture, Berlin supplied clothing for a broader range of income levels. The growth of the clothing industry in Germany received a boost in the wake of the Franco-Prussian War, which interrupted the clothing industry in Paris. International customers in the United States, England, the Netherlands, and Switzerland who had depended on French exports turned to German exports.[21] Berlin developed a wholesale clothing industry, which sold to retailers rather than directly to customers. The clothing produced in Berlin was widely exported, even to Paris.²² While the clothing industry in France was strongly concentrated in Paris, that of Germany was more diffuse. Berlin was the main center of clothing production, but there were also smaller centers in a number of cities including Munich and Breslau.²³

The largest number of these larger-scale retailers in Alsace was in Strasbourg. Even the advertisements for newspapers outside of Strasbourg, such as the *Weissenburger Wochenblatt*, regularly featured advertisements for fabric and clothing stores in Strasbourg. Three businesses in particular were frequent advertisers during the 1880s: Maison Wolff frères, A. Pfister, and J. L. Erlenbach. Each of these stores sold a variety of fabrics and also specialized in a particular range of clothing. While these three businesses advertised fixed low prices, they were not truly department stores. The concentration in a particular specialty was different from the large-scale emporia found in Paris, which would have offered all of these different goods in one store, but typical of stores in Germany. While Strasbourg offered a high concentration of clothing and fabric stores, there were also similar establishments in other towns. Wissembourg had Samuel Gerschel's shop and Fohlen-Troller, while Saverne had A. Erlich's and E Heinrich. The reach of these larger-scale retailers in Alsace was not limited to Strasbourg and these stores would have been accessible to the majority of Alsatians in rural areas.

The sort of large-scale store specializing in dress fabrics that were the forerunners of department stores were not necessarily incompatible with the preservation of traditional styles. In fact, advertisements do reveal that stores sold materials and goods intended specifically for traditional dress. One such example was Michel Biedermann's store in Pfaffenhoffen. According to Biedermann's letterhead from a 1918 correspondence, the store specialized in fabrics for women's and men's clothing, notions, trimmings, yarn, and *Elsässische Trachtenartikel*.²⁴ Biedermann was the uncle of Jean-Paul Sartre. The young Sartre spent the years of the First World War in Pfaffenhoffen with his aunt and uncle. In his diaries kept during 1939–40 when he was stationed in Alsace, Sartre describes returning to look at his uncle's store: "I found myself in front of a big ochre construction, very ugly, with slate roofs, turrets and gables: it was the Biedermann emporium."²⁵ The store was clearly an imposing structure, and the choice of the word "emporium" confirms that it offered a wide variety of goods. The variety of items stocked by the shop suggests that the products were intended the production of clothing, either for home sewers or for professional dressmakers and tailors.

The fact that the availability of materials for regional dress received special mention is noteworthy. Alsatian regional dress was not simply assembled from the same materials as cosmopolitan dress, but the materials were manufactured rather than being homemade. For example, by the early 1900s the ribbons for the headbows were at least a foot wide. This ribbon as well as the ribbon that trimmed the skirts and stomachers would have been specially stocked. One of the popular styles for aprons was composed from a striped fabric with an elaborate woven pattern. This type of weaving was done on a jacquard loom. The photograph by Spindler of the woman in Hunspach shows that although her dress rigorously adheres to the traditional style of dress in the Outre-Forêt, the beautiful apron was woven on a jacquard loom (Figure 3.6). The preservation of regional dress depended not just on its continued production but on the continued production and availability of its component parts.

Many stores in villages across Alsace must have stocked the ribbons, fabrics, and shawls that were the component elements of regional dress. In 1909, Wolff-Liebschütz in Strasbourg took out an ad listing a variety of wares including silks and woolens for women's blouses and clothing, linens, carpets, linoleum, bridal

Figure 3.6 Charles Spindler, Woman in Hunspach wearing apron of jacquard woven textile. Spindler Archives.

trousseaux, cloth for men's suits, and men's shirts.[26] The store also offered a special department dedicated to *Elsässische Landestrachten*. The sales of Alsatian regional dress in the center of Strasbourg at this late date, however, seems less a continuation of a traditional practice than an effort to allow Alsatians to participate in their heritage. This decontextualization of the regional dress into an urban location suggests that it may have been for folk dress rather than for its traditional use in religious occasions such as Sunday services. The final line of the ad reads "*Auch nach Mass*," suggesting that the *Tracht* was available both made to order (*nach Mass*) and ready-made. The availability of ready-made traditional dress was clearly a departure from tradition. The interpretation that this store sold Tracht as a sort of souvenir or costume is confirmed by the last item listed among the store's goods: Alsatian dolls. The folklorization of costume had reached the point where dolls dressed in costumes were sold as tourist souvenirs. The selling of dolls suggests a further level of the commodification of regional dress. In its original usage, regional dress is intended to be worn by the owner and serves an extension and reflection of who they are. However as a costume for a doll the dress does not reflect its owner's identity. The doll's dress is even more decontextualized than folk costume purchased by urban Alsatians for wear in a festival or parade. The dolls were collectibles that allowed the owners to possess a piece of Alsatian culture without presenting themselves as Alsatian. The abundance of goods available in department stores and the resulting consumerism changed the relationship between Alsatians and regional dress.

Although department stores dominated retail in Paris and a number of German cities by the 1880s, at this period in Alsace, the larger stores were only gaining a foothold. Traditional dress practices persisted alongside the reorganization of retail for several decades. The introduction and development of department stores in Alsace were gradual processes as was the introduction of urban, cosmopolitan styles. Between the first department stores in the 1870s and the disappearance of regional dress in the years before the First World War was a transitional period. The specialty stores selling fabrics and trimmings were certainly not inconsistent with distinctive regional dress practices. In fact, the greater accessibility of goods paralleled the growth of the headbows themselves. Although the arrival of department stores ultimately ushered in the introduction of homogenized cosmopolitan fashion, the extravagance of Alsatian costumes reached its peak with the introduction of large-scale retail and industrially produced goods. In this sense modernization through the availability of manufactured goods served to shape regional dress rather than eliminate it.

While the organization of retail in Alsace more closely followed the German than the French model, Alsatians admired French styles and looked to France for inspiration and for imports. The influence of Parisian stores such as *Au Bon Marché* and the *Grands Magasins du Louvre* first reached the provinces through the development of mail order catalogues. By the 1870s, these stores published catalogues that included images and descriptions of various garments. A catalogue from *Au Bon* Marché includes a lengthy explanation of its shipping costs and policies. For shipments to France, Alsace-Lorraine, Germany, Belgium, Holland, Switzerland, England, Scotland, and Ireland, the packages with a value over 25 francs would be sent *franco de port* to the residence.[27] Further precisions covered shipments to the Austro-Hungarian Empire, Italy, Corsica, and Algeria. These shipping policies attest to the extent of the market for department stores. The special mention of Alsace-Lorraine was obviously due to the French reluctance to simply consider it as part of Germany and clearly indicates that Alsatians were customers of Parisian department stores at this time.

Advertisements from Alsatian newspapers attest to the market penetration of these French department stores into Alsace. In 1882 an ad for Au Bon Marché announcing the new catalogue for the upcoming season appeared in the *Weissenburger Wochenblatt*.[28] The ad was written entirely in German as was the rest of the newspaper. Readers were invited to request the catalogue to be sent free of charge and could receive samples of their silk, wool, and printed fabrics for free upon request. The following year, Les Grands-Magasins du Printemps announced in the same paper that it was inaugurating a new store along the rue du Havre and the boulevard Haussmann. This ad offered to send its newest catalogue for free to anyone who requested it by sending a postcard to its offices in Paris. While the terms the two rival department stores offered were similar—free shipping on purchases above 25 francs—the Printemps ad was written in French rather than German. In fact, the ad stands as the only text in French on the whole page, likely in the whole newspaper. Most readers would have been able to read the French text, but they would have been more comfortable with German. The Au Bon Marché ad was more targeted for the Alsatian audience as evidenced not just by the use of German but also by the reference to an office in Germany.

The French model of large-scale department stores spread to Alsace through the establishment of branches. By the 1890s, a branch of Bon Marché opened in Strasbourg by Jacques Koppel. An ad for this store appears in the *Strassburger Post* in 1893.[29] This ad, which is entirely in German, announces its dress fabrics

(*Kleiderstoffe*) in bold, large type. The emphasis in the ad is on the low prices, which are indicated in similarly large, bold font. The buyer is assured that any woman who buys the silk-blend dress fabric, for example, will be able to make an ultramodern (*hochmodernes*) dress from it. This ad, however, is for fabrics and not for finished garments. In contrast, the 1882 ad for the Paris store had offered not simply fabrics but also toilettes, suits, skirts, petticoats, hats, and shoes. A later ad for the Strasbourg Bon Marché which appeared in *Elsässische Nachrichten* in 1901 indicates that the branch expanded its offerings to include ready-to-wear. The listings for the fabrics had been reduced to one small section of the ad while the other sections refer to the ready-to-wear, which was divided by age and gender. For men and boys, the store offered a complete range of clothing including pants, jackets, and suits. Girls were offered a variety of outerwear including jackets and coats, but also dresses, skirts, and underwear. The range of options for women stopped short of complete dresses, but included not just the outerwear such as jackets, coats, and boleros but also suits, skirts, and blouses.

Just as the ads provide insights into the shopping experience in Alsace in the late nineteenth century, they also shed light on the strong association between fashionable style and French culture. Maison Wolff Frères ran a few different ads. The longest ads were bilingual with the full text written first in French and then repeated completely in German. Maison A. Pfister similarly ran ads that presented the information twice: once in German and once in French. The choice to run a bilingual ad is curious because the editorial portion of the newspaper was entirely in German. It is unlikely that the readers would have been unable to read the German section of the ad, so the decision to include French served a purpose other than presenting the reader with the content. In the case of the Wolff ads, many of the fabrics are described using the same French terms in both translations.[30] In fact, the function of the inclusion of French seems to be that the vocabulary for fashionable clothing and fabrics was in French. The bilingual Alsatian community may very likely have used the French terms for textiles rather than German.

By the 1890s larger Berlin-based stores were advertising in Alsatian papers. In October 1894, the *Strassburger Post* ran an ad for the *Confections-Haus Max Vornstein*, which was based in Berlin. The store was opening a branch in Strasbourg in addition to its other branch in Baden-Baden. As dealers in ready-to-wear, they offered a variety of clothing items, which all seem intended for women. The list read: "Costumes—Manteaux—Jaquettes—Capes—Abendmäntel—Regenmäntel—Robe de chambre—Matinées—Jupons—Blousen." Except for the

Abendmäntel and *Regenmäntel*, every one of these garments is designated with a French word. The rest of the ad, however, is written in German. This ad captures the character of the ready-to-wear industry in which the production occurred largely in Germany and yet marketers wished to link the product with France. While cosmopolitan dress ostensibly transcends geographic boundaries, in reality, the conception of Frenchness developed a close association with fashion and everything chic. This aspect of French national identity was seemingly at odds with the persistence of regional dress as well as regionalism within its boundaries.

Introduction of Department Stores into Alsace

Between 1900 and 1914, Strasbourg saw the development of two major department stores. The first was the Kaufhaus Louvre which developed from the gradual expansion of smaller specialty store J. L. Erlenbach. By the outbreak of the First World War, Kaufhaus Louvre grew to occupy the space that had once been filled by two additional neighboring shops. During the war, the store was renamed Kaufhaus Hohen Steg, likely to eliminate the reference to the quintessentially French Louvre. Following the First World War, the former Kaufhaus Louvre became the Magasins du Louvre, which it remained until 1927 when it received the new name, Grandes-Galeries. The second major department store was known first as the Kaufhaus Modern and unlike its competitor was built from the ground up as part of the urban project known as the *Grande Percée*, which reorganized public space in the Strasbourg.[31] With its numerous departments and grand building, the Kaufhaus Modern was a true department store, but plans for its opening were derailed by the outbreak of the First World War. The building was requisitioned by the city and was used for grain storage.[32] Immediately following the war, the store finally opened as the Magasins Modernes or "MagMod."

Even by the 1920s when the full-scale department stores in Strasbourg were open for business, the clothing production for these department stores continued to be done to order. The building records for MagMod contain the plans completed in 1921 for the *Nähatelier* or *atelier de couture* on the fifth floor.[33] The top floor of the building housed a number of ateliers in addition to the offices for the store's management. The large atelier for couture was designed to support fifteen workers. The existence of this designated space indicates that clothes were made to order right on site at the department store.

Although certainly the store would have stocked ready-to-wear, such items had not replaced custom-made items.

The clothing sold at the Kaufhaus Louvre and the Magasins Modernes was certainly fashionable. An advertisement for the Kaufhaus Modern that ran in 1913 in anticipation of its opening the following year attests to the modern style that it sought to sell (Figure 3.7). The two chic women look out at the grand façade of the building from the opposite side of the wide boulevard. The store was intended as the epitome of urbanism and fashion. The design of this ad contrasts starkly with the designs of ads for the large specialty retailers of the 1880s and 1890s. While those had been entirely text based and sought to attract customers through low prices, this ad is almost entirely dependent on the illustration. Rather than appealing to customers' wallets, Kaufhaus Modern shifted to an appeal to desire for glamor, elegance, and modernity. This concept of modernity was diametrically opposed to the rural parochial styles of regional dress. The reference to exaggeratedly high fashion is underscored by the fact that they appear to be in evening dress rather than attire appropriate for a shopping expedition. Although the new grand boulevard in Strasbourg represented a great achievement in the Imperial German building project, the department store retained a strong association with France, with advertisement in both French

Figure 3.7 Advertisement for Kaufhaus Modern, ca. 1913. Archives de Strasbourg, 5 MW 283.

and German. The illustration offered not just a new shopping experience but also a new vision of Strasbourg itself.³⁴ The advertisement for Kaufhaus Modern was aspirational rather than a reflection of the prevailing culture in Strasbourg. The store itself would not open in one year as promised, but rather more than five years. The progress of Strasbourg toward the sort of modernity that emanated from Paris was slow and made slower by war.

Home-Based Industrial Production

The transformation of the clothing industry in Alsace depended on the widespread availability of textiles, many of which were produced in the region. Alsace is widely known as a center for the industrial production of textiles, but the factory-based industrial weaving and printing that had developed in Mulhouse since the late eighteenth century did not eliminate the persistence of home-based textile production throughout Lower Alsace. Among the principal agricultural products in Alsace were bast fibers, such as hemp and flax that were cultivated in order to be transformed into textiles. The prominence of spinning wheels in the popular image of rural Alsatian life attested to the persistence of cottage industries whereby these raw materials were fashioned into textiles. Rural domestic industry continued through the nineteenth century as largely seasonal activities to supplement income during the winter when farming was less productive. A survey of the number of home workers in each district of Alsace in the 1890s noted such seasonal variations in the statistics.³⁵ The most significant industries performed in homes throughout Alsace were textile and clothing production. The textile production included not just weaving but also such tasks as spinning, knitting, and crocheting. The continued importance of home production to the region's economy which resisted competition from industrial production in factories serves as a parallel to the persistence of regional dress when confronted with cosmopolitan dress. Through the early twentieth century earlier rural customs resisted elimination from seemingly more modern alternatives.

Charles Spindler took a few photographs that show Alsatians engaged in these forms of homework such as weaving and knitting. While weaving was an occupation for men, sock knitting was performed by women and even girls (Figures 3.8, 3.9, and 3.10). It is difficult to date his photographs precisely, but these images were probably taken some time between 1890 and 1910. In the photographs of knitting, the young women appear to be making socks. It is

Figure 3.8 Charles Spindler, Man weaving. Spindler Archives.

possible that they were knitting for their own use, but it is very likely that they were engaged in the activity to provide supplemental income for their families. The socks that are being produced by these girls were rather heavy. Delicate knits for fine silk stockings would have been produced elsewhere on mechanized looms. The area around Troyes in the Champagne region, for instance, was a center for the production of hosiery.[36] These photographs attest to the social aspect of knitting. For expert knitters, it is a task that does not require full concentration, so these girls were free to talk. These home industries attest to the general industriousness of rural life where time was not wasted, even by children.

The Spindler photographs provide a clearer image of these rural cottage industries. The production of textiles and socks supplemented the incomes for rural families. The setting for this work was very much within the house and was integrated into the domestic scene. They also represent a middle ground between homespun and homemade textiles and garments and professionally made products. Labor intensive tasks such as weaving and knitting were not performed in every rural household but rather performed by experienced people.

Material Goods 123

Figure 3.9 Charles Spindler, Girls knitting in doorway. Spindler Archives.

Figure 3.10 Charles Spindler, Girls outside while one knits. Spindler Archives.

The statistics show a decline in the number of people throughout the rural districts who were involved in such cottage industries.[37] Although there was a decline in the number of households that were involved in such occupations as weaving and sock knitting, they were still considerable by the beginning of the First World War. The cottage industries that were thriving by the beginning of the First World War were those related more directly to clothing industry. These opportunities were concentrated around the city of Strasbourg. The concentration of clothing production in cities coincided with the similar concentration of clothing retail. The growth of department stores in Strasbourg was accompanied by an increase in homeworkers involved in the piecework of making clothing. The specific example of the development of the clothing industry in Strasbourg corresponds to the broader trend across Germany. Barbara Franzoi pointed out the shift in clothing manufacturing into an urban industry, which in Germany occurred between 1895 and 1907. As production increased in certain cities, it decreased in small and medium cities.[38] Those sorts of occupations of home workers that were disappearing in the rural areas—particularly weaving but also shoemaking and woodworking—were largely male dominated. Those occupations that were growing and concentrating in urban areas were female dominated. While male jobs moved to urban areas and factories, women's occupations remained out of the public eye, but formed an important sector in the modern economy.

Education and Apprenticeship for Craftspeople

The interests of artisans in Alsace were rewarded with the establishment of the Chamber of Artisans (*Handwerkskammer* or *Chambre de métier*). In 1896, the Imperial Governor of Alsace-Lorraine called for a Commission on Artisans. In his address to the Commission's opening session, the governor said: "In the same way, craft has been displaced into a disagreeable position by the development of machinery and equipment. Handwork is getting ever more replaced and restricted by the machine and the activity of craft is being drawn into ever narrower limits."[39] The efforts to preserve craft in Alsace were closely aligned with similar efforts across Germany. In July 1897, the Reichstag passed a law authorizing the establishment of *Handwerkskammer* and at the end of September, the Commission on Artisans in Alsace decided to establish such a chamber for Alsace-Lorraine.[40] While the underlying motivation was the preservation of handcrafts in the face of mechanization and industrialization, the principal function of the Chamber of Artisans was the regulation of apprenticeships and the establishment of qualification for artisans.

Although the Chamber of Artisans had originally served only male artisans, in 1912 after years of debate, it was decided to admit women.[41] Because most of the occupations that employed female artisans were not ones that also employed men, the Chamber had to develop new rules for these exclusively female occupations. The particular occupations that this effected were dressmakers, milliners, and hairstylists. In May 1913, the Chamber published a description of pieces that women would be tested on for qualification as master in each of these occupations.[42] The dressmakers had to produce as their masterpiece an "elegant ladies" dress, party dress, or "ballgown" and complete an "elegant jacket." In addition to being judged on the workmanship of these pieces, they had to demonstrate knowledge of a range of skills and information. They had to be able to distinguish the major sorts of fabrics including both weave structures and the material as well as recognizing differences in quality and colorfastness. They had to be able to determine the amount of material needed for a dress, have mastery of a good system of cutting, know how to steam and iron, be able to match plaids and stripes, as well as make necessary corrections for a final fitting. Additionally, they had to have "an elementary knowledge of beautiful style and form." It is abundantly clear from the list of skills that these women were preparing for making cosmopolitan clothes and not honing their skills at making regional dress. The efforts to protect the interests of artisans and perpetuate the necessary skills were directed toward the creation of custom, cosmopolitan dress.

The system of teaching sewing skills and preparing the next generation of dressmakers and tailors involved a combination of primary schooling, specialized trade schools, and apprenticeships. The curriculum for Alsatian *Volksschulen* specified that girls receive instruction in sewing and knitting.[43] In her analysis of German primary education of sewing skills for girls, Katherine Kennedy addressed both the motivations for such instruction and its effectiveness.[44] The arguments made at the time in favor of teaching girls stitching and knitting was that it would prepare them for domestic life, but also instill "diligence, patience, precision, orderliness, cleanliness and thriftiness."[45] In practice, the coursework provided inadequate time for practice and did not ultimately successfully prepare girls for future employment. In the 1910s as the school curricula were being re-evaluated in Bavaria, school inspectors took note of complaints that rural girls were not capable of basic handwork.[46] The skills that girls developed from these courses were inadequate for either employment in the sewing trades or even making their own clothing. Both the fact that sewing was introduced into primary education and that potential employers were ultimately dissatisfied with girls' sewing skills suggest that learning to sew was not necessarily integral to home life and girls' upbringing. Clearly many women were not able to make their own clothes and depended on professionals. Dressmakers and tailors were not reserved for bourgeois women in large cities—rather they served a wide range of society, across a wide range of social classes.

While elementary education prepared the groundwork for women to learn to sew, the level that was attained simply through school was not necessarily sufficient for gainful employment. Imperial Germany had a system of continuing education programs (*Fortbildungsschule*) that provided classes to instruct in various professional skills. Rather than being products of centralized government efforts, this system for professional education in Alsace was organized by local actors, including private organizations.[47] The development of programs of continuing education for women served to provide education in skills including sewing to provide them with marketable skills. The *Frauen-Industrie und Fortbildungs-Schule* in Strasbourg, which began classes in the fall of 1903, was established through the efforts of the German Patriotic Women's League (*Vaterländischen Frauenverein* or VFV), one of the largest societies for women in Alsace.[48] The VFV worked to improve the conditions of women, in part through education. The efforts to facilitate women's entry into the workforce were not directed by the state but nevertheless were consistent with the aim of encouraging women's integration into the German nation.

Although the development of the school was organized by the women's club, the curriculum was reviewed by the superintendent for schools in Strasbourg (*Kreisschulinspektor*) who outlined a basic program of classes. The principal motivation for the establishment of this educational program was the training of women for sales positions. In the development of the school's curriculum, the chamber of commerce issued a questionnaire to various shopkeepers across Strasbourg to solicit guidance on requirements for female employees. The proposed course of study included three tracks; in addition to the one aimed at forming women for sales positions, there was also a general program of study and a professional program. It was the general course of study that emphasized sewing skills, including not just sewing, but also mending, dressmaking, hat making, and ironing. The women in this program would have been gaining the skills necessary for jobs that could be done by home workers.

One of the skills that was omitted from the general track was French language. While women working in stores would need to interact with customers and would need a grasp of appropriate vocabulary in both French and German, those women preparing for work from home only needed the necessary vocabulary in German. In fact, the need to teach women German suggests that many of the women entering the program were Alsatian speakers who lacked the skills in either formal German or French for tasks such as correspondence, stenography, and typing that were demanded by the workplace. The inclusion of language training in addition to sewing and accounting indicates the extent to which the introduction of women into the workforce furthered the integration into the nation. Changes in consumer practices undermined distinctive local culture not just in the replacement of distinctive dress with urban fashion, but the more widespread adoption of formal French and German. The classes at the women's *Fortbildungsschule* were open to "daughters of all classes."[49]

The skills taught at the Fortbildungsschule went far beyond the basic instruction covered in the Volksschule. The basic education had only covered handsewing and did not move beyond a basic introduction to cutting. In these continuing education programs women learned how to use sewing machines and learned sophisticated techniques for cutting clothes. They learned how to measure the body, cut pattern pieces, and then make alterations for a final fit. They also learned how to create clothes based on fashion plates. In addition to learning the skills for a dressmaker, they also learned the skills used by a laundress (*Wäscheschneiderin*) which included the production of "whites" including shirts and sheets, in addition to starching and ironing. Students were able to complete as much of the program as they chose. Although completing the entire program would take two years, students had the option of selecting just the courses they wanted. Those students who wished to follow the course of studies in order to become qualified to teach had to complete the entire program.[50] The introduction of department stores and ready-to-wear clothing did not simply affect women as consumers, but provided a variety of occupational opportunities. While sewing was viewed as women's work, girls were routinely educated in all of the necessary skills as a part of growing up. The training was supplied or at least supplemented through the educational system, which developed to prepare women for these increased opportunities.

The development of schools to provide preparation for employment in sewing ultimately came into conflict with the traditional system of apprenticeships. One of the issues the Chamber of Artisans debated in the years immediately after the war was whether professional education could substitute for an apprenticeship as qualification as an artisan. The Chamber made a distinction between state schools and private ones. The latter group included the *Première École de coupe et de couture* in Strasbourg, which advertised in the Alsatian magazine for tailors and dressmakers, *Le Tailleur et la Tailleuse d'Alsace*, offering courses to aspiring seamstresses.[51] The Chamber of Artisans refused to accept such coursework in lieu of a formal apprenticeship although it did accept training from schools run by the state. One of the reasons for the establishment of private sewing schools was an increasing number of women entering the field of dressmaking in the years after the First World War.

The war itself proved to be an interruption to the careers of many artisans and the development of a new generation of skilled craftsmen. Both experienced artisans and potential apprentices were called to serve in the war. Statistics published by the Chamber in 1919 attest to the sharp decline in apprentices from 1913 to 1918.[52] After the war, the Chamber put into place certain allowances to accommodate veterans who wished to return to apprenticeships. The length of the apprenticeships could be reduced: for a two-year apprenticeship, six months could be forgiven, while a three- or four-year apprenticeship could be shorted by a full year.[53] A more general change that was a result of the war was the establishment of a fixed salary for apprentices. While young men had been eligible for auxiliary service to perform industrial work for the war effort, artisanal operations had no equivalent means of attracting talent. Following the war, the Chamber proposed a government subvention to encourage rural artisanal occupations.[54]

The situation of the tailoring trade followed the general pattern for skilled craftsmen overall. In 1913, there were 466 young men apprenticed to be tailors in the Strasbourg district and 734 apprenticed in all of Alsace-Lorraine. By 1918 the number in Strasbourg had dropped to 113 and the overall number had fallen to 172. On the other hand, the statistics for female apprentices showed a very different pattern. While in 1913, Strasbourg had 270 young women apprenticed as dressmakers, by 1918, that number had risen to 360. The number of women apprenticed as milliners showed a similar increase. While male apprentices and masters were called away to the front, women were increasingly needed to work. The period of the war followed soon after women's first admission to the Chamber of Artisans so their numbers may very well have grown through this period regardless of the war; however, the discrepancy between the situation of those trades performed by men and those performed by women is striking. In fact a discrepancy in the number of tailors and dressmakers would persist throughout the interwar period. The survival of custom-made clothing for women but the loss of artisanal tailoring for men underscore the divergent course for men's and women's wear more generally. The two industries were largely separate; custom-made men's clothing was made by men and women's clothing by women. As men left the tailoring trade, the production of clothing for men also became the domain of female workers. The move to ready-to-wear occurred sooner for men than for women; this trend corresponded to the greater persistence of regional dress for women as well.

Apprenticeships in the Interwar Period

Following the Chamber of Artisans' reorganization under the French regime starting in 1919, a principal theme in the annual reports is the declining number of apprentices. The discourse in the first years of French rule was on the tremendous interruption due to the war on the preparation of the next generation of artisans. However, while there was a correction of this problem under peacetime, the 1920s saw a continued decline in artisans. The report from the Chamber of Artisans for 1930 included statistics marking the declining number of apprentices.[55] These statistics do not break down artisans by urban or rural; however, the decline in dressmakers and tailors corresponded with a growth in department stores and ready-to-wear which would have been concentrated in urban areas. The lists of artisans maintained by the Chamber attest to the continued presence of clothing makers in rural villages during this period, but the lack of apprentices meant while these artisans continued their work through the 1930s and 1940s, the next generation would see a significant decline.[56]

The declining number of artisans overall disguises a very different reality for male and female workers in the clothing trades. Between 1913 and 1922, the number of men had fallen by half, but the number of women had doubled.[57] The figures for women would reverse course in the next decade as the number of dressmaking apprentices declined between 1922 and 1930, but there were still nearly twice as many as there had been before the war. The introduction of ready-to-wear and the decline of traditional dress occurred in men's wear well before it occurred in women's wear. Correspondingly women's occupation in custom clothing production persisted and even grew in significant numbers well after comparable men's occupations declined.

The survival of traditional artisans in Alsace through the 1920s and 1930s was supported through the efforts of the Chamber of Artisans as well as the French government. One of the tangible forms of support were monetary awards to needy boys and girls to help defray the expense of an apprenticeship. The grants were given to children of families in difficult circumstances to pursue a rural occupation. In particular many of the recipients came from families with many children. Apprentices in both dressmaking and tailoring were supported through these grants. The process of apprenticeship enabled the preservation of skills across generations. By the 1930s the persistence of these skills was considered in doubt, in part because of difficult economic circumstances.

By 1934 the ongoing efforts to support rural artisans, though grants to apprentices, had shifted to an explicit project to preserve regional dress. At the General Council of the Bas-Rhin, M. Heil offered an amendment to the measure allocating 2,500 francs for encouraging rural artisans, so that special consideration would be given to those tailor apprentices who would learn to make local Alsatian costumes. In his argument for such consideration, Heil contended:

> Our costumes run a certain danger, not because our peasants no longer want to wear them, but above all, because the artisans, that is to say the tailors, no longer want to or are no longer able to make them. Yet when there are no longer tailors in the countryside to cut our costumes, they will cease to exist.[58]

His assertion that the disappearance of regional dress was due to a lack of people willing and able to make them rather than a lack of demand from consumers is provocative and points out the importance of the knowledge and skills of the artisans in saving the disappearing styles. Another member of the Council, Dr. Schalck, agreed that only the older generation of tailors would still accept to make traditional costumes, while the "young refuse to pure and simple."[59] The amendment passed with everyone in agreement.

While the debate in the General Council was expressed in exclusively male terms such as *tailor*, there were female applicants for the grants who were rejected on account of learning ready-to-wear rather than custom-made production techniques. Such rejections confirm that the program to support rural artisans was not simply an effort to provide economic support for those in difficult financial straits but was designed to preserve disappearing trades. The economic challenges that practitioners of these traditional crafts faced were confirmed by comparing the advantages for the girls who chose to work in ready-to-wear where the apprenticeship was shorter and better paid. The intervention of the government in defense of traditional crafts was too little too late. The pressures against the continued practice of rural crafts were numerous and a few hundred francs here and there were inadequate to support rural families' resistance.

Tailoring and Dressmaking in Literature

The clearest view of changing retail experience comes not from government archives and business records but from contemporary literary works. Alsatian theater served as a vehicle for preserving the Alsatian dialect but also captured scenes of daily life. The prominent role filled by tailors and dressmakers as central characters in plays written in Alsatian during the 1920s and 1930s both provides a window into the organization of the trades associated with clothing production and attests to the important place that they held in the Alsatian imagination. The play *Zwei Schweschtere*, which was published in 1926, presents a picture of dressmaker shops in the interwar period.[60] In the play, the shop run by the dressmaker, Madamme Walther, employs four additional women: two workers, Marguerite and Aline, and two apprentices, Lücie and Maria. Marguerite and her younger sister, Charlotte, who does not work in the shop, are the two sisters of the title. The dressmaker shop is furnished with a large cutting table, but it also contains two or three sewing machines, a dress form with a black suit on it, hooks for clothing, and shelves with fabric and boxes. The walls are decorated with fashion plates and patterns. It is clear both from the props such as the sewing machines and fashion plates and from the dialogue itself that the clothing made in this shop would have been cosmopolitan, urban dress. The customer who visits the shop and whose clothes are made and discussed during the course of the first act, Madamme Savalle, is French. The other characters speak amongst themselves in Alsatian but speak with Savalle only in French. The clothes are also described with French expressions such as being *"le dernier cri"* even while the characters are otherwise speaking in Alsatian. The language of the play underscores the complicated navigation the Alsatians made between their local culture and their French nationality. When Savalle is presented with the suit that has been made for her, she complains that the jet buttons are not at all chic. In response to Marguerite's insistence that she had bought the buttons from a Parisienne, Savalle declares *"à moi, elle ne l'aurait pas vendu."*[61] Despite the ostensibly fashionable styles of clothing made by this dressmaker shop in Strasbourg, the Frenchwoman fears that by shopping there she risks wearing out of date styles.

The second act of the play takes place in Marguerite's home and focuses on her sister, Charlotte, who is sewing when the scene opens. The stage directions indicate that there is a sewing machine in the house. Later in the act, the dressmaker, Madamme Walther, brings the work that Marguerite is supposed to finish sewing. The allure of France continues in the second act as Marguerite's sister hopes to get a job in France. She finds a posting in the *Journal des Modes* seeking girls for positions as domestics in Paris. Her mother adamantly opposes her plans to leave Alsace and find work in Paris. The tension in the first act between Parisian style and Alsatian production becomes an even clearer tension between staying in Alsace and leaving for the capital.

In *D'Hochzittshose*, which is set in a tailor's shop, Meckerle, the master tailor, runs a shop that is supported by three employees: Stipfler, the journeyman (*Gsell*) and two apprentices (*Lehrbüe*), Schakoebel and Gueschtl.[62] The set for the tailor shop includes a large worktable strewn with articles of clothing with additional men's garments hanging from a rack (*Kleiderstände*). The plot of the play centers around the eponymous pair of wedding pants that were 10 cm too long. Each of the workers in the shop takes it upon himself to shorten the pants without alerting the other characters, with the result that the pants end up 30 cm too short. The comedy in the play also depends on the tensions and miscommunications between master and apprentices. In light of the sharp decline that had occurred to the tailoring trade following the First World War, it is likely that this play is as much a nostalgic look at traditional life as it is a window into the operations of a tailors shop as late as the 1930s. The comedic village scenes were an idealized vision of life in rural Alsace that was in decline by this period. The tailor's shop which was the main gathering place in this play was a central element in the traditional life of these villages, and its disappearance marked a change in sociability as well as dress practices.

Of the two plays, *Zwei Schweschtere* more accurately captured the contemporary realities of the clothing industry. The play highlighted the powerful tensions between city and country or at least periphery. Despite the recent introduction of department stores into Strasbourg, the small shops with a qualified dressmaker who employs not simply assistants but also apprentices were the predominant source of clothing for Alsatians in Strasbourg as well as in smaller towns and villagers. The young women who were directly employed by the dressmaker and work in the shop were responsible for making the clothing. This organization of labor, however, also depended on work being completed at the home. The world of clothing production was clearly divided into women's work and men's work and this gendered division corresponded to the gender of the customer. Women's clothes were made by women and men's clothes were made by men. Whereas all of the characters in *D'Hochzitthose* were men, all of the characters in *Zwei Schweschtere* are women. The latter play also underscores the widespread circulation of French fashion periodicals in Alsace. Paris loomed large in the public imagination as the center of fashion, at least in the interwar period upon Alsace's return to France. These small shops that operated in the interwar period were a continuation of the means of clothing production that had prevailed in the region throughout the nineteenth century. During Alsace's integration into France in the interwar period, clothing designs increasingly reflected cosmopolitan styles but the intimate, domestic spaces in which the clothing was produced continued through the interwar period. In the economic sphere French nationalism favored cosmopolitan dress while in the realm of propaganda regional dress was presented as a symbol of Alsatian loyalty to the nation.

Conclusion

The disappearance of regional dress was only the most visible component of the transformation in how clothing was bought and sold in rural Alsace. Below this superficial evidence of change, there were profound, systemic changes from how textiles were produced and distributed to how clothing was sized and fitted. The introduction of new retail practices began in large urban areas, particularly Paris and Berlin. While these early stores affected rural areas initially through mail order business, ultimately branches began to open in provincial cities such as Strasbourg and even smaller cities such as Saverne and Wissembourg. As a Reichsland, Alsace was subject to German laws regarding commerce and its experience of these changes in consumption practices closely followed the German model. Despite these structural congruencies with Germany, Alsatians continued to place high value on French goods and style. Even though department stores and ready-to-wear had become established in the opening years of the twentieth century, the prevalence of dressmakers and tailors making custom-made clothing persisted well into the interwar years. In particular women continued to rely heavily on custom-made dresses and the production of such clothes employed a significant number of women. Within organizations such as the Chamber of Artisans that sought to promote the interests of artisans, women were important beneficiaries. Although the number of independent tailors declined sharply in the years following the First World War, women's jobs as dressmakers did not follow a similar pattern. Just as women continued to wear traditional dress well after men had abandoned it, women continued to pursue the traditional craft of dressmaking well after men stopped working as independent tailors.

4

Museum Objects

In 1907, the Musée Alsacien in Strasbourg opened to the public with the stated goal "to assemble objects of all types relating to Alsatian art and popular traditions, to group these objects, to oversee their maintenance and to display them to the public curiosity in a setting specifically set aside for that purpose."[1] This project, initiated by members of the Cercle St.- Léonard, including Pierre Bucher and Charles Spindler, literally took regional dress out of rural Alsace and situated it in the middle of Strasbourg. This decontextualization of rural costumes removed them from their original relationship with their wearers and reframed them in a narrative about the distinctiveness of Alsatian culture. Ultimately, the museum's activities expanded from simply assembling and displaying Alsatian art and popular culture to actively producing and developing it. While certain aspects of modernity such as mass production and department stores threatened the continued existence of folk dress, the development of the museum was itself a product of modern understandings of space, entertainment, tourism, and display.

The idea of a museum that collects humble, everyday objects seems contradictory to the more traditional conception of a museum as the assembly of objects inspiring wonder through their rarity, beauty, and value. The founders of the Musée Alsacien were by no means the originators of the idea of a museum of everyday life. The folk museum draws not from the tradition of art museums but rather is an ethnographic museum, which developed as an offshoot of World's Fairs in the mid-nineteenth century.[2] In fact, museums showcasing regional culture are just one of the many types of museums that owed their introduction or at least, proliferation, to the expositions of the second half of the nineteenth century.[3] The shift toward celebrating quotidian, rural life was a development of the late nineteenth century. The growing acceptance of popular culture as appropriate for museum collections occurred alongside the movement to preserve disappearing rural cultures across Europe.

The origin of the Musée Alsacien is at once representative of the wave of museum building at the turn of the century which resulted in folk museums across Europe while at the same time particular to the unique political situation of Alsace. The generally accepted history of the Musée Alsacien emphasizes the loyalty of the museum's founders to France and their decision to celebrate Alsatian culture as a form of allowable resistance to German authority.[4] They cultivated a uniquely Alsatian regional character as distinct from German allegiance because they could not openly proclaim their loyalty to France. While it is true that the strength of this movement owed much to the highly contested political situation, it is a misrepresentation to characterize it simply as a proxy for suppressed French nationalism. The efforts by locals to preserve and celebrate their regional culture were not effectively leveraged in support of one or the other nation. In fact, the agenda of the museum's founders was at odds with the French use of folk culture that appeared in the national museums.

The political situation of Alsace cannot be ignored when seeking to understand the movement to celebrate traditional culture, but it is not sufficient to understand why the resistance would take this particular form of expression. Both France and Germany proved fertile ground for museums organized on both the national and local level that preserved rural culture widely seen as disappearing. This disappearance was alternately viewed as a sign of progress or regretted as a loss of defining components of local and national character. The competing national and local interests motivating the collection and preservation of rural culture ultimately contributed to the changing meaning of regional dress and its association with political rather than religious affiliation.

Roots of Folk Museums

The critical role of international expositions in the development of ethnographic museums underscores the complexity of the relationship between regional and national identity. World's Fairs represented a scene of competition where each nation defined itself through the display of its industrial products and cultural achievements. They primarily served as showcases for nations to display their technological and industrial progress. The 1867 Exposition Universelle held in Paris was one of the first exhibitions of traditional European costumes and the precursor of museums of European ethnography. On this occasion, in addition to the central exhibition hall, the nations also erected pavilions in the surrounding park.[5] These national pavilions, which would become a standard element in future World's Fairs, provided an opportunity for more elaborate visual displays of architecture as well as material culture such as costumes. Bjarne Stoklund argues that "the international exhibitions were not only a competition in goods, but also in culture."[6] Although the appropriation of regional culture to serve a national agenda may not have originated with the World's Fairs, it certainly received great reinforcement from this forum in which regionalism was displayed as evidence of national character.

The World's Fairs were an opportunity for people from many different nations to gather in one place. It was an environment designed for spectacle and entertainment that presented the diversity of national origins into a tangible, visual display. This very "progress," however, threatened the continued existence of traditional rural life and led to movements throughout Europe to preserve and celebrate these seemingly endangered practices. In 1867, many nations including Prussia, Great Britain, and Spain did not present their vernacular architecture and traditional costumes. Instead, they represent their modernity and progress in their pavilions.[7] The pavilions representing various North African and northern European nations prominently featured traditional architecture. The World's Fairs, in fact, juxtaposed the products of industrial products with those of the disappearing rural cultures. The clash between traditional and industrial culture was visually represented through architecture and display. The context of the World's Fair transformed culture and history into entertainment and something that could be consumed, sometimes quite literally. The experience of foreign cultures was designed to appeal to all the senses. Alongside the pavilions arose restaurants and bars that offered the food of the nations represented.[8] The presentation of the traditional, rural culture was heavily influenced by the desire for spectacle and entertainment shaped by the modern age. Ultimately, the fairs' format for presenting culture effected a transformation in the discipline of anthropology, specifically folklore studies. During the early nineteenth century, folklorists had focused on the less tangible elements of popular culture that made up folklore such as songs, stories, and dialects, but by the second half of the century this emphasis shifted to more tangible elements such as clothing and architecture.[9]

Following up on the popularity of their displays in the fairs, several nations transformed their temporary exhibitions into permanent collections. World's Fairs were ultimately connected to the establishment of national museums with collections of folk costume including ones in France and Germany. The pioneer in the establishment and design of these museums was Artur Hazelius (1833–1901) who built the first permanent museum of folk costume in Stockholm in 1873 and provided a model for countless folk museums that followed.[10] The museums inspired by the folk displays at the World's Fairs continued to ascribe a national character to the traditional culture. The opening of folk museums, however, occurred concurrently in nations across Europe. Even though traditional culture corresponded more to regional divisions rather than national, its incorporation into national collections encouraged the absorption of regional allegiance into a national framework. In essence, the World's Fairs contributed to the development of a transnational vocabulary of folk culture. Despite the ostensible similarity of their missions, however, the national institutions reflected different underlying philosophies.

National museums in both France and Germany assembled representative objects from regions in a manner that reflected conceptions of national identity. The national museum in France that included traditional regional costumes was the *Musée d'ethnographie du Trocadéro*, although its principal focus was on non-Western cultures. The museum was founded in the wake of the success of 1878 Paris Exposition's display of ethnographic objects. One month before the exposition's closing, a commission was put together to consider the creation of a permanent ethnographic museum.[11] The official opening of the museum occurred in 1882. The museum's Hall of Europe opened two years later and included objects and costumes from Greece, Italy, Portugal, and Russia as well as from France.[12] The rest of the European collection combined, however, was significantly smaller than that from France. The French collections numbered roughly 2,000 objects in 1889 but grew rapidly through a combination of collecting missions, gifts, and exchanges.[13] By 1896, the French collection included more than 2,700 objects. Objects from Brittany made up nearly a quarter of the early collection. Besides the heavy concentration of Breton objects there were also a substantial collection of pieces from Auvergne. The collection also included objects from Provence, Normandy, Maine, as well as Alsace and Lorraine.[14] The inclusion of Alsatian and Lorrain objects in the French national collection clearly indicated the political claims that the cultural institution made on the disputed region.

The curator of the museum's "Salle de France," Armand Landrin, was trained as a geologist, but worked first in a natural history museum. Even beyond his indirect work shaping the national identity through the presentation of regional culture, Landrin was involved more directly in national politics. He was close to Jules Ferry and served as the delegate to the ministère de l'instruction during the 1878 Paris exposition. Landrin's commitment to French ideas of progress and its civilizing mission were clear in his writings and in his organization of the exhibitions. He published a number of essays of instructions on collecting ethnographic materials in which he made clear his understanding of ethnography, which he defined as "the study of the mores and customs of various peoples in order to determine their line of descent [*filiation*], character, origin, migrations, social state, and degree of *civilisation*."[15] As Daniel DeGroff argues, the degree of civilization that Landrin felt the French peasants demonstrated was below that of Parisians. Rather than providing testimony to an essential Frenchness that had deep cultural roots, Landrin presented traditional dress and other elements of rural culture as a baseline to demonstrate the remarkable progress achieved by modern France. The Paris public was invited to the Trocadéro to satisfy their curiosity about the strangeness of more primitive peoples, including not just colonial subjects but rural French peasants.

At the same time that France was developing an ethnographic museum at Trocadéro, Germany also developed a national museum that featured folk costumes. The collection of German folk dress was originally part of the larger Museum für Völkerkunde in Berlin, but in 1889 the collection found a new home within a separate building and became the *Museum für Volkstrachten und Erzeugnisse des Hausgewerbes*. The driving force behind this museum was Rudolf Virchow (1821–1902), the eminent pathologist. Virchow was a widely known and respected medical researcher and scientist who also held a seat in the Reichstag from 1880 to 1893.[16] As a pathologist, Virchow's interest in the study of human culture favored physical anthropology, particularly the evolution of man.[17] In 1874, he attended a conference in Stockholm about archaeology and physical anthropology where he had the opportunity to meet Hazelius and visit the new Swedish museum, which gave him the idea to construct a comparable institution in Berlin.[18] Just like its counterpart in France, it included costumes and objects from Alsace in its collection. While the French museum was making a political claim to Alsace through its inclusion in the Salle de France, the inclusion of the Alsatian room in the German museum was not simply a legitimate political claim, but also a deeper cultural one. A plan of the museum from 1908 shows that the museum displayed objects not just from areas of the German empire but also from neighboring German-speaking countries in Switzerland and Austria.[19] The German concept of nation depended on deep cultural and linguistic roots, which were clearly translated into the selection of German-speaking nations in the museum of folk costumes. The development of a museum of folk costumes was more consistent with German ideological foundations of the nation than it was with the French counterpart.

The construction of these national museums in the 1870 and 1880s was followed by the development in the subsequent decades of a number of smaller museums within the regions themselves. The shared history between World's Fairs and folk museums does not automatically impart the latter with the same nationalist spirit of the former. These regional museums were established through the efforts of local leaders and elites whose agenda was different if not directly at odds with that of the national leaders. Despite the support of French nationalism expressed by many of the founders of the Musée Alsacien, their agenda was firmly in opposition to the civilizing mission of progress put forth by Landrin at the Trocadéro.

Founding of the Musée Alsacien

Under the section heading of "Chronique" of the July 1900 issue of the *Revue Alsacienne Illustrée*, there appeared the first public announcement of the plan to found the Musée Alsacien in Strasbourg.[20] The fact that the museum's founding was first announced in the *Revue* was not coincidental; rather, many of the museum's organizers were closely associated with the publication as well. Pierre Bucher, along with Leon Dollinger, served as the director (*gérant*) of the committee. A committee was formally organized in 1902 to begin planning in earnest and the supervisory board included Robert Forrer, Anselme Laugel, and Charles Spindler.[21] The establishment of the museum grew out of the same movement that had been working to establish an Alsatian artistic movement. The *Revue Alsacienne Illustrée* became the mouthpiece for the museum's founding and promoted a vision for the museum that aligned with that of Bucher.

By the time that plans for the Musée Alsacien were first announced, Pierre Bucher had begun to take control of the *Revue Alsacienne Illustrée* and transform it into an instrument for the promotion of French nationalism in Alsace. The Dollinger brothers who shared leadership of the Musée Alsacien also shared Bucher's political ideology. Bucher was close friends with Maurice Barrès who had throughout his writing espoused a political view that celebrated tradition and regionalism as a rejection of universalism. He articulated a view of nationalism that depended on regionalism.[22] Barrès wrote an article for the *Revue* in which he identified the Museon Arleton, founded in 1896 by the Provençal poet, Frederic Mistral, as the inspiration for the Musée Alsacien.[23] In his article, Barrès included the text from a letter Mistral wrote to him of the satisfaction he felt in having created the museum in Arles:

> And I do not regret my time because the people, the true people, that flow on Sundays into our halls, finding themselves there moved, religious, triumphant,

in the awareness of their race and their personality. This creation should be repeated in all of our villages of France. It is the best lesson of history and of patriotism and of attachment to the soil and of ancestral piety that one can give to all.[24]

Mistral saw this form of museum celebrating the objects from daily life that were unique to the region as a model for other regions. Even in his expression of the conviction that regional culture was distinctive, Barrès argued for a celebration of heritage that could be applied with slight modifications to different regions.

> To give us the sense of this permanence and of our slow preparation across the centuries, the most humble objects are worth almost as much as the most magnificent. It is thus that next to Munster, a museum of ordinary objects, a house full of old witness to the local and regional customs manifest Alsatian tradition, would give more of the conscience of this *"petite patrie."*[25]

Barrès, a native of Lorraine, expressed one vision of the political implications of museums of regional culture. Bucher agreed with Barrès on this model for the establishment of the Musée Alsacien modeled after the Museon Arleton in Provence. In following the ideology of Barrès, he worked to adapt the particularities of Alsatian culture into a sort of mold for a folklore museum.

Although Bucher's control of the *Revue Alsacienne Illustrée* helped him shape the message that was communicated about the mission and inspiration for the museum, the project was the work of many men each of whom had his own motivations and vision. One of the first prominent advocates for a museum of Alsatian culture was Robert Forrer. As early as 1900, Forrer published an article in the *Strassburger Post* advocating for the establishment of an Alsatian museum.[26] Originally born in Switzerland, Forrer was an antiquarian and archeologist who settled in Strasbourg in 1887.[27] While he was a collector of Alsatian art, antiques, and even costumes, Forrer's interest in traditional culture was not restricted to Alsace. In the 1880s, Forrer had collected the Alsatian costumes and other objects for the *Elsässisches Stube* in the *Museum für deutsche Volkstrachten* in Berlin. In 1889, Forrer also offered the government of Baden to engage in a collecting mission in preparation for the establishment of a museum of Badisch costume.[28] Although his offer to Baden was declined, it demonstrates that Forrer's commitment to collecting traditional costumes was not bound by political borders or agendas. While Bucher identified Mistral's museum in Arles as the inspiration for the Musée Alsacien, the museum also followed the precedent set by the museums throughout Germany.

The Musée Alsacien was organized and funded by private individuals rather than any government body. The original statutes of the *Société du Musée Alsacien* were written in French and describe it as a "*Société à responsabilité limitée*" or SARL, although legally it was a GmbH or *Gesellschaft mit beschränkter Haftung*.[29] The *société* may have grown from a social organization, but the establishment of the GmbH in 1902 created a business. In so doing the founders faced the pressure to make the museum a profitable enterprise. To participate in this Société the members made contributions of 500 or 1,000 marks. Although those initially credited with founding the museum drew from the same artistic group that founded the *Revue Alsacienne Illustrée*, a significant percentage of the members of the Société were in business, finance, or industry. An additional third of them were simply listed as landowners.[30] Out of a list of thirty-eight members, fifteen were listed as living in Strasbourg, while an additional eight were from elsewhere in northern Alsace (Bas-Rhin). There were eleven members who lived in southern Alsace (Haut Rhin), all of whom were in industry. The three members who were not listed as living in Alsace were native Alsatians who had left and resettled in Nancy or Paris. The only woman included on the list was the Comtesse de Pourtalès. While the initial impetus for the founding of the museum seems to have come from the artists and intellectuals who gathered around St. Léonard, the funding for the museum drew from a wider swath of Alsatian society—or rather a wealthier swath. While the supervisory board included two medical doctors, an archeologist, a notary, and an artist, the remaining members were businessmen or landowners rather than professionals. Furthermore the Cercle St.-Léonard focused largely on the traditional culture of Lower Alsace, while a significant proportion of the museum's supporters hailed from Upper Alsace. The proliferation of industry in Upper Alsace, particularly textiles, since the early nineteenth century explains both the erosion of traditional culture in that area and the relative predominance of capital from there. In drawing support from Upper Alsace, the Musée Alsacien did contribute to a cultural coherence across the entire region.

The museum founders' decision to create a limited liability company could suggest that the members were hoping for profit, but the motivations were presumably to protect the contributors' financial interest in the event that the enterprise failed. In such an event, any member's liability was limited to the amount of their initial contribution. In theory they could receive returns on their investment but would not have to cover losses greater than they had pledged. In his memoir, Spindler describes the statutes as having been drawn up in such a way that they should protect against "all governmental interference." While it is clear that the museum's organizers took care to protect their interests through the creation of a GmbH, they did allow for the possibility of government involvement. The final statute that they drew up stated: "In case of the dissolution of the Société, the funds (*fonds social*) must be offered and transferred to a municipal Alsatian museum."[31] The decision to remain independent of government control demanded that the directors became particularly concerned about profits.

The first significant financial decision the founders made was the selection of a building. Bucher recommended the purchase of the building in Strasbourg where the museum was founded in 1907 and remains to this day[32] (Plate 14). In February 1904, the Société purchased a house at 23, quai St.-Nicolas as the site of the museum.[33] The building is typical of early-seventeenth-century houses in Strasbourg. The building faces the Ill, affording views of the river and the Ancienne Douane from its front rooms. When entering the building from the street, one passes through a long corridor into the courtyard, which separates the front building from a second building. Two three-story galleries that flank the courtyard connect these two structures. The rear building includes a basement intended as a storeroom for the merchants who originally occupied the house.[34] The mortgage the Société took out for the property states the amount of the loan as 80,000 Marks.[35] Spindler placed the cost for the building at 100,000 Marks.[36] The latter figure includes not only the cost of the buildings but also expenses related to its renovations. The Alsatian architect Théo Berst was in charge of the renovations, which involved the restoration of historic character of the house and courtyard as well as the adaptation of the space to make it suitable as a museum.[37]

The selection of a historic residential building in the heart of Strasbourg came to be critical to the development of the museum, but it was not the only possible option for the museum. Rather than the central bourgeois venue that was chosen under the direction of Pierre Bucher, Charles Spindler had advocated a group of modest buildings scattered throughout rural Alsace that would provide visitors with a fuller experience of immersion in traditional culture. The two conflicting plans for the museum represented very different visions of the function and significance both of museology and of Alsatian regional culture. The house in the center of Alsace was the more accessible option, and it was also grand and imposing. When filled with objects, the museum evoked a sense of wealth and abundance. The beauty of the building imparted a sense of value to the objects that a humbler setting would lack. The bourgeois setting was consistent with the vision of Mistral for the Museon Arletan, which ultimately occupied the palais de Laval-Castellane, a former *hôtel particulier*. In contrast, Charles Spindler had a vision for the Musée Alsacien that drew much more heavily on the distinction of Alsatian culture. He said of the Museon Arlaten:

> I have a horror of museums of that sort that are the consecration of that which is definitively dead and out-dated, a cemetery; that is why I never showed great enthusiasm for the project ... I, on the other hand, wanted a thing that was livelier and more within reach of the people.[38]

He argued in his memoire, and presumably in person at the time, that rather than have a single Musée Alsacien in Strasbourg, they should have established a *Société des musées alsaciens*, which could have purchased a typical house in each canton of Alsace. These houses could be inhabited by people who would dress in costume for visitors in those cantons where the costumes were still in use. Once the houses were purchased and restored, their care and maintenance could be entrusted to the community.[39] Spindler clearly put serious consideration into these plans that he offered to his fellow committee members. He gave examples of two houses in Boersch, the town nearest St. Léonard, that were available for sale at the time. The first could have been purchased for 3,000 Marks, the other for 7,000. Based on these numbers, Spindler speculated that the amount of money spent for the house in Strasbourg could have purchased ten houses in the countryside.[40]

Spindler presented a model for the museum that drew heavily from the model of Skansen, the open-air museum in Stockholm. Artur Hazelius constructed Skansen in 1891 after having developed the Scandinavian-Ethnographic Collection in 1873. Just as the Swedish display at the 1867 had provided the model for folk costume displays, Hazelius' Skansen proved just as inspirational for future open-air museums.[41] It was located in Djurgården which was a peninsula that was easily accessible to the city, yet far enough from central Stockholm that it felt a world apart.[42] Spindler's plan likewise depends on a sense of separateness from the city, although the locations he favored would have been difficult for city dwellers to access at the time. The sense of immersion into the experience of the museum could be a legacy of the popularity at the time of spectacle. The experience of the World's Fairs had introduced travelers to a form of entertainment that emerged the spectator into an entire world complete with architecture, objects, smells, sounds, and tastes. Spindler had an artistic vision of creating a world for the visitor rather than simply presenting objects that had been removed from their original context and function.

Spindler believed that the museum's funds would be better spent on the rural houses because he saw the traditional culture that the museum sought to preserve and celebrate as essentially tied to its rural surroundings. The architecture of the Strasbourgeois house was fundamentally different from that of a house of a fisherman or a winemaker (*vigneron*) or a dairy farmer (*marcaire*). He pointed out that "a house in the city was not suited for the placement of peasant furniture. The peasants' room always had two facades with windows, this configuration couldn't be found in a house hemmed in between the neighboring houses."[43] Spindler recognized the rural architecture itself as a critical component of traditional culture and believed that it was integral to both preserving folk culture and educating the community about it. His name was listed in these early records as one of the members of the supervisory board; however, his participation began and ended with his attendance at the founding meeting, because he had serious objections to the mission and location of the museum.[44] The main reason that Spindler distanced himself from the enterprise was his disapproval of the idea of situating the museum in an urban setting.

Spindler's alternative proposal for the Alsatian museum calls attention to the extent to which the form that the museum ultimately took was neither inevitable nor uncontested. Furthermore, it suggests a diversity of opinions about the museum's purpose and function. Bucher's interest in the museum and in traditional culture drew from ideological commitment to French nationalism. He, like Barrès, viewed regional particularities as the components that built the variety and character of France. This nationalist fervor was not shared by all of the proponents of traditional culture and founders of the museum, however. Spindler represented those adherents who loved Alsatian culture for its own sake rather than as a proxy for French nationalism. His vision for the museum depended on immersing the visitor in the most authentic experience of traditional culture possible. Each of these plans encapsulated dominant contemporary trends in museum practices. Bucher's plan assembled various materials from different localities in an urban center for best access. Spindler preferred to emphasize the vitality and diversity of traditional culture by retaining the lived experience. His approach drew from the modern practice epitomized first by the pavilions in the World's Fairs and later by the Scandinavians.

The Collection and Its Acquisition

The Musée Alsacien was not founded in order to house a collection; rather the collection was assembled to fill the museum. When the *Sociéte du Musée alsacien* was established in 1902, the collection did not yet exist. The founders of the Musée

Alsacien, however, began collecting objects before they had secured a building. The same article in the *Revue Alsacienne Illustrée* that announced the formation of the *Société du Musée Alsacien* also called for contributions, both of money and of objects. In describing the desired objects, the passage states, "The most humble will be worth almost as much as the most magnificent, and there is nothing, no matter how simple, that doesn't represent a precious record."[45] While this call for objects certainly resulted in numerous donations, there were two additional ways in which objects were added to the collection. The first method was for collectors to donate their collections to the museum. The second was for the museum's founders to acquire them during their travels through the Alsatian countryside. These methods came to shape the collection and, by extension, the museum.

The first waves of interest in traditional dress across France and Germany in the 1830s had been led by artists. The documentation had largely been in the form of two-dimensional representation, such as the works of Emrich and Lewicki. Artists such as Théophile Schuler and Frédéric Lix had collected costumes as part of their efforts to accurately portray them in their art. By the 1880s, collecting had taken on scientific methods and purposes. Folk museums organized collecting missions that reshaped the understanding of costumes and other materials as objects. At the national level in France, Landrin himself directed and participated in collecting missions. His primary focus was on Brittany to collect objects for the Trocadéro.[46] He was meticulous about recording the details such as usage, Breton name, locality, and name of donor and believed that collecting should be done by experts. In order to instruct others in the systematic methods he followed, he wrote a detailed set of instructions as did others including Paul Sébillot, the general secretary for the *Société des traditions populaires*.[47] Together Landrin and Sébillot published "Instructions sommaires relatives aux collections provinciales d'objets ethnographiques" which divided ethnographic objects into a number of categories: habitation, furniture and interior, outbuildings, agriculture, alimentation, non-agricultural occupations, clothing, the human life (*la vie humaine*), children's games, adult games, vigils, religion, superstitions. For example, under the heading of clothing follows:

> Past local costumes: their geographic range.
> Description of their various parts.
> By whom they were woven, cut or sewn. Former local makers.
> Drawings, photographs or dolls representing them.[48]

Despite being entitled "Instructions," this document is simply a list that includes not just actual objects but also customs and practices.

While the constraints of museum practices demanded that traditional culture be represented by actual objects, these instructions maintained an emphasis not on things but on practices. While there was a section in the instructions dedicated specifically to clothing, it also appeared in many of the other categories. Under *la vie humaine* it appeared repeatedly: under birth, baptism, marriage, and death. Clothing also appeared under non-agricultural occupations: "Dress or ornaments particular to an occupation." These instructions clarify the categorization that ordered the collecting of the Musée d'ethnographie du Trocadéro. The collections of the national museum were assembled through a combination of missions by its own staff and through the assistance of designated collectors familiar with the particular regions.

When the founders of the Musée Alsacien set out to amass their collection, they found themselves on a well-trodden path. The Museon Arlaten also amassed its collection, thanks to such collecting missions. In fact, right around the time that the museum was founded in 1896, one of its founders, Emile Marignan, wrote *Instructions pour la récolte des objets d'ethnographie du pays arlésien*.[49] This work enumerated eight categories of objects as follows: Anthropology; Food, agriculture, livestock, hunting, and fishing; Family life, habitation, furniture, costumes, games; Religion, traditions, superstitions, sorcery; Sciences, arts; Industry, commerce; Social life, customs, *fêtes populaires*; and Bibliography, iconography.[50] Marignan, who would become the first curator of the Museon Arlaten, was trained as a doctor, and his classification system for ethnographic objects reflects his scientific training. By the time he was involved in the establishment of the Provençal museum, he had already participated in the collection of objects for the Provence/Languedoc section of the Musée d'ethnographie du Trocadéro a decade earlier.[51]

Like the folk museums of France, both regional and national, their German counterparts amassed collections through a similar blend of donations and collecting missions. When the *Museum für Volkstrachten und Erzeugnisse des Hausgewerbes* was in its development stages, the area of Mönchgut was chosen as the location for the first collecting mission. Rudolf Virchow traveled to the peninsula at the tip of the island of Rügen at the extreme northern edge of Germany in order to collect representative objects including costumes. The residents of the area, whose economy was largely dependent on fishing, had been known for their distinctive costumes.[52] Virchow had made an earlier visit to the region within the context of an excursion of the Anthropological Society (*Anthropolgischen Gesellschaft*) in 1886 and had been particularly struck by the women's costumes.[53] These expeditions were comparable to the sorts of scientific and anthropological missions that were launched to study the cultures of Asia, Africa, and the Americas.

Not only did Virchow directly participate in collecting expeditions, but he also put out a call for experts in different regions to collect for the museum. The financing for the museum was in large part provided by the banker Alexander Meyer-Cohn, himself an amateur of traditional culture. Meyer-Cohn traveled around the German-speaking world on behalf of the museum. Rather than purchasing items for the museum himself, he provided credit for young researchers, including Robert Forrer, to choose the objects.[54] By the time Forrer explored the Black Forest in search of costumes, the villagers were already aware of the value of their costumes for collectors.[55] As the customs of wearing the clothing were disappearing, the objects were becoming collectibles, thus affecting their value. The movement to create folk museums was inextricably linked to efforts to collect the elements of traditional culture. The desire to collect had existed within certain individuals who had amassed their own personal collections, but the larger motivation of creating museums had spurred on this practice into a veritable crusade starting in the 1880s. These efforts at creating a typology for folk collections helped construct a carefully defined notion of "folk." This period also saw a change in the notary inventories noted in Chapter 3 as descriptions for clothing switched from listing individual pieces to listing them by function.

Just as the founders and collectors who contributed to the early folk museums in Germany and France comprised an assortment of people with a wide range of knowledge and education, those people responsible for creating the Musée Alsacien had diverse backgrounds, ranging from scientists and doctors to artists and poets. The list of donors that appears in the Rapport des Gérants of 1908 drew from a more diverse segment of the Alsatian population than the list of financial contributors. While all of the latter were men, there are a number of women who are listed as donors. The donors ranged from clergymen to noblewomen. Diverse though the group of donors may have been, few seemed to be from rural villages. A full two-thirds of them were residents of Strasbourg. The objects were as diverse as the donors; they ranged from medical supplies to prints and paintings to doors and ceilings. The costumes were not simply rural dress but also a variety of historic garments such as the "*costume de bourgeoise époque Louis XVI*" donated by Dr. Thomas of Strasbourg. The donors were not restricted to people living in Alsace; there were also a number of donors from Paris as well as one from Nice. The eclectic assortment of goods offered by the public were by no means limited to the sorts of rural items generally associated with folklore. The openness of their collecting mission and the variety of donors created a somewhat hodgepodge collection, which had as a unifying theme that all of the pieces were from Alsace.

While many of the donors gave just a few items, there were a number of prominent Alsatians who contributed all or some of their collections to the Musée Alsacien. An additional substantial gift came from Mme Pierre Schlumberger who contributed thirty-nine items from her late husband's collection. Pierre Schlumberger was an industrialist in Mulhouse and also made significant financial contributions to the fledgling museum.[56] Unsurprisingly, there are a number of names that were important in the preservation of traditional culture including Hans Haug, who went on to become curator of the museum, as well as the wife of Théophile Schuler who had been an artist who painted traditional costumes. The list also includes a number of artists associated with the Cercle St.-Léonard including Josef Sattler and Gustave Stoskopf, who each contributed drawings.

The variety of backgrounds of the collectors paralleled a range of motivations and ideologies that inspired these people to collect. The largest single gift to the museum came from Paul Westercamp who gave 145 pieces including furniture, dishes, lamps, pottery, jewelry, and bonnets. Westercamp was a notary whose family was originally German but settled in Wissembourg, a city at the extreme northern edge of Alsace, near the German border. He was a collector of antiques who donated only a small portion of his collection to the Musée Alsacien. In 1913, a group of men in Wissembourg founded a separate museum of Alsatian culture, which they named the Musée Westercamp. This group, the *Altertumsverein*, differed in their political ideology from the dominant philosophy of the founders of the Musée Alsacien in Strasbourg. The collections of the two museums had some overlap in that both were dedicated to collection Alsatian art and popular culture. While the Musée Alsacien emphasizes Alsatian particularism, the Musée Westercamp explores the way Alsatian culture, particularly on the northern border, is a product of the intersections between French and German influence and conflict. The Westercamp concentrated on military and lithographic print collections, although it also included many other collections including costumes. The fact that the Paul Westercamp's collection formed the foundation of two separate museums with two distinct missions underscores the role of the museum in constructing meaning through the assembly and presentation of objects.

Another notable collector who made a significant contribution to multiple museums, including the Musée Alsacien, was Robert Forrer. His donation to the museum comprised over a hundred carved wooden pieces including chair backs, canes, doorknobs, and barrels. Primarily an antiquarian and archeologist, Forrer was not simply a connoisseur but actually a dealer in antiques. His collection included prehistoric, Coptic, and medieval objects as well as jewelry, coins, and arms. His interest in cultural institutions in Strasbourg did not end with the Musée Alsacien; he was instrumental in the establishment of the Musée archéologique as well as the Musée historique, not to mention his leading role in the *Société pour la Conservation des Monuments Historiques d'Alsace*. Forrer's passion was for antiquities and collecting with a remarkable disregard for national borders. His own neutrality on questions of Alsatian national allegiance echoed the neutrality of his native country, Switzerland. His expertise and company were sought out by both Kaiser Wilhelm II and Georges Clémenceau.[57] As mentioned earlier, Forrer had helped collect objects for the *Museum für Volkstrachten und Erzeugnisse des Hausgewerbes* in Berlin. In fact, he worked to gather not only Alsatian objects but also those from the Black Forest and from Switzerland. Like Westercamp, Forrer did not share the political views of Pierre Bucher, those views that ostensibly motivated the establishment of the Musée Alsacien.

Forrer went on collecting missions through rural Alsace along with other members of the Cercle St.-Léonard including Charles Spindler and Auguste Laugel whose enthusiasm for the hunt he described: "Spindler and Laugel liked to discover the rarest pieces of old regional costumes and we saw them more than once set chase to a frightened young woman who feared for her virtue, when they wanted nothing but her clothing."[58] The pair had collected pieces while they were working on compiling *Costumes et coutumes d'Alsace*. Eventually Spindler donated the collection, which he appraised at 1,000 francs, to the Musée Alsacien. In his memoire he admitted that he bitterly regretted having made the donation.[59] Evidently Spindler went on to develop a strong difference of opinion regarding the direction that the museum would take, but during the initial planning stages, he supported the efforts through substantial donations.

August Kassel (1862–1930) like Spindler was a collector who focused almost exclusively on Alsatian traditional culture. He rode his bicycle through the countryside around Hochfelden as he got to know the villagers, listened to their stories and songs, and collected their objects, including costumes.[60] Kassel wrote a book about Alsatian traditional costume that was published the year the Musée Alsacien opened, 1907.[61] Unlike Spindler whose analysis of costumes largely centered on entire ensembles, Kassel's interest focused on details, such as the stomachers, stockings, and headdresses. He analyzed the evolution both of the styles and of the words for them. In keeping with his training as a doctor he maintained a nearly scientific precision in his attention to detail. His systematic methods more closely resemble those of Landrin at the Trocadéro or Marignan in Arles who was also a medical doctor. Also remarkable about his book, *Über Elsässische Trachten*, is that it is entirely in German. In fact, his concentration on the Alsatian words for various accoutrements underscores the link he creates between oral culture of the Alsatian speakers and their clothing. His collecting habits reflected his interest in details as he focused particularly on stomachers and stockings. His collection of costumes that was given to the Musée Alsacien was comprised of a nearly comprehensive array of clothing pieces.

While the collectors who provided the objects that would make up the Musée Alsacien came from a range of backgrounds—ideological, political, and intellectual—they all shared a common love of Alsatian culture. While a pro-French political agenda is frequently ascribed to the museum's founders, a closer look at the actual men whose connoisseurship, scholarship and collecting shaped the institution's holdings highlights the limitations of such a characterization. Those people who actually scoured the countryside for objects showed a greater interest in the people and culture that created those things than in the construction of a national character. In fact, the interest of collectors such as Forrer transcended national boundaries in recognition of the commonalities of rural cultures. While the Musée Alsacien's institutional mission may have served a nationalizing purpose, such was not the intention of those who played such a critical role in its foundation.

In the years immediately following its founding, the Musée Alsacien lacked a consistent system of tagging and cataloguing the items in its collection. The institution's founders were not trained museum professionals. As a result of the haphazard way in which incoming objects were recorded and described, many significant facts about them have been lost. The first systematic inventory of the costume collection was not performed until 1917, ten years after the museum first opened. At that time, the information was recorded by the daughter of an Austrian doctor named Braun. The resulting inventory was handwritten in German. The records she made for the bodice shown in Figure 4.1 provides a sample of the type and extent of information that was known about these pieces. Braun noted that the bodice was similar to another bodice in the collection and she indicated that the word "Hunspach" had been written in blue inside. This writing on the lining is the only documentation indicating the bodice's origin. There is no record of who donated the item, when it was made or worn, what other items would have been worn with it.

Figure 4.1 Bodice from Hunspach. Collection of the Musée Alsacien de Strasbourg.

While the general system for processing new items in the collection was not rigorous, there were exceptions. For instance, the collection of costumes donated by Spindler was carefully documented. In a letter dated January 27, 1903, he wrote to the Musée Alsacien to announce the delivery of costumes.[62] He also described the system that he instituted to label each of the costume pieces: "The first thing to do would be, in my opinion, to stitch in the interior of each garment [*défroque*] a little piece of white fabric, for putting the number. The numbers will correspond to a future catalogue. I have started to do it but want for time."[63] These tags still remain in those items Spindler donated to the Musée Alsacien and facilitate the identification of pieces from his original collection (Figure 4.2). This system instituted by Spindler contrasts with the limited identification of other items from the original gifts to the collection. The record for the bodice shown in Figure 4.2 includes a description of the object such as the color, material, trim, and closure as well as its dimensions in centimeters. Demoiselle Braun also indicated that the bodice bears the label (*Innen Zittel*) that reads "B39" and she noted the corresponding description in the *Zittelkatalog*, which was written in French. In addition to noting that the bodice was of red wool with blue silk trim, the original catalogue indicated that the piece originally belonged to a peasant

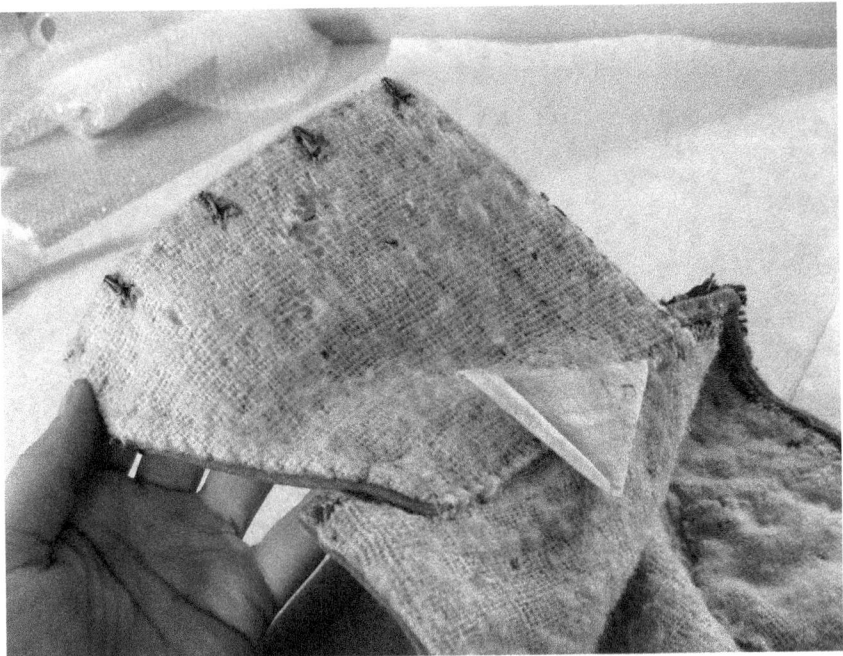

Figure 4.2 Bodice donated by Charles Spindler. Collection of the Musée Alsacien de Strasbourg.

from the town of Geispolsheim and dated it to around 1850.[64] The record of another bodice in the museum's collection that was not part of the Spindler donation reveals less information. Because most of the objects were donated by collectors rather than the original owners, even identifying the donor would not provide critical information about the piece. Traditional dress is generally classified according to the village of origin. The role of bourgeois intermediaries in the establishment of the museum obscured some of the information about the objects. The resulting record keeping provided geographical information about the pieces but little chronological information. Any exhibition or research based on these objects could not shed clear light on questions of how these pieces changed over time.

Nature of the Early Displays

Just as the idea of folk culture was defined through the selection and collection of objects by museums, the manner of their display was also fundamental to its construction. The idea of recreating domestic interiors as exhibits originated

Figure 4.3 Room from Winzenheim from *Images du Musée Alsacien à Strasbourg*, 1912. Musée Alsacien de Strasbourg.

with the folk costume exhibits in the World's Fairs. In German, these interiors are referred to as *Stube*, which is a specific type of room centered around the heat source. Martin Wörner traces what he terms the "*Stubenprinzip*" to the Swedish presentation in the 1867 Paris Exposition. A similar technique had been seen in Crystal Palace exhibit in 1851 for the Tunisian and Indian exhibits. Beyond the arrangement of furnishings to evoke an interior, the Swedish exhibit in 1867 was notable for the skillful way the mannequins in costumes were incorporated into the scenes. The realistic mannequins were sculpted in wax by the sculptor Carl August Söderman and the arrangements were based on popular paintings showing rural life.[65] The artistry of the presentation was arguably more critical to their appeal than their accuracy. In fact, these scenes were very similar to a wax museum such as the Musée Grevin which appealed so strongly to Parisians. Although the Musée Alsacien did not go as far as Spindler advocated in reconstructing the typical Alsatian house, the lower floors were designed as recreated interiors. The Rapport des Gérants describes the museum's exhibits room by room. For example, the first room was an alchemist's laboratory, which was filled with a variety of flasks and bottles as well as traditional medicines including a lizard suspended from the ceiling. The next room was a rustic chapel, which was reproduced "as faithfully as possible," down to the wooden sculpted Christ, the altar, offerings, and votives.[66] In 1912, the museum transported an entire room with its typical wood beams and recessed bed from Winzenheim in the Kochersberg (Figure 4.3). While the Musée Alsacien adopted the well-established display techniques in evoking a variety of different rooms, these vignettes were not the only form of display.

While the lower floors were arranged in a series of vignettes, the rooms on the upper floors housed certain categories of objects, which were arranged in multiples to showcase variations rather than recreate scenes evoking their original usage. The collection of Jewish antiquities for instance was not arranged in the same way the Catholic objects were in the rustic chapel but were rather grouped with like items together. For example, the lamps were together, then the portraits, the embroidery, and the torah pointers. Rather than being laid out as they would be used they were arranged to showcase the distinction of the individual items. The report describes the collection of Judaica as "curious," whereas the rustic chapel was a reconstruction of the oratories that "everyone was familiar with."[67] Rather than creating a tableau to reproduce a scene where Judaism was practiced, the exhibit introduced the visitors to the objects associated with Jewish worship. Other rooms throughout the museum also assembled collections of similar pieces, including one room filled with various objects carved from wood and another room full of prints and paintings. While an actual interior would only have a small number of chairs, this second manner of display could highlight the countless variation among chairs or stoneware or cake molds.

The exhibit of costumes followed the second type of display strategy. No pictures survive of the early costume displays but the description suggests that the mannequins were just lined up rather than arranged in a scene. Three of the rooms on the second floor were dedicated to costumes. The report lists sixteen complete costumes, which were joined by mannequins displaying various individual pieces "from the 18th and 19th centuries," as well as several cases containing assorted accessories such as stomachers and bonnets.[68] The description of the costume display simply lists all of the complete costumes, which suggests that they were not arranged in vignettes but rather the mannequins were simply lined up. The individual costumes are identified simply by their place of origin:

1) A complete costume of a woman from Schleithal.
2) A complete costume of a woman from Oberseebach.
3) and 4) Two complete costumes of a woman from Mietesheim.[69]

Starting from the museum's inauguration, the costumes on display are described according to their place of origin rather than by their date. Besides the categorization according to village of origin, these descriptions divide the costumes into men and women; the numbering suggests that the men's and women's costumes from the same towns were shown separately. The man from Oberseebach is number ten while the man from Mietesheim is number thirteen. The arrangement of the men and of the women follows a generally geographic order from north to south. The women's costumes from the Outre-Forêt, Schleithal, and Oberseebach are followed by the costumes from the area around Strasbourg and finally the costumes from Metzeral in the Vallée de Munster. The men's costumes follow the same general organization. The only costumes with descriptions that make reference to their date were a man's costume worn for the parade celebrating Gutenberg held in 1840 (which is discussed in Chapter 5) and the costume of a "Strasbourgeoise of the 18th century." In other words, the rural costumes were described simply by their place of origin while the urban costumes were described according to date. This museum display reinforces the narrative that rural costume was timeless and fixed in contrast to urban costume, which changed over time.

For the women's costumes, the geography is almost the only descriptive information provided, while men's are almost all described by their function. Only one of the women's costumes makes any mention of the occasion for its use: "6) A complete costume of a bride from Obernai." In contrast most of the male costumes are described according to the wearer's occupation: a shepherd from Hunspach and a conscript from Mietesheim. Curiously two of the costumes that are described by the wearer's occupation were worn for festive occasions rather than for work. The miner's costume from Sainte-Marie-aux-Mines is described as a *"costume de fête"* while the final costume was the costume from the Gutenberg parade worn by a cooper. The presentation of men's and women's costumes highlights the difference in the messages communicated by their clothing. The women's clothing reflected her village and marital status while the men's costume reflected his occupation. Even for festive occasions the men's costumes continued to make such distinctions. Interestingly the description of the costumes does not mention the wearer's religion. While Catholicism and Judaism were the subjects of their own galleries, the implication of religious differences was not reflected in the presentation of the costumes. The differences in the costumes were implicitly linked to religious affiliation, while the exhibition, as reported in the *Rapport des gérants*, did not make these distinctions explicit but instead focused on geography and occupation. Rural costume was not viewed as religious dress, despite the fact that the festive occasions for which much of it was worn were integral with religious observation.

The prioritization of geography over chronology in the display and analysis of costumes had a number of shortcomings. While the distinctions among different villages were defined according to stylistic differences, the variations within villages were not explored. Instead, these costumes become a simplified code to represent a village. To a certain extent, the limitations of museum displays favor such simplifications. In the case of costume, there are a number of different organizing schemes besides geography. For instance, the pieces could be organized chronologically or according to religion. However, it is challenging to simultaneously explore all of these different variables in a coherent display. The nuances and complexity of costumes are difficult to display within the limitations of the space and the holdings of the collection. While the museum ostensibly sought to explore variations within costumes, the ultimate result of the exhibits is the construction or reinforcement of stereotypes.

Producing and Reproducing the Image of Regional Culture

While the mission of the Musée Alsacien was to save elements of traditional culture from oblivion by gathering them and presenting them to the public, the founders actually played a bigger role in protecting and encouraging the preservation of traditional culture. In order to promote the museum and its activities, the museum produced related materials, including images, which they offered for sale. Despite his lack of active participation in the museum's development and operations, Spindler played a central role for the museum because he provided both its content and image. He developed the design that would be used for the certificates (*diplômes*) given to each member of the Société du Musée Alsacien (Figure 4.4). Bucher wrote to Spindler to thank him for so generously offering to produce these certificates. Evidently the pieces were hand-colored lithographs, which had to be made for each of the thirty-three *sociétaires*.[70] The design that Spindler arrived at prominently featured a woman dressed in the quintessential black headbow. The figure is seated off to the side of the image and is surrounded by numerous objects meant to represent the sorts of items collected by the museum including pottery, furniture, wooden clogs, and a tricorn hat. Almost as prominent as the figure, however, is the enormous window that overlooks a typical Alsatian village. While the outside scene reveals characteristic half-timbered architecture and mountains, presumably the Vosges,

Figure 4.4 Charles Spindler, "Diplôme de sociétaire". Musée Alsacien de Strasbourg.

even more evocative of Alsace is the ornamentation and carving on the frame of the window. The choice of setting perhaps refers to Spindler's insistence on the centrality of the house itself and its location to the museum's function. Through the distribution of this certificate to all of the members of the museum, Spindler's portrayal of Alsatian culture became an iconic imagery for the museum. Bucher considered the certificate a means of gaining new members.[71] Despite the strong denunciation Spindler made of the Musée Alsacien in his writing, he could not undo the stronger link forged through his illustrations.

The founding directors of the museum clearly realized the power that images of traditional culture had in shaping the public imagination. They also issued a series of photographs entitled *Images du Musée Alsacien*, which were delivered to subscribers every two months. Publication of these images began in 1904, even before the museum opened its doors and continued uninterrupted until the outbreak of the First World War.[72] Each biweekly installment comprised four prints for a total of 24 prints a year and a complete run of 262 prints. The high-quality prints were printed at a size of 30 × 40 cm and were photogravures (*héliogravures*) either in the original black and white or colored (Figure 4.5). The range of subjects included posed figures in costumes, assorted objects in the collection such as hand towels or baskets, scenes of marriages or festivals in villages, and architectural details. The *Images* effectively were the successors to the earlier series of images produced by Spindler and the other members of the Cercle St.-Léonard including the similarly titled *Images Alsaciennes*. Considering the relationship between the museum and the *Revue Alsacienne Illustrée*, which had been including many images very similar in subject and composition, the idea to sell a series of print images is a natural corollary.

The *Images* were deployed as both a reward for members and an incentive to lure new members. An annual subscription to the *Images* cost 12.50 francs for residents of Strasbourg and 15 francs elsewhere, which entitled subscribers to free admissions to the museum in addition to receiving the bimonthly *Images*. In effect, they gained membership to the museum. Members of the *sociétaires*

Figure 4.5 Late-eighteenth-century farm in Imbsheim from *Images du Musée Alsacien à Strasbourg*, 1914. Coll. et photogr. BNU, Strasbourg.

received the *Images* as a privilege of their membership, while *membres associés permanents* received a discount—they were charged 6.25 francs that is to say half price. As a privately funded venture, the museum had to find support from the public so the development of various avenues of fundraising was vital. The Rapport des Gérants touted the *Images* as "sought after by collectors and lend themselves very well to being framed."[73] In fact, a museum catalogue from 1985 confirms that the *Images* would become sought after by collectors who wished to acquire a complete set.[74] Furthermore, certain plates proved to be more popular than others, particularly those featuring traditional costumes.[75] Beyond simply collecting items of traditional culture in order to preserve them, the museum began to produce items, which in turn became objects to be collected.

The *Images*, in fact, were only one of the items developed for the museum to sell. Another lucrative venture was the sale of postcards. The postcards were produced as photogravures, just like the *Images*. In contrast to the larger *Images*, which documented the same elements of popular culture that the museum set out to collect, the postcards documented the museum's displays (Figure 4.6). The first series had sold out by the time the Rapport des Gérants was issued in 1908, which is to say in the museum's first year. The second series included the following ten scenes of the museum: the façade, the sign, the entrance, the

Figure 4.6 Postcard from the Musée Alsacien showing exhibition. Archives de Strasbourg, 5 MW 275.

courtyard, the eighteenth-century gallery, the Jewish antiquities, the laboratory, the bell ringer, the sculptures, and the roofs with the Cathedral's spire in the background.[76] These postcards were meant to serve as souvenirs of a visitor's trip to the museum and remain a record of the early display techniques.

The Musée managed to profit from the sale of not just these visual representations of traditional culture, but also through the reproduction of "traditional" goods. The founders explicitly stated their view of the place of commerce within the museum:

> We think that the Musée Alsacien is within its role in directing the taste of the public towards those objects having an essentially Alsatian artistic character, and that it works thus in an effective manner to maintain Alsatian tradition.[77]

They created a series of children's toys including a peasant family made out of hand-painted wood that reproduced "the most characteristic costumes."[78] Each member of the "family" wore the costume of a different village. While the wooden peasant family was basically two dimensional, there were also three-dimensional Alsatian dolls offered for sale. Village dressmakers created the costumes of the dolls with a "rigorous exactitude." The description of the toys suggests that their primary goal was to provide souvenirs for visitors and thus raise money and promote the museum.

The museum also commissioned products for sale that served a more complicated function of promoting traditional crafts. In order to "encourage the work of village embroiderers," the museum offered various embroidered items including tablecloths, napkins, and hand-towels.

> These models, modified or transposed following the taste of the rustic embroiderers, make a beautiful impression, and do not at all spoil the entryway to the dining room of our bourgeois homes.[79]

Continuing along the idea of creating souvenirs that depicted Alsatian costumes, the directors of the museum went so far as to sell actual "traditional" costume. The directors explained that they had been motivated by the rapid disappearance of the costumes in the countryside. The fabric known as *bombasin* that was used to make the skirts was becoming difficult to find, so the museum arranged to have the textiles woven specifically for them by village weavers. The report repeatedly emphasizes the authenticity of the costumes. It also indicates the occasions for which the "gracious Alsatian costume" might be worn including "all imaginable *fêtes*, costume balls, charity events, processions ..."[80] The museum clearly crossed the line from preserving traditional culture to producing it. As a private enterprise that needed to raise money to continue its operation, it faced pressures to appeal to public taste. The museum did not simply respond to the contemporary fascination with traditional culture, it also worked to create a market for traditional goods. The founders saw their function of preserving traditions as extending to supporting the continued wearing of traditional dress, which could not continue without the continued production of the necessary elements. In selling this "authentic" culture, the museum played a curious dual role in preserving traditional methods but also profiting through their continued sales.

Kermesse: Masquerade and Commerce

The Musée Alsacien did more than simply selling objects to its visitors; it sought to sell them an experience. Beyond selling costumes that could be worn to charity events, it actually went so far as to stage an event where traditional costumes could be worn. In fact the full-scale launch into commerce in the Musée Alsacien began with its grand opening in late May 1907, when it hosted a *kermesse*. On the occasion of opening a museum of popular culture, the people of Strasbourg were invited not only to see characteristically Alsatian objects displayed in a series of renovated houses, but they were also encouraged to dress up as Alsatian peasants and attend a fair inside the museum (Figure 4.7). This transformation of traditional culture into an experience for tourists has a clear precedent in the World's Fairs. Taking a cue from the pavilions where visitors could buy food and souvenirs from costumed participants, the museum became a scene of immersion into the culture it showcased. The event was not merely an occasion for dress-up in the manner of a masquerade but was a kermesse, or fair. The intention of the activity was commercial, albeit charitable. Beyond simply allowing people to sell things in the museum, the museum as an institution entered into the production of "traditional" goods.

Both the courtyard and the galleries were decorated in a *"villageoise"* manner. The visitors could participate in games as well as visit stands where goods were for sale. The Rapport des Gérants emphasizes the participation of women from the "best Alsatian families" both as volunteers and as visitors. The booths were run by the wives of the museum founders including Ferdinand and Léon Dollinger. In fact, the section on the kermesse was the only part of the Rapport des Gérants that discusses women's participation in the museum. While women were critical in the production of traditional culture, they played little role in

Figure 4.7 Kermesse at the Musée Alsacien, 1907. Coll. et photogr. BNU, Strasbourg.

its preservation in the museum. Rather than highlight their significant role as organizers and sellers at the Kermesse, the report emphasizes their charming appearance. "One can see a crowd of the gracious young peasant girls, dressed in the most becoming finery of our villages, stocking the counters, artistically decorated and copiously provisioned with all that is attractive in a bazar."[81] The founders of the museum were without exception men. The prominent role of women in the kermesse illustrates their role as consumers rather than producers of the modern iteration of folk culture.

While the kermesse was a remarkable demonstration of the conflation of museum and market, it also suggested the reach of interest in folk culture across regional and even national boundaries. The word itself is Dutch from *kerk* or church and *mis* or mass. Such festivals originated in Flanders, including northern France. While the word itself was long since adopted into the French language, its application in this instance is worthy of attention. Alsace has comparable traditional festivals known as *messti*. The local term may have been forsaken instead of the more widely used word because of specific connotations of the two words. Although both basically originated as religious observances, "kermesse" came to signify a festival organized for charitable purposes. The irony of adopting a general term for a popular festival from the Flemish rather than taking inspiration from local traditions underscores the generalization of folk traditions regardless of political boundaries. The opening of the Musée Alsacien combined general references to a transnational vocabulary of folk culture with very specific elements of local traditions.

The goal of encouraging the continuation of traditional production methods underscores the fundamental difference between the efforts of the Musée Alsacien and the agenda of the national museum of folk culture in Paris. The Trocadéro displayed objects with the clear message that the tools and costumes were relics of a fast disappearing past. An article in *La Nature* about the exhibit of French regional costume in Paris discussed the obsolescence of the objects:

> It is not without difficulty that we were able to collect these objects, out of use now for the most part, having been replaced by newly perfected and patented instruments. They are rare, the peasants who have kept the costumes of their fathers instead of wearing the horrible blouse.[82]

Spindler directly contradicted such sentiments when he wrote:

> In Alsace, the peasant has preserved the sense of his worth, and this sentiment translates into a certain dignity in his bearing. He is proud to affirm it through his costume and if he abandons it, it is because of reasons independent of his wishes. That is why I believe that the resurrection of costume is not a utopian dream.[83]

Rather than viewing the traditional culture as obsolete, the founders of the Musée Alsacien, including Spindler, hoped that the museum would not just provide a space for traditional culture including dress to be saved on shelves but serve as a vital link in its continued production, reproduction, and even performance.

Conclusion

The proliferation of museums of traditional life and folk culture at the turn of the century is often seen as a manifestation of a wave of nationalism at the time. Although this movement had a clear political agenda on the national stage in France and Germany, as a political movement at the regional level the agenda was much more fluid. A closer examination of this trend, specifically focusing on the Musée Alsacien in Strasbourg, suggests that a number of other forces played as salient a role in their development as nationalism. The Musée Alsacien was a private institution that arose from the efforts of a core group of patrons and collectors. Rather than maintaining a coherent political ideology, the motivations of these founders varied fairly widely. While the initial directors, Pierre Bucher and the Dollinger brothers, were strongly pro-French in their views and likely envisioned the museum as a form of resistance against German rule, other critical supporters of the museum did not agree with this vision. The Francophiles were instrumental in the organization of the institution, but they were not the participants with the strongest connection to the objects the museum would collect. The people who formed a critical link in the drive to preserve folk culture by establishing contact with those who continued to produce the objects and maintain the traditions were the collectors. The urges that led men such as Charles Spindler, Robert Forrer, Paul Westercamp, and August Kassel to seek out and purchase objects ranging from clothing to dishware to furniture were varied, but a passion for the objects themselves rather than loyalty to France predominated among their motivations. The role that these men played as intermediaries in the acquisition of objects obscured the connection between these objects and their original owners and users. The loss of information about when these objects, particularly the costumes, were made undermined efforts to establish a chronology for their use. Ultimately rather than educating the public about the original context and function of Alsatian dress practices, the early exhibitions contributed to an understanding of rural dress that emphasized fixedness and rules while discounting change over time.

The transformation of ordinary, everyday objects from rural homes into museum displays for the entertainment of an urban public is the compelling drama behind the establishment of the Musée Alsacien. Such a displacement was a byproduct of a variety of modernizing forces, including growing urbanization and the rise of department stores. This same urbanization along with improved transportation and increased leisure time allowed for the development of an audience for the museum. Furthermore, this audience had developed a taste for spectacle and immersive museum experiences through the precedent of the World's Fairs. The form the Musée Alsacien took was strongly influenced by the general museological trends of its day. The museum, in turn, had a significant influence on the traditional culture it purportedly preserved. Founded through private initiative, the Musée Alsacien needed to raise revenue to support its operations. As a result, the museum created a number of items for sale ranging from images and postcards to dolls and even costumes. The museum participated not only in the sales of objects but also into the experience of traditional culture more generally. In seeking to preserve the performance, production, and representation of traditional dress, the museum played a critical role in its transformation into folk dress.

5

Living History

While the survival of pieces in museums transforms them into literal relics of a bygone era, regional dress's continued deployment as costumes for folk groups reframes it as a dynamic aspect of contemporary regional culture. By the early twentieth century the earlier religious uses had widely given way in favor of performances for tourists or for political rallies. The performers who continued to dress in these costumes were generally members of groups who organized in large part to continue to preserve the dress practices as well as the songs, dances, and other elements of rural culture. While this attention to maintaining cultural heritage reflected an interest in tradition and history, the changing circumstances for wearing regional dress reflected distinctly modern political and social realities. In fact various governments and officials deployed folk groups and folk dress in performances that used history for their own agendas. Many who study folklore have dismissed the twentieth-century manifestations of folk culture as "folklorism" or even "fakelore."[1] However, there was a meaningful evolution of these forms of sociability, which developed even as the religious occasions became disassociated with the forms of dress. In fact, the changing use of regional dress may have varying functions and may involve material changes to the style and production, but these later iterations have important value in their community.

Despite the clear evolution of usage and the subtle progression of the styles themselves, historians studying regional dress have focused on the way that regional dress reflects an understanding of the past as unchanging.[2] Malcolm Chapman, for instance, sought to explain why regional dress froze the styles at particular moments of time: namely the eighteenth century for Scotland and the late nineteenth century for Brittany.[3] While certainly the continued use of distinctive regional styles now demands a reference to earlier dress practices, the performances when these styles were worn underwent noteworthy changes over time. The evolving contextualization of these styles deserves study and recognition. More recent scholarship in folklore studies has re-evaluated folklorism, which Regina Bendix defines to as "folklore out of context," to recognize the value of continued relevance of elements of folk culture such as regional dress in modern Europe.[4] While folklorism studies have been valuable in describing the adaptations that cultural forms such as dress have undertaken due to societal changes, these adaptations do not make these later interpretations less significant or even authentic.

Regional dress is a manifestation of local culture. Through the nineteenth century it became mobilized as a demonstration of regional character in parades which often had political meaning. While the basic chronology of the development of regional dress in Alsace is typical of regions in France, the German-speaking regions of central Europe progressed along an earlier timeframe. This chapter will compare the gradual politicization of regional dress in Alsace as well as the emergence of organized folk groups to cases elsewhere in Europe, particularly in Germany and France. Throughout the nineteenth and early twentieth century, regionalism played a complicated and evolving role alternately as an obstacle to and a building block of nationalism in France and Germany. While the conventional view of regionalism in France has been that the national ideology favored a universalist, centralizing agenda which had little place for regional difference, the proliferation of folk groups and their continued popularity through the twentieth century and into the twenty-first suggests a reconsideration of this reductive view.[5] The history of folk groups in France, particularly in Alsace, in many ways parallels developments in Germany where regional dress or *Tracht* was mobilized to demonstrate loyalty to the nation as well as the distinctive character of the individual region.

In the early twentieth century, intellectuals and artists increasingly sought to preserve regional dress which they recognized as disappearing. The dress became linked to appreciation for natural beauty, pride in peasantry, attachment to the land, and the value of domestic production. These ideas became influential in the 1930s and were actually shared across national boundaries. For instance, the 1937 World's Fair in Paris was a celebration of French regional culture. However, this celebration of peasantry and folk culture saw its culmination in the ideology of the National Socialists in Germany. Ultimately in the aftermath of the Second World War, the close association between Nazism and folklore led to the subsequent distancing from folk dress and a decline in the perceived legitimacy for the discipline as a whole.

The history of folk groups further complicates the dichotomy between regionalism and nationalism as they both reflect attachment to subregional, local areas and operate on a transnational level. As evocations of local and regional identity, folk groups drew together people not just in one nation but across national boundaries. Folk festivals provide opportunities for people from villages across Europe to gather, share their own cultures, and learn from others. At the same time the members of the folk groups are active in their local communities and promote regional tourism. The agenda of many organizers of festivals during the late nineteenth and early twentieth century could be interpreted as making tourist attractions out of local residents. By the later twentieth century, the members of the folk groups themselves took on a greater role in controlling their own image and ensuring a benefit for the participants.

Non-Religious Festivals

While regional dress had its origins in religious dress as discussed in Chapter 1, it gradually lost its religious connection as the dress became used in secular parades and festivals. Across Germany in the early nineteenth century festivals would be held to honor events such as royal marriages. The most well known of these events was the festival held in Munich in October 1810 to celebrate the wedding of Crown Prince Ludwig of Bavaria (later Ludwig I) to Princess Therese of Sachsen-Hildburghausen. This celebration developed into an annual event known as Oktoberfest. As part of this first observance, participants in the various events such as the horse races and the shooting competitions proceeded from the town to the site of the fair in the meadow, which came to bear the name *Theresienwiese* (Therese's meadow) after the bride. This procession took on an organized quality for a royal homage in which children representing each of the eight districts of Bavaria presented gifts to the royal family. According to the analysis of Gerda Möhler, these children dressed in clothing that was distinctive to each of their districts. She argues that these costumes presented an allegory in which the kingdom of Bavaria was portrayed through the clothing of its people.[6] Unfortunately there is no record of what this clothing looked like.

Although there was a component of the parade in 1810 that did include regional dress, it was the parade in 1835 for the twenty-fifth anniversary of the first Oktoberfest that is considered the forerunner of the modern costume parades. The procession was depicted by Gustav Kraus, so the appearance of the participants is clear. One of the elements of the parade was a sequence of eight wagons which represented each of the eight administrative divisions of the Kingdom of Bavaria (Plates 15 and 16). These eight wagons were led by a wagon carrying an allegorical figure representing Bavaria as a woman in a plumed gold helmet dressed in classically inspired blue robes and holding a lance and shield. The wagon containing Bavaria was filled with two groups of young women dressed in white gowns holding ribbons attached to two flagpoles. The blue and white flags were the banners of Bavaria and were included on virtually all of the wagons in the procession. The costumes worn by the passengers in the eight subsequent wagons reflected the distinctive dress from each of the different areas of Bavaria. As in the Oktoberfest procession of 1810, these wagons paid homage to the king and represented a means of making the diversity and richness of the kingdom tangible. The wagons themselves were festooned with greenery and bore the coat of arms of their respective districts. The green bedecked wagons filled with figures in regional dress became a fixture of parades and festivals throughout Germany during the nineteenth century.

The written descriptions of the parade refer to the dress worn by these passengers as *Nationaltracht*,[7] which translates into the expression national dress, one way that regional dress continues to be described. This term connects the distinctive dress which corresponded to very local usage in specific villages to the nation state. The organization of this series of wagons suggests that it is not the individual style of dress by itself that represents the nation, in this case the Kingdom of Bavaria, but rather the assemblage of the distinct local styles. It is this coming together of different styles that enables the local styles to stand in for the collective identity of the nation. In this early period, the unit of political organization represented by the "national dress" was Bavaria. Following the establishment of a unified Germany in the 1870s, Bavaria itself would become one state in the larger German nation. Bavarian culture in turn would play a role in constructing a coherent German identity.

The dress of the passengers in the eight wagons that Gustav Kraus depicts resembled the styles of dress seen in the illustrations of regional dress that were popular in the 1830s. All of the wagons included both men and women as passengers. The costumes showed clear differences from wagon to wagon, but there was also variety within individual wagon for both the men and women. Some of the men wore dark jackets and top hats which resembled fashionable, urban dress while others wore three-cornered hats. The variation in the men's costume is noteworthy because it reflects a general transformation that was occurring in men's fashion. The transition from the eighteenth-century styles with three-cornered hats and breeches to the nineteenth-century style of top hats, trousers, and suits of plain black wool is usually considered to have been complete by the 1830s. However, this illustration reveals that in the areas represented, some men continued to retain the older styles. The variability of the styles depicted suggests that the dress associated with each district or village was not fixed but was changing and adapting with the times. The inclusion of these wagons of regional dress did not represent a historical view of a nostalgic past; instead, they were a depiction and celebration of contemporary life in Bavaria.

While the Bavarian Oktoberfest may have been the earliest example of a folkloric parade in Germany, other regions soon held their own. In 1838 the earliest known procession of folk dress in Baden took place in Karlsruhe at a festival organized for German farmers.[8] The meeting took place over three days and included exhibitions, concerts, and theatrical performances as well as a parade. Young men and women from across the Grand Duchy of Baden attended dressed in their regional costumes. The Karlsruher Zeitung of September 14, 1838 describes the procession:

> In addition to the whimsical, brightly colored costume of the Hauensteiner one saw the dainty inhabitants of the former county of Hanau-Lichtenberg, the yellow straw hats of the Black Forest women next to the shepherd's headwear, red skirts and white aprons of mowers or reapers of the lower Murgthal, the black, ribbon-flying hoods of the daughters of the district of Lahr and the almost sought after finery of the members of the Schwetzinger or Wiesloch district, one saw the stocky raftsmen of the Enzthales in their high water boots and with their raft rods next to the hops farmers of the Palatinate, the herdsmen of the Black Forest valleys next to the dark miners of the pit works.[9]

The descriptions of the regional dress of these parts of Southwest German concentrated on occupational dress. The different costumes were defined by the people's work as shepherds, reapers, raftsmen, hops farmers, or miners. This was fitting as a parade of costumes occasioned by an agricultural festival. The description of the event continues on with a description of the grapes, the hops, the turnips, the grain, the wool, as well as the cows and oxen that were also displayed at the festival. The celebration of these products was linked with a recognition of the agricultural customs including dress that defined the different regions. Significantly the people who attended the event and paraded in their festive dress represented the different areas of Southwest Germany and testified to its richness. The Grand Duchy of Baden had only existed as such since 1806 when the Holy Roman Empire was dissolved. Thus in 1838 its component parts were only recently coming to understand themselves as belonging into a single unified whole.[10] The assembly of folk peoples from the region became a means of visualizing at once the diversity of the region as well as its coherence.

Alsace also saw parades which celebrated occupations through their distinctive dress. On June 24, 1840, the city of Strasbourg presented a parade in honor of the inauguration of a statue of Gutenberg in the city's square that bears his name. The parade celebrated the industrial sector of the city through representations from a vast array of different occupations. While this parade stood in sharp contrast to the more agricultural focus of the earlier festivals in Bavaria and Baden, it did include a wagon that represented gardeners and farmers (Plate 17). While the vast majority of wagons were all men or else included girls and young women who served a decorative function rather than being workers themselves, the wagon of gardeners prominently featured women who seemed to be the representatives of the occupation. These young female gardeners all wear small bows on their caps, which were the forerunners of the enormous headbows that would come to dominate Alsatian regional dress. Women also feature prominently in the wagon described as "Inhabitants of the Robertsau" (Plate 18). Robertsau is an area at the northern perimeter of Strasbourg, bordering the river Ill that was very marshy and agricultural in the nineteenth century. The women in the wagon representing the area wore very broad-brimmed straw hats rather than the caps with headbows. Like the earlier Bavarian wagons, the wagons for the gardeners and the inhabitants of the Robertsau were decked with greenery. Just as in Bavaria where the blue and white flags showed allegiance to the kingdom, all of the groups participating in the Strasbourg procession flew the French tricolored flag. The industrial parade took place on the second day of festivities in honor of Gutenberg that were organized by the city.[11] While the procession of the first day featured the city's dignitaries and thus had a more political function, the industrial parade also paid homage to the government through the display of flags. The representation of Alsatian society focused on a more corporate conception of the populace through the divisions of its residents by occupation.

While as in the Munich parade five years earlier, men rode and directed the horses, the wagons in the Strasbourg procession were filled only with women. The dress of the participants in the Alsatian parade reflected the gendered divisions in how men's and women's dress were represented in performances involving regional dress. Men were clothed according to their profession, but only women in agricultural work were represented according to occupation. Otherwise women's dress and thus the women themselves represented a geographic area. This distinction in which women come to symbolically represent their region continues in parades from the late nineteenth century through to the present day.

Wedding Processions

These urban parades in Strasbourg and Munich carefully documented the use of wagons filled with men and women dressed in regional dress as early as the first half of the nineteenth century. In both Munich and Strasbourg, these styles of decorated wagons likely developed from local usage related to weddings which included enthusiastic procession through the village streets. An illustration of a village procession appeared in 1855 in a book by Frédéric Piton describing Strasbourg and its surrounding area. The illustration by Alfred Touchemolin discussed in Chapter 2 shows a wagon festooned with garlands filled with young women dressed in regional dress[12] (Figure 2.9). The accompanying text describes the scene as the preparations for a wedding. The groom has traveled to his bride's farm and picked her up in a wagon into which she piles all of her belongings including her spinning wheel with a distaff wrapped in flax or hemp. Her maids of honor accompany her in the wagon while the friends of the groom ride alongside. Piton describes the procession:

> The hurrahs, the rifle and gun shots salute its arrival, and the cavalcade makes its solemn entrance to general acclamations, until the large courtyard of the farm receives them, and then begins the cortege on foot to the church, likewise accompanied by detonations of firearms.[13]

Although the church was the final destination of this nuptial cortege, the celebrations along the route were boisterous. The style of wagon adorned with garlands and filled with young women dressed in regional dress closely resembles the floats in the 1835 Munich Oktoberfest as well as the 1840 industrial parade in Strasbourg.

The influence of rural wedding processions on urban folkloric parades was made explicit in the 1842 Munich Oktoberfest which coincided with the wedding of Crown Prince Maximilian (later King Maximilian II) to the Prussian Princess Marie Friedrike. To celebrate the wedding, thirty-five couples from each of the eight administrative districts of Bavaria were invited to get married as part of the festival. The brides and grooms dressed in the regional dress of the area they were from. Gustav Kraus documented the parade just as he had the earlier one in 1835[14] (Figure 5.1). For those who came from parts of Bavaria where no regional dress survived by the 1840s, the couples wore historic dress. For instance, the representatives of Regensburg wore "old Regensburger Tracht" which for the men resembled eighteenth-century suits with tricornered hats and breeches and for the women resembled seventeenth-century dress with wide lace collars and cuffs.[15] Each couple along with a small bridal party to serve as witnesses

Figure 5.1 Gustav Kraus, Procession of thirty-five wedding couples at Oktoberfest in Munich on October 16, 1842. Münchner Stadtmuseum, Sammlung Graphik/Gemälde.

took part in grand procession through Munich. The Catholic and Protestant couples diverged as they headed to the churches for their respective confession for the marriage ceremony. Then the procession resumed as the wedding parties proceeded to the Theresienwiese where they paid homage to the royal family.[16] The illustration confirms that many of the bridal parties rode in wagons bedecked with greenery. The costumed parade was an actual wedding procession although on a grand scale transposed to an urban setting. The original religious context for the parade was preserved along with the political implications and tourist appeal.

Turn-of-the-Century Festivals

The growing development of secular festivals that featured regional dress, which had clear precedent across Germany, also developed in Alsace. Villages across the region would hold annual celebrations known as *messtis* that had lost their association with the church by the late nineteenth century. Charles Spindler photographed a number of messtis in villages around Alsace in the 1880s and

1890s in which regional dress continued to be worn. Even the still photographs conveyed the liveliness and excitement of the events (Figure 2.12). These festivals often included carousels and other elements of fairs as well as musical performers who marched through the streets accompanied by dancing.

One of the best-known messtis was that held in Schiltigheim, a town that lies just north of Strasbourg. The earliest recorded messti in the town was in 1738 as a festival for the patron saint. By the 1880s, the little parade featuring local personalities grew into the *Messtizug*, a grand parade with floats, marching bands, choirs, and various clubs.[17] As the scale of the Schiltigheim messti grew, the character of the event changed. By 1895, the messti was held in conjunction with an industrial and trade fair that was also held in Schiltigheim.[18] The religious origins of the celebration had completely disappeared in favor of a link with industry and commerce.

The transformation of the messti from a small local festival into a much larger regional event paralleled the changing place of regional dress. The program for the festivities of 1895 included a *Trachtenfest*. Rather than being worn as best dress for a special occasion, the *Tracht*, or regional dress, served as the costume for a party that was held several days after the main parade. The Trachtenfest that took place in Schiltigheim in August of 1895 was one of a number of similar events at that time. In fact, just one month later a larger Trachtenfest took place in Strasbourg. Like the event in Schiltigheim it was held in conjunction with the city's industrial and trade fair. The intentions of the festival's planners were at once to attract people to the exposition and also to encourage the preservation of regional dress.[19] Wagons representing different villages in Alsace were decked out as parade floats and filled with villagers in their regional dress. The villages that were represented were those where the costumes continued to be worn and were exclusively in Lower Alsace.

Shortly after the event took place, August Kassel published a full description, which focused primarily on the float from Alteckendorf, the closest village to his native Hochfelden in the Pays de Hanau.[20] Kassel describes the wagon as being adorned with garlands and flowers and each side bore inscriptions celebrating the industriousness and self-sufficiency of the peasants while attesting to their underlying faith in God. They attributed the pride they took in their own handiwork to the grace of God. Although the Trachtenfest was anything but a religious occasion, the inscriptions indicate that the villagers continued to find a close affinity between their rural culture and their religion. These folk festivals at the turn of the century marked a critical step in the disassociation of regional dress from religious observation. The villagers wore the costumes for an exposition celebrating industry and commerce. Furthermore, the intention was to attract and entertain curious spectators rather than to worship and honor their faith. At the same time, those who created and appeared on the float made their faith plain through not only their dress but also their words. Even though the occasion for wearing the costumes was not religious, they still demonstrate the underlying faith that continued to be fundamental to their village life.

The Trachtenfest in Schiltigheim had its counterpart in Munich held the same year, 1895. There had actually been a more modest parade of costumes included in the 1894 Munich Oktoberfest, organized by the Gebirgstrachtenerhaltungsvereine (Group for the Preservation of Mountain Costume). However while the 1894 parade included about 700 members of the groups, the event was not included on the official Oktoberfest schedule.[21] The committee formed to organize the 1895 Trachtenfest invited Bavarian poet and novelist, Maximilian Schmidt, to a meeting where he presented a program that he had first proposed in 1884. Schmidt celebrated and researched the region's dialect but also took a keen interest in preserving the region's dress. Schmidt along with Professor Sepp was elected to the board to organize the event. For five months he traveled around Bavaria in search of disappearing regional dress. He encouraged the participation of far-flung residents and encouraged them to gather their old dress. He depended on the cooperation of teachers, clergy, and officials in various villages who supported the efforts. In his autobiography, Schmidt singles out one particular young woman from the Bavarian forest who wore an outfit made up of sixteen pieces assembled from thirteen different houses.[22] Ultimately Schmidt boasted of the participation of over 150 groups made up of 1,400 people.[23]

The effort that Schmidt made to present Bavarian dress was actually an effort to reconstruct as well as preserve the distinctive dress practices. It is clear through both the description of Schmidt's campaign to bring to light surviving examples of regional dress and the very existence of the Gebirgstrachtenerhaltungsvereine dedicated to protecting Tracht, that regional dress was widely viewed as at risk of disappearing. The organization of folk groups appearing in parades at agricultural and folk festivals represents a shift in the occasion for which the dress is worn. Rather than religious in function, the dress became part of a performance of regional identity but also a means of holding on to a disappearing culture. Wearing them became re-enactments of earlier practices as well as shifting part of the contemporary rural and even urban culture.

As the wearing of regional dress for occasions such as religious festivals was waning in the late nineteenth century, folklorists and ethnographers began to intervene for the preservation of these practices they valued. Just as the poet Schmidt took a leading role in preserving Bavarian customs, one of the pioneering intellectuals whose efforts on behalf of regional culture served as a model for other regions across France was Frédéric Mistral. In 1903, Mistral organized what he called a Festo Virginienco (Virginal Festival) held in the Museon Arlaten. The first occasion of the festival showcased twenty-eight young women from Arles and the surrounding area known as the Crau.[24] Each participant received a beautifully designed certificate with an illustration by the Arlesian painter Lelée and a verse by Mistral. The second annual festival drew 370 women from across Provence in their regional dress. Just as importantly, twice as many visitors flocked to attend the event. The wearing of regional dress became an occasion for curious onlookers rather than a simple act of putting on one's clothes for attending services. As Jules Charles-Roux describes the success of the event in his book on Provençal costume: "the organizers were overwhelmed by this enthusiastic crowd, who had hurried in from across Provence to celebrate the costume of the region and the beauty of the young Provençales."[25] The value of the region's culture was assessed according to its aesthetic qualities. Its beauty or rather the beauty of the young women was equated with its worthiness of being preserved and celebrated.

Mistral intended the Festo to be a model for villages across Provence, which it was. Some towns presented festivals for just a few years, while the town of Saintes Maries de la Mer has continued the practice into the twenty-first century. The event begins in the church where a mass in Provençal is observed. Then the participants form a procession and pass from the church to the arena. The ceremony in the arena begins with events featuring bulls and a small herd of Camargue horses, the breed of horses indigenous to the area. Then the young women dressed in their regional dress as well as members of folk groups file into the arena. In keeping with the practice of awarding prizes for women who are celebrated for their beauty, there is the election of a queen of Arles.

These customs which emerged in Provence had their equivalents in other regions of France as well as Alsace. In Brittany, in particular, a number of festivals began to be organized in the first decades of the twentieth century. The earliest Breton folklore festival began as the Fête des Fleurs Ajoncs in Pont-Aven in July 1905.[26] This festival was organized by Théodore Botrel, who like Mistral was a poet who celebrated his native region, in this case Brittany, in song and verse. Botrel reflected the influence of regional literary interest in Paris. He found fame in the capital where he explored his Breton origins in poetry and song.[27] The event's organizers identified it as a "Grand Pardon" to connect it to the festivals deeply entrenched in the area's devout religious practice. The Fête des fleurs indeed include a procession and mass but was focused on the secular component of crowning the "Queen of the Ajoncs." The queen was elected from young women from Pont-Aven and the surrounding towns and villages.[28] The event culminated in competitions as well as music and dance performances at the city hall. The biannual occasion of the Fête des Fleurs became a successful event and attracted an audience in the thousands.

The festivals in France were similar to the German examples with their presentation of regional dress but differed in their lack of political symbolism. Unlike the Oktoberfest organized around paying homage to the king and the royal family, these French festivals were purely municipal activities. Lacking a monarchy and minimizing any official sanctioning of regional distinction, France did not incorporate regional dress into any political program. However, despite their differences in political ideology, folkloric festivals and parades developed along a similar trajectory in both France and Germany. Spearheaded by poets and artists, the parades were organized to preserve customs which were at risk of disappearing. In so doing new customs were established and the function of the dress traded its religious function for an aesthetic one. The appreciation of these beautiful dresses and the women who wore them served to attract crowds of tourists.

Folklorization of Fête-Dieu

The ambiguous status of the Fête des Fleurs as a religious ceremony categorized as a Grand Pardon, and incorporating a mass is similar to one of the most celebrated religious processions in Alsace. The preservation of the Fête-Dieu procession in Geispolsheim highlights the underlying tensions between its original motivation as an expression of a community's faith and its popular appeal to visitors as a picturesque display.

In *Costume et Coutumes d'Alsace*, Laugel describes Geispolsheim's Fête-Dieu thus:

> It is impossible to not be touched, to not be seized by the grandeur of this spectacle at once magnificent and naive: magnificent in its aims and naive in the manifestations that take place. One can barely, in fact, imagine the touching thoughts that come to the brain of these good people when they want to celebrate the glory of God.[29]

The description of the ceremony extols the beauty of the event yet is strikingly dismissive of its reverence. While acknowledging the solemnity of the event, the description focuses on the sensory experience—the colors and sounds—while completely discounting the spiritual importance. In fact, Laugel goes on to critique the costumes of the children dressed as lambs and shepherdesses as being "bizarre" and inauthentic because they are insufficiently rustic. He contrasts the costumes of the younger children with the dress of the older girls whom he describes as charming and compares to paintings by Velasquez because of their stiffness, solemnity, and superb finery.[30] The blatant preference for the costume that was distinctly Alsatian over the religiously symbolic dress of the lambs and shepherdesses attests to Laugel's experience of the event being shaped by his own conceptions of Alsatian rural life. Laugel selectively saw the beauty of the quintessentially Alsatian costume while dismissing the religiously symbolic elements of the event. The vision of rural Alsace that was captured and conveyed to the outsider downplayed the intense piety and religious conflict in favor of beauty and pageantry. While the image of the young Geispolsheim maiden in her red "butterfly bonnet" became emblematic of the region, the underlying religious act that its wearing represented was minimized. The significance of the procession differed between the interpretation of the liberal, secular folklorists and the devout participants. Folklorists were spectators and passed the perspective of the spectator down to future generations.

Spindler also took particular note of the ceremony in his memoire. He attended the procession sometime around 1890 and he reported that he was the only spectator:

> Nothing like what one sees now could give the idea of the spectacle that was offered at that time. All the female peasants in red dresses, the majority of the little girls with the red or colored bow on the head, and the male peasants in their long frock coats, all perfectly natural, without affectation.[31]

Spindler was so impressed by his experience in Geispolsheim that he told several of his friends who made a habit of attending every year. In fact, he claims responsibility for transforming the quaint observance into the folkloric spectacle that it would soon become:

> Thanks to our recommendation this procession soon became a destination for the lovers of 'folklore.' … The old peasants of Geispolsheim became bit players delivered up for the curiosity of tourists and the indiscretion of photographers.[32]

Spindler's description of the ceremony focuses entirely on the visual spectacle of the event; he disregards any of the significance or ritual of the occasion beyond the stunning costumes. His keen observation suggests his interest in capturing the scene in a painting. While he adopts a tone of regret for the loss of the original naiveté (real or imagined) and purity of the customs, he played no small part in the transformation. By documenting for the purpose of preserving customs and bringing greater awareness to the beauty and pageantry of Alsatian customs, he invited curious onlookers. Spindler articulated the narrative that comes to define the Fête-Dieu—preservation in the face of disappearing customs. Essentially, this reframing from a long-held custom to a spectacle for curious tourists represents the transformation of religious devotion. In seeking to preserve the custom, Spindler lost sight of the profound cultural significance of the event itself.

Interventions to preserve the Fête-Dieu went beyond simply encouraging spectators. By the turn of the century, fewer and fewer young women were wearing their regional dress in the procession. By 1909, the leaders of the Musée Alsacien decided to intervene. They had the broad red ribbons produced and sold them at cost. Then they provided a gift of pottery to the girls who wore complete costumes. As a result of the efforts, the number of young women in regional costume went from twelve the year before to seventy-four once the museum intervened. For several years the museum promoted the event through announcements that included train schedules, recommended lodging, and descriptions of the ceremony.[33] The event attracted thousands of spectators and became a popular attraction. The museum encouraged the use of regional dress for its original function, the celebration of a religious event; however, the promotion transformed the religious event into a form of tourism. The museum's role in preserving regional dress practices fundamentally changed their meaning and audience.

Folk Dress in Political Rallies

While in France the events where regional dress was worn were increasingly secular and touristic by the turn of the century, they lacked the political implications of such events in Germany. However, following Alsace's incorporation into the German empire, parade floats full of girls in regional dress were included in political events as early as the 1870s in Strasbourg. The politicization of regional dress in these parades reflected the direct influence of German culture in the region. When the Kaiser visited Alsace in 1877, he was greeted with a parade through the streets of Strasbourg, which he observed from a balcony.

> The cheering ovations of the young men and girls, who continuously waved their hats and scarves up to the Kaiser, touched even those who had witnessed the

scene at the Veste Kronprinz. From the vinedressed green arbors, into which the festival wagons had been transformed, stout young peasant girls, some of them remarkably beautiful, in their various impressive costumes of Lower Alsace, sent their greetings up to the Kaiser; a picture filled with colorful, folkloristic Impressions, as one can rarely witness.[34]

An illustration of this same event shows the women in regional costume seated in a wagon decorated with garlands that is pulled by a team of draft horses[35] (Figure 5.2). The wagon and the entire parade bore a close resemblance to the earlier illustration by Touchemolin of a rural wedding and of the processions in the Munich Oktoberfests. The green garlands on the wagons were supplemented with German and Alsatian flags. In this example, the Alsatians have simply repurposed their clothing and wagons for political celebrations, rather than their more usual local celebrations. Kassel later wrote of the great interest Kaiser Wilhelm I had taken in regional dress and that the rally in which hundreds of young Alsatian women greeted the aging ruler had left a lasting impression.[36] In this description of the event, Kassel only mentioned the women in regional dress and not the men. Although in these parades that developed out of the village corteges included both men and women, the women were the focal point.

Figure 5.2 Parade of Alsatians greeting the Kaiser on his visit to Strasbourg from Bernhard Friedrich Wilhelm Rogge, *Kaiserbüchlein: 1797–1888. Zur Erinnerung an Deutschlands Heldenkaiser Wilhelm I*, 1888. Widener Library, Harvard University.

Alsace was hardly unique in presenting women in regional dress to welcome visiting royalty, nor in fact was it unique to German-speaking lands. In his biography of Willem II who was king of the Netherlands from 1840 to 1849, Bosscha relates the anecdote that when the king visited Friesland he was asked what would be most pleasing to him and replied that he would like to be greeted by Frisian beauties dressed in their regional costume.[37] The deployment of women in their regional dress as a sort of spectacle arranged for the pleasure of the sovereign suggests the way in which rural women were viewed as representatives of their region. Their beauty stood for the value of the territory they represented.

The gendered nature of the display in which women served to gratify the male sovereign becomes apparent when the tables are turned and the sovereign herself was a woman. In the Netherlands there were a succession of female sovereigns and rather than women dressed in regional dress appearing for the queen, it was the dress itself that was presented. An early example of this occurred when Willem II's wife Anna Pavlovna and daughter Princess Sophia visited Friesland in 1841. The princess attended a ball on July 21 dressed in Frisian dress, then the following day both mother and daughter appeared outside for gathered crowds dressed in the regional costume.[38] In 1892, Queen Wilhelmina and her mother Emma made a visit to Friesland. The women and girls of Friesland presented as a gift to the twelve-year-old queen a complete Frisian costume. When she visited the region again in 1905, Wilhelmina arrived dressed in Frisian costume. It is clear that in Friesland as in Alsace it was the women's costumes that became a political symbol used to represent the region. The presentation of the costume, whether on young women or as the physical costume itself to the national leader, becomes a symbolic act of allegiance and of regional pride.

Once the French returned to power in Alsace at the conclusion of the First World War, wagons full of women in regional dress rolled out to greet the victors. A photograph of a wagon festooned in garlands filled with young women from Geispolsheim shows the celebration that followed the French victory.[39] French flags have replaced the German flags, but the entire presentation of the wagon closely adheres to the model established earlier by the nuptial cortege and the Kaiser's rally. The enthusiasm the residents of Geispolsheim and other Alsatian villages felt at end of the First World War naturally found expression in a very similar form of celebration to that which had accompanied weddings and messtis.

On Bastille Day in 1919, Strasbourg hosted a tremendous celebration which included women and children outfitted in folk dress. Photographs of the event indicate that the festivities included a sort of pageant in Strasbourg's main square, Place Kléber, in addition to the parade of French troops. One of

Figure 5.3 Girls in Bastille Day parade in Strasbourg, 1919, auteur non mentionné. Archives de Strasbourg, 1 Fi 1 / 2.

the photographs shows a formation of young girls dressed in folk costumes marching and carrying flags (Figure 5.3). Most of the girls visible in the photograph are dressed in Alsatian folk costume, but one of the girls in the front row is wearing the costume associated with Lorraine, which features a white mobcap rather than the large black bow of the Alsatians. These girls were not wearing the clothes they would have worn to church or to a festival. Instead they were dressed up as representations of Alsatians. The girls carried flags to symbolize their incorporation, which is to say the incorporation of Alsace into the French nation.

Unlike festivals such as messtis, these political rallies included only women in regional dress. For political purposes women became the symbolic representation of Alsace. In fact, in this case, young girls, who promised to be future of the region and the nation, became the standard bearers. Another photograph of the event shows even more clearly the allegorical tableau performed for these festivities (Figure 5.4). On an elevated platform kneels a French solder, a *poilu*. To his right stands a woman in Alsatian dress and to his left is a woman in the dress of Lorraine. These two women are each at a higher level than the man, and directly behind him and a step up from the first two women is a woman dressed as Marianne, the allegorical representation of the French Republic, in a

Figure 5.4 Allegorical tableau at Bastille Day in Strasbourg, 1919, auteur non mentionné. Archives de Strasbourg. 1 Fi 1/3.

loosely draped garment and Phrygian cap. In contrast to the men throughout the audience who are dressed in French uniforms, the figure in this tableau wears the uniform of the poilu, a member of the infantry. His round Adrian helmet contrasts with the stiff kepis worn as part of the dress uniform by the other men attending the ceremony. The utilitarian uniform of the poilu evoked the physical challenges faced by the foot soldiers who served in trenches through the recent bloody combat.[40] The figure of Marianne standing at the apex of the tableau had its origins in the figure of Liberty and thus represented the abstract ideals for which the nation stood.[41] By contrast the figures of Alsace and Lorraine, were synecdochical, individual citizens who served to represent the whole population of the region, rather than the embodiment of abstract principles. In this particular performance, Alsace and Lorraine have been rescued and reunited with the nation, Marianne, who stands above them. This was an enactment that resolved the narrative that had played out through wartime propaganda in the form of postcards and posters portraying Alsace and Lorraine as lost sisters who needed to be saved.[42]

The selection of women to symbolize Alsace (and Lorraine) was in accordance with the convention of representing nations as women; however, the exclusion of

Alsatian men from the pageantry is worth examining. The fact that thousands of Alsatian men had worn the German uniform and fought against the poilus made their inclusion in the festivities deeply problematic. While it was reasonable to depict Alsatian women as sustaining loyalty to France despite German rule, a parallel depiction of Alsatian men must have seemed inappropriate. The allegiance of the young girls who played such a prominent part in the ceremonies was less ambiguous than that of their parents. They retained the potential to become loyal Frenchwomen through proper schooling.

The inclusion of women in regional dress for ceremonial political events continued through the interwar period. For example, when Maréchal Foch visited Strasbourg in 1920 he posed with young women dressed in folk dress (Figure 5.5). Other ceremonial occasions for wearing folk dress included ribbon-cutting ceremonies and dedications. These events were political stagecraft in which the enacted scenes performed the types of propagandistic use of folk dress that had been depicted by artists for decades. Photographs from these scenes reveal that each woman had affixed a cockade onto her headbow to demonstrate her loyalty to France. The introduction of cockades onto the headbows followed the model introduced in the painting *Elle Attend*

Figure 5.5 Visit of Maréchal Foch to Strasbourg, November 21, 1920. Archives de Strasbourg, 1 Fi 1 / 26.

by Jean-Jacques Henner as well as the work by Hansi as we saw in Chapter 2. The presence of these women in folk dress to greet visiting dignitaries served as a symbolic welcome from the Alsatian people shaped in no small part by decades of propaganda.

While these ceremonial instances for wearing regional dress do correspond to its original function of marking special occasions, the introduction of rural villagers into official ceremonies in Strasbourg was a noteworthy innovation. Rather than serving an integral part in the community activities, these ceremonies were well outside of the villages and separate from the community. Rather than serving as a part of religious observation such as Sunday services or weddings, the costumes were worn for political purposes. Furthermore, the women who were wearing these costumes would not have worn them for any other purpose. The usage in these political events replaced the original religious usages.

Organization of Folk Groups

While the participation of women dressed in regional Alsatian costume became a common part of political demonstrations and parades in the years after the war, the groups of costumed women began to organize into formal associations starting in the first decades of the twentieth century. The Exposition Internationale de l'Est de la France took place in Nancy in 1909. As the largest city within the area of Lorraine that remained part of France, Nancy held an important situation on the French border. The exposition was an effort not only to showcase the rich cultural value of the city but also to foster relations with German controlled Alsace-Lorraine as well as other neighboring countries including Belgium, Luxembourg, and Switzerland. People in Alsace who continued to encourage close ties with France wished to send representation to Nancy. The festival committee invited 204 Alsatians dressed in their regional costumes to attend the exposition. Dr. August Kassel, who was instrumental in organizing the 1895 Trachtenfest, continued his organizational efforts for the Alsatian delegation sent to the 1909 International Exposition held in Nancy. Kassel contacted the mayors of villages across northern Alsace to organize groups who would travel to Nancy and wear their regional dress.[43] Ultimately villagers from Mietesheim, Engwiller, Uhrwiller, Hoerdt, Geudertheim, Hunspach, Oberseebach, and Schleithal, the principal villages where costume continued to be worn at that time, represented Alsace in Nancy. The Alsatians participated in a parade through the streets of Nancy and arrived in a section of the park decorated for dancing. In his description of the Alsatian delegation to the Nancy exposition for the *Revue Alsacienne Illustrée* Leon Dollinger concluded that "before the sympathy and admiration towards them that one could not skimp on, our peasants could realize that respect for tradition is a force, that it is an element of their patrimony. From this point of view, the Alsatian festivals of Nancy are a regionalist manifestation of the first order."[44]

While the description of the costumed villagers at Nancy from contemporary sources such as the *Revue Alsacienne Illustrée* makes it seem that the participants simply came together for the occasion of the exposition, some groups were becoming more formally organized. Similar occasions for costumed performances followed, including an Alsatian festival in Vichy in September 1924 and the *Fête de la Presse* in Strasbourg in November 1924, which featured a *Grande Kermesse Alsacienne* complete with parade.[45] The groups who participated in such festivals and parades across Alsace in the first quarter of the twentieth century were only loosely organized or were affiliated with musical groups that had more formal associations. For instance the Harmonie de Furdenheim was one such musical group founded in 1920.[46] The all-male musical group first came together on Bastille Day 1920 and held its early performances for weddings and family festivities across the Kochersberg.[47] The musicians wore uniforms that corresponded to the village's regional dress and were accompanied during their performances in parades and festivals by a group of women also outfitted in regional dress. In 1934, the entire folk group, including both the musicians and the women, traveled to Nice for the *Fête des Provinces Françaises*.[48] This national festival was evidence of the growing regionalist movement across France during the 1920s and 1930s.

In 1935 the Federation for the Conservation of Alsatian Peasant Costume officially formed for the purpose of ensuring the continued survival of regional dress. Gustave Stoskopf who was an artist and playwright who wrote in dialect was the force behind the organization as well as its first president. Stoskopf was joined in his efforts by the mayors of a number of villages and cities primarily across northern Alsace such as Wissembourg, Haguenau, and Geispolsheim as well as Louis Philippe Kamm, another artist whose work often featured Alsatian regional dress. As outlined in its statutes, the Federation was dedicated to "the country life in its entirety (peasant house, habits and customs, traditions, popular art, songs, dances, etc.)."[49] The members traveled around the region on a campaign of propaganda showing movies and giving talks.

The Federation's most significant activities revolved around their work as a governing body for the folk groups in the region. In part the Federation worked with existing musical groups already organized in the villages in order to encourage them to adopt regional dress as their uniforms.[50] It also registered folk groups and then served as an intermediary when organizers of events such as expositions and fairs sought the participation of Alsatian folk groups. One of the first events the Federation became involved was a festival held on the Monday of Pentecost in Wissembourg. Although the festival had been held annually since the nineteenth century, in 1936 the Federation assumed an active role in coordinating the participation of various costumed groups.[51] In particular the Federation insisted that the only participants could be groups from the villages where the costume was worn. This excluded groups of Alsatians not only from outside of Alsace but even those based in Strasbourg.[52] The Federation sought to guard against what they termed "abuse of the Alsatian costume" wherein city dwellers who had never worn the Alsatian costume took part in festivals dressed in inauthentic, "*fantaisiste*" costumes.[53] The role of the Federation in screening groups for festivals was to ensure authenticity which consisted both in accurate costumes and in restricting the wearing of costumes to the villagers themselves.

The efforts to control how folk groups maintained and presented their costumes occurred not just at the regional level with organizations such as Stoskopf's Federation in Alsace, but with larger national umbrella organizations that governed folk groups from across France. Stoskopf was a member of the Fédération des Groupes Folkloriques des Provinces Françaises founded in 1935 by Léonce Armbruster. This national group hosted festivals which brought together folk groups from across France. Armbruster's support of regionalism put him closely in line with the efforts of the Fédération régionaliste française (FRF). Founded in 1900 by Jean Charles-Brun, the FRF opposed centralization not only political but above all cultural in France. The organization advocated for teaching local history and folklore in the hopes of developing children's respect for their ancestors and pride in their native land.[54] The FRF popularized the term *regionalism* which the Académie française defined as the "tendency to favor the distinctive, autonomous development of the regions and to preserve the physiognomy of their manners, customs and historical traditions, while still maintaining national unity."[55]

Charles-Brun took a leading role in organizing the section of the 1937 Paris World's Fair dedicated to the regions of France. While many proponents of regionalism were conservative, the movement was not directly linked to a particular political leaning and drew adherents from across the political spectrum.⁵⁶ In fact the 1937 Paris World's Fair was associated with the policies of the left-wing Popular Front party which came to power in France in 1936. Unlike previous French universal expositions, the 1937 World's Fair included a "Regional Center" featuring the distinctive culture of twenty-seven different regions of the country.⁵⁷ The World's Fair brought national prominence in France to the regionalist movement and also linked its proponents with their international counterparts. In conjunction with the World's Fair, the noted French folklorists Georges-Henri Rivière and Paul Rivet organized an international conference on folklore held at the École du Louvre. The gathering of intellectuals as well as the displacement of folk groups and vernacular rural architecture into the urban setting of Paris called into relief the divide between the curiosity about regional dress and rural culture and its continued production in the provinces.

The establishment of folk groups in the 1920s but particularly through the 1930s reflected the fact that the celebration of the provinces and regional culture was not simply an intellectual exercise for elites but was supported by rural residents across France. While the records of the intellectuals who organized the governing Federations survive, few records remain of the individuals who took part in the festivals dressed in their regional costumes besides photographs. One article in the *Elsass-Lothringer Zeitung* from November 1936 does address the motivations of the folk group members. The writer welcomed the dedication of the members to reviving the clothing of their ancestors: "Only proud peasants can find their way back to the traditional costume, self-aware peasants who are not ashamed to show by their appearance daily and hourly: 'I am a peasant, I want to be.'"⁵⁸ The writer went on to decry the other motivations of the group members, which were centered around the appeal of traveling around the world and getting to see many things that would otherwise be inaccessible. While the writer was critical of bathing resorts, which were often the destinations where folk festivals in the 1930s were held, certainly the appeal of travel to cities such as Nice and Vichy for rural Alsatians was clear. Participation in folk groups served both as a means for members to celebrate their cultural heritage and as an opportunity to travel and share their culture with people from other places.

Another newspaper article, which reported on the 1936 Pentecost Monday parade in Wissembourg, revealed the perception of the participants in these sorts of productions.

> In Wissembourg, yesterday there was no disguise, nothing theatrical. These young women and men who paraded before our enchanted eyes were truly of the land [*terroir*]. Solid peasants, robust workers of the fields and the farms, all

of these people in jubilation showed their joy to wear and to honor the costumes that must remain those of the populations proud of their past and confident of the future.[59]

The audience understood the participation of rural villagers in the folk groups as an expression of pride in where they came from and their connection to the land. They established a connection between the land or terroir and these distinctive dress styles, much as a wine came exclusively from a particular locale. The people themselves were discussed in similar terms to a crop or produce from the soil. The festivals served as a way for urban Alsatians and perhaps Frenchmen from farther away to feel they understood and appreciated rural Alsace. At the same time as their gaze was admiring there is a distancing in the word choice of "solid peasants, robust workers."

Just as Stoskopf's Federation sought to ensure the authenticity of costumes that appeared in folk festivals, the national Federation wished to regulate how the member groups presented themselves during festivals. As part of the international conference held in 1937, Armbruster's Federation issued instructions that member groups would "submit themselves to a severe discipline and maintain everywhere abroad through their excellent apparel the prestige of France and in France the good reputation of their province."[60] The costume was not to be seen as a disguise, but to be treated with respect. "In taking on the costume of a province, one had to take on the soul." Those groups from regions such as Alsace where the costume was still worn had to dress the way it was currently worn without any reconstitution of historic styles. For those groups from provinces where costume was no longer worn there were two options: either wear the authentic costume as it existed at the moment it disappeared or wear costumes composed of new elements inspired by historic costumes. The latter style had to come as much as possible from rural artisans. Beyond these general guidelines, the instructions went on to specifically address how women could adhere to regional styles of coiffure if they had cut their hair into the hairstyles fashionable in the 1930s. Furthermore, women were forbidden to smoke, to remove their headdresses, to paint their fingernails unnatural colors, to go without stockings, and finally to dress in masculine costumes. There were no specific rules addressed to men. From the rules relating to short hair, painted nails, and makeup, it is clear that regulators believed these symbols of modernity to be at odds with their desired presentation of traditional village life. However, as men were evidently permitted to smoke or take their hats off, clearly the concerns about patrolling members' behaviors were directed prejudicially against women. The virtue of women and their performance of traditional values were viewed as necessary complements to the authentic presentation of regional dress.

The instructions further forbade any of its member groups from participating in any competitions where Queens of the Provinces were elected. The groups were also not allowed to participate in any festivals entitled "Fêtes des Provinces" which would have entailed appearing alongside carnivalesque performances and groups dressed in fancy dress. The concern was that the character of the folk group's performances, intended to showcase the rich cultural heritage of rural life in the French provinces, would be demeaned by an association with carnival-style amusements. The instructions read as a reaction against situations that clearly had arisen in the presentation of folk groups. Many groups existed outside of the affiliation with governing bodies such as the Fédération des Groupes Folkloriques des Provinces Françaises. The proliferation of folk festivals that culminated in beauty contests with the selection of a queen has already been outlined in the example of "Queen of the Ajoncs" at the Fête des fleurs in Brittany. The vision of the intellectuals and folklorists who sought to preserve regional dress and customs through performances at folk festivals came to be at odds with festival planners who sought to attract and entertain audiences.

The costumes served as an emblem of Alsace's integration in the French nation and much of the coordination of the folk groups centered on activities within France. Stoskopf's Federation did have contact with corresponding organization in other countries, however, notably Switzerland. Stoskopf corresponded with the chairman of the Schweizerische Trachtenvereinigung (Swiss Federation for Tracht) who reached out to Stoskopf upon learning of the establishment of the Alsatian group. The Swiss group had been established about ten years earlier and had similar aims to Stoskopf's.[61] The efforts to preserve regional dress occurred across Europe and the leaders of the movement had much in common. Similar groups to Stoskopf's organized across Germany. For instance one formed in Baden as early as the 1890s and there were similar groups in the 1880s in Bavaria.[62] Despite the existence of these comparable organizations in Germany, Stoskopf's personal archives do not reveal any contact with German groups. He was closely linked with his colleagues across France but despite being fluent in German did not correspond with any German folk groups or folklorists. Born in 1869, Stoskopf lived through the entire period when Alsace was German territory, but upon the return to France, he completely allied himself with French interests. The development of folk groups in the 1930s occurred in an increasingly volatile political period. Despite the potential for folklore to bridge national borders, it largely had more polarizing effects.

Nazi Influence on Folklore

During the 1930s in Germany, Nazi ideology profoundly influenced how folklore generally and folk costume more specifically were studied and understood. In Germany and the German-speaking countries of Europe, *Volkskunde* or folklore was more deeply established as an academic discipline than its equivalent fields in France. This interest in German popular culture with its emphasis on the distinctive character of the *Volk* had powerful resonances with the agenda of the National Socialist party. Many folklorists across Germany in the 1930s reshaped the discipline into an instrument of the *Blut und Boden* (Blood and Soil) propaganda which promoted the preeminence of the German peasantry. Hitler himself in *Mein Kampf* had called the peasant the "foundation of the entire nation" and this emphasis led to an embrace of elements of peasant culture including their distinctive dress styles.[63]

Hans Strobel, a leading National Socialist folklorist in the 1930s, wrote an essay on the relationship between fashion and regional dress published in the Nazi journal *Nationalsozialistische Monatshefte*. The journal disseminated the work of leading Nazi academics for a popular audience. Strobel sought to reframe regional dress not as a derivative holdover of once fashionable urban dress but rather as a direct legacy of ancient Germanic cultures. Because they were shaped by the local community, they were more appropriate and morally righteous than foreign-inspired fashions.[64] Regional dress was particularly appealing to adherents of National Socialist ideology because of its celebration of peasant classes and supposedly indigenous German cultural production.

On the other hand, regional dress highlighted local differences and marked the divisions between Catholics and Protestants. In their desire to unify Germany under their nationalist agenda, National Socialists chafed against the parochial distinctions of regional dress. Their tributes to Tracht downplayed the religious circumstances that originally occasioned its wearing. Their deployment of Tracht replaced religious significance with political pomp. In her book *Nazi Chic?*, Irene Geunther reveals how popular Tracht became in Germany and Austria in the 1930s. She found ample material espousing the virtue of *Trachtenkleidung* with "its rich Germanic history, its deep symbolic significance as a metaphor for pride in the homeland and the importance of its revival."[65] Rather than the highly variable regional dress styles, more generic styles of dirndl were promoted by magazines and other media for not just rural but even urban women.[66] The popularity of these dirndl-styles entailed a rejection of foreign fashion. The fashion industry in the 1930s was dominated by design from France, seen as an affront to the nationalist regime. Just as notably, the industry employed a significant number of Jews from tailors and dressmakers to department store owners. The celebration of Tracht was not simply for its aesthetic appeal but because of its domestic production. Rural women, in particular, were encouraged to produce raw materials such as flax and sheep for wool in addition to performing the related labor of spinning and handweaving.[67] The celebration of peasant culture attempted to elevate certain clothing styles while serving an underlying agenda of reshaping the German economy around self-sufficiency and locally made goods.

Along with clothing styles, the movement in support of Tracht celebrated natural beauty as opposed to fashionable "foreign" beauty enhanced by cosmetics. The ideal "Aryan-Nordic" type was strong and healthy as well as fertile. This natural style of beauty became conflated in the Nazi propaganda with rural culture along with clothing style such as dirndls. This association with regional dress with natural beauty was not in fact unique to Nazi Germany as it can also be seen in the rules forbidding smoking and nail polish developed by the Fédération des Groupes Folkloriques des Provinces Françaises founded in 1935 by Léonce Armbruster. It is likely that in both France and Germany the desire to preserve a conception of natural femininity stood in resistance against the potentially corrupting influence of Hollywood starlets with their heavy eye makeup, lipstick, and cigarettes. However, the Nazis' promotion of natural beauty went to a further degree with its underlying racial ideology which viewed physical beauty as a sign of genetic superiority.

While political parades had a long tradition in Germany, the Nazis drew from the long precedent to create tremendous pageantry. One of the most prominent occasions for a parade was the Nazi party rally held each year in Nuremberg between 1923 and 1938. The rally held in 1934 was notable both for its spectacular light display design by architect Albert Speer and being the subject of Leni Riefenstahl's film *Triumph of the Will*. The award-winning documentary includes footage of the parade of men and women in regional dress from across Germany. Some of the people wear more generic styles of rural dress and carry farm implements such as rakes while others are in very elaborate Tracht. Prominent among the women in their distinctive dress are ones from the area around the town of Bückeburg in Lower Saxony. The enormous beaded crowns and swooping stiffened ribbon caps worn in that region are singled out not only by Riefenstahl in her film but by Strobel in his analysis of German Tracht. Although he critiques what he terms the *Bückeburger Flügelhaube* (winged bonnet) as being an exaggerated reinterpretation of a foreign style, the region's dress is paraded before Hitler and the Nazi Party as the embodiment of German distinction.[68] In one scene from the movie, Hitler shakes the hands of a line of young women dressed in their various regional dress. They also offer the Führer baskets full of vegetables from the season's harvest. The women along with the produce represent the bounty of the German soil.

Following the Nazi annexation of Alsace in 1940, parades of women in Alsatian regional dress began to be incorporated into German propaganda. For instance, groups of young women posed with uniformed Nazi soldiers in the streets of Strasbourg in 1940 (Figure 5.6). Another scene juxtaposing Alsatian headbows and banners bearing swastikas appeared in the main Strasbourg newspaper, the *Neueste Nachrichten*, on October 20, 1941. The caption to the photograph suggests that the costumes signal that the "old German Alsace is reawakening under the influence of the National Socialist idea." The Alsatian attachment to Tracht was viewed as evidence of its German heritage and thus region's rightful place in the Third Reich.

The visual evidence linking Alsatian regional dress to the Nazi regime, however, is relatively scarce. While it was documented as signaling allegiance to the German government during the Second World War, the styles have been

Figure 5.6 Nazi soldiers with women wearing Alsatian dress in Strasbourg, 1940. Archives de Strasbourg, 1 Fi 134.

much more widely used to demonstrate allegiance to the French government. In fact not long after Alsace returned to French control after the war, women adorned in their headbows appeared at ceremonial occasions to greet visiting French dignitaries. When Charles de Gaulle visited Alsace in October 1945 he was photographed for the *Neueste Nachrichten* shaking hands with a women dressed in the costume of the Outre-Forêt.[69] Again in 1946 when President Félix Gouin visited Strasbourg, he was greeted by young women in their regional dress.[70] The presentation of these young women in their Alsatian dress was deliberately staged by municipal authorities. By the 1940s regional dress only continued to be worn on a regular basis in a few remote villages—certainly not in Strasbourg or Wissembourg. These women donned the costumes in order to perform the welcoming of French authorities in the guise of Alsace. Just as they had after the First World War, the costumed women came to stand in for the region as a whole. Once they were French again, Alsatians performed their allegiance through regional dress, being quick to indicate that their cultural heritage, in this case dress, was not proof of their Germanness or adherence to Nazi ideology. As political theater, regional dress proved remarkably flexible and was able to accommodate allegiance both to Germany and to France. The ideological framework that Nazis had developed to explain and appropriate folk culture was not inherent in the dress itself. However, the strong association between Nazism and folk culture did lead to a decline in participation in folk groups.

Re-Emergence of Interest in Folklore

The disinterest in folklore held until the 1960s when the series of performances described in the introduction of this book were first organized. In the summer of 1963, M. Gugumus proposed a series of Sunday morning performances that would include music, singing, and dancing to be held in a variety of locations around Strasbourg.[71] Gugumus was a functionary with the Council of Europe as well as the director of the folk group Fischer Kapell based in Schiltigheim. The municipal office in charge of tourism organized the festivities and provided each participating group with 200 F. The first year, the performances were held every other Sunday in July and August. Following the first performance on July 7, the *Dernières nouvelles du Lundi* reported on the success of the presentation by the group from Berstett that "gave tourists the opportunity to take magnificent photographs."[72] The whole series of performances was so well received that the city continued to organize them in the years that followed and expanded the schedule to run from June through September.⁷³ The official support provided by the city of Strasbourg attests to the value that folk costumes have provided for the encouragement of tourism and development of unique experiences for visitors to the region. The activities of the folk groups demonstrate the continued relevance and adaptation of Alsatian folk dress more generally.

The launch of these regular summer performances in Strasbourg marked a renaissance for interest in folk costumes and participation in folk. By this time, the folk groups of Alsace were governed under an umbrella organization, the Federation des groups folkloriques d'Alsace which itself was part of a national confederation of French folk groups. In 1968, key organizers of the Strasbourg performances met to discuss improvements to the program.⁷⁴ The attendees included the vice-president of the Federation of as well as representatives of folk groups and the city. They proposed to provide paid instructors who would meet with each of the different folk groups "in order to develop the presentation and choreography."⁷⁵ The music and steps for the dances were "established in documentation made available to all of the groups." The folk groups were not able to pay for the instructors, so the city was asked to step in and provide the funds. Another recommendation from the meeting was that M. André of the Office de Radiodiffusion Télévision Française should develop the script for the presentation to be read by one or a couple of the participants. The text would preferably be in three languages and provide a greeting as well as an explanation of the costumes and dances. Through the 1960s the presentation of these performances came to include an elevated stage, microphones, and even refreshments. Effectively by standardizing the instruction and dances for the folk groups and writing the script, this intervention sought to enforce a coherent image for Alsatian folk dance and costume.

The number of folk groups across Alsace has continued to increase. During the summer of 2007, nine different groups performed in the Place Gutenberg, including the Groupe folklorique du Pays de Hanau de Bouxwiller (GFPHB), which was founded in 1978 (Plate 1). For their performances, the women of the group wear the regional costume of the area including the large black headbow, colorful wool skirts, stomachers, and aprons, while the adult men wear the red vests with black hats and pants. The group now consists of around thirty children between five and twelve years old, twenty adolescents, and twenty adults.⁷⁶ The group's website describes their mission:

> We aim to maintain the cultural heritage of our region, the "Pays de Hanau" by keeping its manners, customs, dialect, traditional dress, songs, counting

rhymes, country dances and by digging out other aspects of its past and have them revived.

A key part of preserving our linguistic and cultural identity lies in sharing it with others abroad and at home.

The challenge of the group since its creation has been to allow our young dancers to discover and appreciate the habits practiced by their Hanau ancestors, to instill in them an admiration for their roots, and to give them the opportunity to exchange with young people from other countries and cultures.[77]

In keeping with their stated mission, the group not only gives public performances but arranges workshops for members of the local community in such activities as basket making, resist dye techniques for decorating Easter eggs, and baking *Bredele*, Alsatian Christmas cookies. In cooperation with the Office for the Language and Culture of Alsace, the group also conducts an annual event for children entirely in the Alsatian dialect. The members also run a booth at the Christmas market in Bouxwiller. The group's principal purpose is not to entertain tourists but rather to educate young people about not just regional dress but also Alsatian language and practices.

In addition to the annual weekend performance in Strasbourg and the local workshops, each July the group hosts an international festival in the small village of Imbsheim just outside of Bouxwiller. Groups from across Europe come and perform over the course of the two-day festival. In 2007, groups from Bulgaria as well as the French regions of the Vendée and Savoie took part in the festival. The visiting groups stay with host families in Imbsheim and have the chance to travel by bus along the *Route des vins* through the Alsatian countryside. The members of the GFPHB, in turn, have the opportunity to participate in exchanges and explore regions of other countries as well. During 2007, for example, the group traveled to six different departments of France in 2007 as well as to areas of Switzerland, Germany, and the Netherlands. These exchanges provide opportunities for residents of these small villages to meet people from across Europe as well as to travel. The festival is open to the public and primarily attracts people from the surrounding area, particularly aficionados of folk culture. The audience for the event forms an interest intersection between the local community in Alsace and communities in various countries across Europe. The centrality of travel and cultural exchange for these folk groups is in direct continuity with motivations described for members of folk groups in the 1930s. These organizations allowed people from rural communities across Europe to interact through their shared love of their own heritage. The attachment to the local became an opportunity for engagement across national boundaries.

Conclusion

The evolution of regional dress into costume for folk groups clearly reflects the tension between modernity and tradition. The growing separation between the wearing of regional styles and the religious observances where they first emerged is ostensibly consistent with secularization which is one of the cornerstones of modernity. While some of the occasions such as the Fête-Dieu or Breton pardons maintained their original piety and purpose, at the same time even these events increasingly served as attractions for tourists. Religious devotion became an element of rural culture recast as spectacle. The sites for these performances also moved from small villages into larger cities, echoing the larger relocation from rural to urban areas. From the Munich Oktoberfest in the early nineteenth century through the folk dancing in the center of Strasbourg which continues during summers in the twenty-first century, folk performances represent a demonstration of rural life often targeted toward urban audiences. While the folk groups also serve important functions within their local communities, they are most prominent as ambassadors of rural life for city dwellers. In many ways it is the process of urbanization including the depopulation of the countryside which threatened rural traditions including dress. However, it is this very disappearance which created a value and nostalgia for regional dress which motivates its wearers today.

The deployment of regional dress for political purposes began as early as the beginning of the nineteenth century. Parades featuring rural residents dressed in their distinctive splendor served as a means of visualizing the region whether a duchy, a principality, or even a kingdom. The clothing appeared alongside the region's bountiful harvest and attested to the fertile countryside. While political circumstances changed dramatically with the consolidation of nations, the deployment of regional dress proved flexible and accommodated nascent nationalism. In the case of Alsace, floats filled with women in regional dress greeted Kaisers and French presidents in their turn. However, the widespread use of Alsatian regional dress by France both in performances and in artistic representations during the First World War shaped the lasting association with French loyalty. This link did not prevent Nazi incorporation of folk dress into their own parades and propaganda. While essentially tied to the local community and varying from village to village, rural dress worn for parades alternately displayed diversity but increasingly served to represent larger regions. The performance of regional dress reflected the tension between regionalism, nationalism, and transnationalism. While folk performances and parades began as a means of making regional culture visible, they have become a means of creating bridges between regions. Just as Europe has established political cooperation among nations through the European Union, these folk groups represent a means of cultural exchange at the level of the people.

Conclusion

The challenge of writing about the broad phenomenon of regional dress as it emerged across Western Europe is that it is inherently local. In light of this book's focus on the particularities of its emergence and evolution in Alsace, it is valuable to conclude with a reflection on how this particular case is representative of the broader implications of regional dress. Each of the chapters of this book has addressed a different facet of how regional dress appears—as a religious performance, as a rendering by artists, as a material good which is produced and consumed, as an object in a museum collection, and finally as a costume worn by members of folk groups. In each of these forms, regional dress remains relevant today as a means of remembering the past and of continuing to shape an understanding of regional identity.

Fête-Dieu continues to be observed annually in the Alsatian town of Geispolsheim with a procession incorporating regional dress (Plate 19). While the beauty of the ceremony continues to attract tourists as it did in the years when it was promoted by Charles Spindler and the Musée Alsacien, it remains a solemn observance intended primarily as a religious observance rather than a popular attraction. Residents of the village deck out the streets with flowers and palm fronds. The beautiful red bows and skirts of the young women carrying the gilded statue of Mary further enhance the picturesque scene. The attendees, however, do not simply watch the ceremony. In the appropriate points of the mass, they drop to their knees to kneel in prayer. While the uniform regional dress of the women in their red bows provides a visual form of unity and coherence, the collective movement to kneel in the streets also brings together the Catholics in attendance. The regional dress in this ceremony serves as a further reinforcement of the sense of community gathered in shared devotion.

The young women in their red bows and white lace aprons who carry the statues are not the only attendees in costume. The procession includes members of the local band who wear their uniforms which consist of red vests and black pants typical of the male costume worn in folk groups. Additionally members of the folk group Coquelicots de Geispolsheim also attend in their costumes.[1] The women in the group, regardless of age and marital status, wear the red bows which originally signaled the wearer was unmarried. The folk groups, which continue the practice of wearing regional dress, merge seamlessly into the original religious circumstances of the costumes. This religious event continues to be central to the character of Geispolsheim and its observance integrates members of the community including musical groups and folk groups. The line between religious observance and tourism is not a sharp break but a continuum in which the beauty of regional dress complements the decoration from flowers strewn in the streets and filling the window boxes. The village's distinctive heritage and beauty attract onlookers who seek the distinctive character of the region.

A similar sense of community is created in Catholic towns and villages across Europe that also continue to celebrate the Feast of Corpus Christi with processions featuring regional dress. The procession in Bavaria's Seehausen not only navigates the village's streets but continues on to the lake. The boats filled with the faithful include men, women, and children dressed in their local styles of regional dress (Plate 20). The situation of the procession as it passes from the land to water highlights the distinctive geographic features of the village. The local specificity of the festival's setting is echoed in both the distinctive dress and the unique landscape. The dress functions as a means of creating an outward harmony which ties together the people of the village. While the vestments worn by clergy transform the wearers into representatives of the Church, the regional dress worn by the villagers emphasizes their belonging in the community as the members of the congregation. The vocabulary of Catholicism echoes the tension between the universal ("Catholic") and the local ("parochial"). The persistence of local festivals featuring regional dress appeals to a popular love of pageantry but also a form of attachment to the community which exists as through shared religious faith. The continued use of regional dress in its original context for religious festivals undermines the argument that the widespread abandonment of regional dress reflected a loss of faith in face of growing secularization.

Few villages in France mark the occasion with a procession, although religious festivals for other occasions continue to take place in Brittany. The distinctive Breton festivals are known as pardons and like Geispolsheim's Fête-Dieu, the stunning appearance of the assemblage of men and women in their distinctive dress creates a convergence of religious observance and popular attraction. The Grande Tromenie which is held around the village of Locronan every six years attracts thousands of pilgrims, many of whom don their regional dress. The participants follow a path winding around the countryside for over 7 miles as they follow the circuit walked by the local saint Ronan. The pilgrimage honors local sacred spots and connects the participants with the land. The tenacity of Catholicism in Brittany becomes intrinsically linked to the countryside through the walk around the village. The participants' choice of distinctly local outfits further enforces the link between faith and the local village. While many folk festivals in Brittany have referenced pardons, the religious core of the ceremony continues to be observed in events such as the one in Locronan. The ensuing scenes of faith remain attractive to tourists and photographers in no small part because of these costumes.

While the intervention of artists who have documented such religious scenes did not eliminate the religious core in a select few of these festivals, ultimately their work has profoundly influenced how regional dress is understood. The most prominent representations of regional dress now appear across a variety of commercial goods and in retail spaces. The distinctive character of Alsatian culture has been widely mobilized for advertisement. While Hansi originally created political satire so scathing that he was imprisoned several times by the Germans in the years leading up to the First World War, his images of children in regional dress now grace an array of products including tins of cookies and jars of jam. Hansi's work adapts naturally as advertisement because of its inherent cuteness and his own participation in commerce as a graphic artist. His work in advertising includes the logo for Potasse d'Alsace which features a stork and a silhouette of the Strasbourg cathedral. Hansi's work is now maintained as a brand *marché de l'Oncle Hansi*.[2] Hansi consciously sought to promote his concept of Alsace. He created a visual identity for the region which depended on his distinctive artistic style but more importantly on the integration of distinctive elements of regional design and culture—the half-timbered houses, the cathedral, storks, kougelhopf, and most importantly *Alsaciennes* with their large headbows.

While Hansi's work now extends to products such as tableware and stationary, it is most visible in its association with food products. The jams under the label feature distinctly Alsatian fruit such as the quetsch (a type of plum) and the baked goods include such regional delicacies as Kougelhopf, bredele, and pain d'épice. Hansi's *Alsaciennes* also adorn a line of wines, the product with arguably the closest link to the terroir. The connection drawn between the region's wines such as crémant d'Alsace and Riesling and its distinctive dress styles further reinforces a construction of regional identity. The headbow is a visual incarnation which pairs with the physical sensation of taste derive directly from the region's agricultural products. Alsace becomes a concept through the deployment of the senses.

Just as Alsace is constructed through the link between regional dress and foods, a similar process has occurred in regions across Europe. Dutch cheeses are branded with the image of a woman in an adaptation of regional dress. For instance, the brand Cheeseland has a variety called "Dutch Girl" which features an image of a woman dressed in the costume from Volendam with its iconic winged lace cap and wooden shoes on its label. The association between a woman in regional dress and cheese is not simply local in its reach; it is prominent on exported goods. The Dutch Dairy Organization (NZB) introduced the character of Frau Antje to promote their products in Germany (Plate 21). The name actually derived from a young woman from the Hague named Antje who was working at a cheese booth at an agricultural fair in Berlin in 1959. Her popularity led the NZB to engage an actress to model for the character of Frau Antje who came to represent Dutch cheeses for the German market.[3] The character's costume was not specific to any region of the Netherlands but was a generalized impression. The distinct winged bonnet, however, closely resembles the cap from Volendam. The woman in a loose interpretation of regional dress came to represent not a specific region at all but an entire country.

A similar amalgamated costume has come to represent Germany in the popular imagination. St. Pauli Girl beer is instantly recognizable for the image of a woman in a dirndl holding several steins of beer in each hand. The beer brand is now under the ownership of the international behemoth Anheuser Busch InBev. The identity of the brand remains distinct and recognizable by its exploitation of the image of a woman in a variation of regional dress. The dirndl immediately connects the brand to its roots in Bremen, Germany even if it is currently brewed in St. Louis, MO. In a world of global consolidation, the dirndl creates a feeling of *Gemütlichkeit*, the distinctly German sense of conviviality, comfort, and good cheer. The most recent iterations of the St. Pauli Girl label, however, lean more heavily on appealing to lust than thirst. The depiction of the dirndl emphasizes the model's bust and seems to be offering herself as much as the beers in her hands. The sexualization of regional dress with the suggestive depiction of a lusty barmaid to sell beer contrasts sharply on the image of the youthful, innocent *Alsacienne* used in Alsace to sell wine. However, it does have its counterpart in the logo used for the beer L'Alsacienne sans culotte which shifts the emphasis from the chest to the bare rear end. In promoting products, the appeal of a woman in regional dress has conceded over time to the adage in advertisement that sex sells. The deployment of regional dress in advertisement has ultimately veered well away from its religious origins.

The popularization of the image of a young woman in a dirndl as seen in the St. Pauli Girl mascot is accompanied by a market for such costumes. These costumes have proliferated in Germany since the early twentieth century and are now available across the country in specialty shops. Despite their association with Bavaria and the Alps, dirndls as well as the male equivalent, lederhosen, are sold in shops across Germany including from Berlin to Frankfurt. The styles are not linked with a particular village or geographic region and have no association with religious events. Dirndls have evolved from their appearance in the early twentieth century when they were emphatically modest to feature short skirts and low decolletage. The shops that sell them feature an array of products that create the complete style including not just the dirndl dress, blouse, and apron but also appropriate bras and jewelry. For men there is a similar diversity of products including not just the leather shorts, suspenders, jackets, and shirts but also shoes, socks, and even the knit gaiters known as *Loferl*. Some of the stores such as Moser Trachten which has shops across Bavaria have a significant web presence for online shopping.[4] The widespread availability of this form of Trachten as ready-to-wear is distinct from the way that most regional dress is available elsewhere in Europe.

The proliferation of folk groups continues to generate demand for the production of folk dress. Much of this production is done at home by one or more of the members of the group; however, there is enough demand to support a shop in Strasbourg that continues to produce Alsatian regional dress. According to its website, the Maison Bossert has been in business since 1825, although the operation has changed hands several times.[5] Charles Spindler noted that in 1937 there was one remaining shop in Strasbourg that specialized in the supplies associated with traditional dress including red and black bows, aprons, collars, corselets, although he described their quality as "detestable."[6] It is quite possible that Spindler was referring to Maison Bossert which was founded in 1825. M. Stein began running the shop in 1945 after he had traveled around villages across Lower Alsace to purchase garments and learn how the garments were constructed.[7] In 1986, he passed the shop on to Marie Rose Allard, who continued the operation until 2010, when it was bought out by the Groupe Paul Kroely Automobiles. Allard continued to follow the techniques that she had learned from her predecessor.

The current operation at the Maison Bossert is run by Anne Wolff, a historian who worked with the textile collection at the Musée Unterlinden in Colmar.[8] Wolff is dedicated to the preservation of Alsatian dress, and her boutique continues this mission in a number of ways. Beyond simply selling new costumes, the boutique also stocks the materials necessary for its production. Many folk groups make their own costume which means they need to acquire the distinctive materials: the wide ribbons for the headbows, the jacquard woven materials for the aprons, and the sequins and thread for the embroidery. This home production depends not only on these materials but also on know-how. Wolff recognizes the centrality of passing on the specialized knowledge. The boutique hosts a series of ateliers in order to assure that this knowledge is maintained by future generations. According to the website, the boutique is also involved in the restoration of historic garments. It depends on a network of experts who perform work on historic pieces. The continued operations of Maison Bossert reflect the changes that have occurred in the market but attest to the evolving needs of aficionados of regional dress. It serves a material need but also reflects the centrality of continued production and availability of goods for continued performances and representations.

The preservation of historic garments occurs within a commercial context under the auspices of the Maison Bossert but is also central to the mission of museums such as the Musée Alsacien. Museums do not simply house collections but care for them with the help of conservators. This form of care serves to maintain the region's cultural heritage. Some museums go beyond preserving historic items and depend on demonstrating how goods were made in the past. The Ecomusée d'Alsace is just that sort of museum that instructs visitors on Alsace's rural culture through demonstrations and costumed interpreters. The museum which opened to the public in 1984 is in the village of Ungersheim in the middle of the southern Alsatian countryside. The Ecomusée was close to the plan of a museum Spindler had suggested at the time of the founding of the Musée Alsacien; it brings together historic structures typical of rural Alsatian architecture in order to demonstrate aspects of rural culture. The Ecomusée includes livestock and agriculture as well as elements of the built landscape. Visitors are introduced to Alsatian regional dress through a combination of displays of historic pieces and the costumes worn by interpreters. While the displays highlight the quintessential bow and the distinctive special occasion dress, the interpreters wear costumes that reflect everyday wear.

The Ecomusée d'Alsace boasts of being the largest Open Air museum in France, although it is far from the only one. Skansen, founded by Artur Hazelius in 1891, is widely considered to be the first of its kind, but this model of museology has been widely copied across Western Europe. A more modest example in Brittany is the Village de Poul Fetan which is a restored hamlet which showcases peasant life in the nineteenth century. The region's office of tourism describes the scene: "Elegantly dressed as in days gone by, the smiling people of the village greet the visitors, and tell the story of 'Brittany of yesteryear,' that of the work of the fields and the buckwheat porridge."[9] In evoking days gone by, the costumes are an essential element of the reconstruction. Living history museums depend on an immersive experience in which clothing is a central element in evoking the past.

Just over the border from Alsace is the Open Air Museum Vogtsbauernhof in the Black Forest. Designed to explore the cultural heritage of rural areas throughout the Black Forest, it claims to be one of the most visited open-air museums in not only Germany but throughout Europe, having attracted over 16 million visitors since its opening in 1964. The museum encourages visitors to experience with all your senses and incorporates workshops and demonstrations to give visitors a hands-on visit beyond simply observing. The museum is located in Gutach which is where women wear the hats adorned with a pile of bright red pompoms. The pompoms featured prominently in the museum's publicity, website, and brochures. The open-air museums integrate the region's distinctive dress styles with its characteristic architecture, although most of these operations, such as the Ecomusée d'Alsace and the Vogtsbauernhof, have moved most of the buildings from their original locations across the region to be reconstructed on the museum's campus. The museum experience assembles experiences that evoke the past through artful reconstitution and reenactment.

The respect for the variety and richness of Alsatian regional dress reflected at the Ecomusée d'Alsace is also shared by a growing number of the region's folk groups. While the traditional dress worn by folk groups in the 1960s widely conformed to the stereotype with the red skirts and black headbows, more recently many groups' costumes reflect a greater desire to not just show the diversity but even change over time. The Kochloeffel de Souffelweyersheim is one of the groups that is particularly dedicated to recreating with exactitude a variety of different costumes such as the dress of wealthy bourgeois of the late eighteenth to early nineteenth century as well as working dress down to the work blouses, straw hats, and coarse aprons. These groups no longer associate the distinctions between different dress styles with the attributes of the wearer. Women do not necessarily wear the color of bow associated with their confession or marital status. For instance, all of the women of the Coquelicot de Geispolsheim wear the red bows worn by unmarried women from village. The attention to the particularities of dress disregards the underlying significance of the performances. The costumes are reenactments of earlier ways of life.

The social function of these costumes is fundamentally different from their original function, but they continue to reflect the wearers' deep attachment to the community. Rather than an obligation for residents of the villages, these costumes are a choice. In contrast of the urban perception of rural life as backward and parochial, the participants of folk groups find positive value in life in rural Alsace, which is expressed through and derived from these traditions.

The folk groups form associations which are active in benevolent activities within their local communities. They also serve as representatives for their villages and regions in events which bring together people from across not only their own country but across Europe and beyond. As a simple tourist attraction, they provide a vision for visitors of what the local culture is—whether in Alsace, Brittany, Baden, or Bavaria. But many of the festivals that the groups organize and attend bring about remarkable levels of intercultural exchange. When the Groupe Folklorique du Pays de Hanau de Bouxwiller (GFPHB) hosts their annual festival Portes Ouvertes in Imbsheim, they welcome groups from countries as far away as Bulgaria and Mexico not only to their village but into their homes. Members of the folk groups have the occasion to travel extensively and truly experience different cultures: through music, costumes, drinks, and meals. The transnational exchange occurs between members of different groups as well as for the curious tourists who manage to catch a folk performance.

The commercial and touristic uses of regional dress in the twenty-first century have largely diffused the political charge that the dress had for much of the twentieth century. While members of folk groups such as the GFPHB participate in local observances on May 8 to honor the French victory in the Second World War, political occasions for the regional dress are rare. Since the Second World War, the tensions between France and Germany no longer defined the political climate of Alsace. Instead, the two countries became two pillars of the emerging European Union with Strasbourg selected as the seat of the European Parliament to symbolize the resolution of conflict between the neighboring powers. Folk costumes rarely appear on the occasion of state visits in Alsace, as they would have in the aftermath of the First World War and even the Second World War. For example when US President Barack Obama visited Strasbourg for the 2009 NATO summit, he was not greeted by young women in headbows. This omission stood in sharp contrast to his arrival in Kehl, Germany where he was met with girls wearing the distinctive traditional dress of Baden[10] (Plate 22). Despite the exceptions to French centralization that the nation continues to extend to Alsace-Moselle, official state visits correspond to the French model, which does not promote regional dress in the context of national politics.

This divergence in how regional dress is deployed diplomatically by Germany and France demonstrates that regional dress does not appear in exactly the same way across Europe. Just as regional dress varies from village to village it functions differently according to country. It retains its local and national particularities. Oktoberfest in Munich in the twentieth century welcomes visitors from around the world, many of whom dress in dirndls and lederhosen. Visitors and locals alike wear forms of folk dress that define a particular aspect of Germanness. In contrast, visitors to Strasbourg's Place Gutenberg in July enjoy a very different vision of folk costume. In these performances, residents of rural villages present their cultural heritage to tourists and city residents. While the dancing and music is entertaining, an explanation of the costumes provides instruction and context. Like food, regional dress is readily accessible for newcomers to an area in contrast to language and dialect, which are essential elements of local culture unintelligible to outsiders. Regional dress may not convey the same meaning to tourists that it does to the original wearers, but it provides a visible signal of local and regional identity that is comprehensible. Its meanings and uses have changed over time from religious to political and then to touristic and commercial. Throughout this evolution, it retains the capacity to serve a religious and political purpose even as it appeals to tourists. In representing local culture these different facets are often overlapping and simultaneous. Regional dress has a history, but its current iteration as folk dress is form of history of remembering and of understanding regional culture that is distinctly modern.

The clear distinction between tradition and modernity becomes complicated with a closer examination of the phenomenon of regional dress. Considering the hallmarks of modernity as secularization, urbanization, mass production, and nationalism might lead one to the facile conclusion that regional dress is in direct opposition. Rising from religious performances in rural areas, made by hand according to styles handed down through oral history and representing local identity, regional dress represents a hold-over of traditional culture. However, this very process of holding over depended on the very aspects of modernity that it ostensibly defies. Coopted for tourism and advertisement, the dress has lost much but not all of its religious associations. Frequently worn for performances in urban areas, it serves as a link between urban and rural. Sold in department stores or still made by trained hands in specialty shops, the garments make up a very niche market but can still be procured. Even its link to regionalism stands as a complement rather than a simple antagonist to nationalism. Repeatedly regional dress has served as an emblem of national identity or loyalty. Since the middle of the twentieth century nationalism in Europe has increasingly confronted pressures to cooperate in transnational bodies such as European Union. Regional dress and participation in costume folk groups have evolved to remain relevant in events that span national boundaries and bring together people from across Europe and around the world. The history of regional dress is the history of the tensions between traditional rural culture and the homogenizing effects of modernization. The persistence of these distinctive styles attests to the capacity of modern life to not simply accommodate but to foster and valorize elements of the past.

Notes

Introduction

1. For a typology of comparative histories see Heinz-Gerhard Haupt and Jürgen Kocka, eds., *Comparative and Transnational History: Central European Approaches and New Perspectives* (New York: Berghahn Books, 2009), 2–10.
2. Eugen Weber, *Peasants into Frenchmen: The Modernization of Rural France, 1870–1914* (Stanford, CA: Stanford University Press, 1976).
3. David Harvey, *Paris, Capital of Modernity* (New York: Routledge, 2006), 1.
4. Hugh McLeod, *Secularization in Western Europe, 1848–1914* (New York: St. Martin's Press, 2000), 1–3.
5. Weber, *Peasants into Frenchmen*, 492.
6. Harvey, *Paris, Capital of Modernity*, 1.
7. Caroline Ford, *Creating the Nation in Provincial France: Religion and Political Identity in Brittany* (Princeton: Princeton University Press, 1993); Anne-Marie Thiesse, *Ils apprenaient la France : l'exaltation des régions dans le discours patriotique*, vol. 17 (Paris: Editions de la Maison des sciences de l'homme, 1997).
8. Stéphane Gerson, *The Pride of Place: Local Memories and Political Culture in Nineteenth-Century France* (Ithaca: Cornell University Press, 2003), 4.
9. Celia Applegate, *A Nation of Provincials: The German Idea of Heimat* (Berkeley: University of California Press, 1990); Alon Confino, *The Nation as a Local Metaphor: Württemberg, Imperial Germany, and National Memory, 1871–1918* (Chapel Hill: University of North Carolina Press, 1997).
10. Eric Hobsbawm, "Introduction: Inventing Traditions," in *The Invention of Tradition*, ed. Eric Hobsbawm and Terence Ranger, Past and Present Publications (Cambridge: Cambridge University Press, 1983), 2.
11. Hugh Trevor-Roper, "The Invention of Tradition: The Highland Tradition of Scotland," in *The Invention of Tradition*, ed. Eric Hobsbawm and Terence Ranger, Past and Present Publications (Cambridge: Cambridge University Press, 1983), 15–41.
12. Hobsbawm, "Introduction: Inventing Traditions," 2.
13. Regina Bendix, "Diverging Paths in the Scientific Search for Authenticity," *Journal of Folklore Research* 29, no. 2 (1992): 104; Bendix credits this phrase to the German linguist Uwe Pörksen, *Plastic Words: The Tyranny of a Modular Language* (University Park, PA: Pennsylvania State University Press, 1995).

14. Siân Jones, "Negotiating Authentic Objects and Authentic Selves: Beyond the Deconstruction of Authenticity," *Journal of Material Culture* 15, no. 2 (June 1, 2010): 182, https://doi.org/10.1177/1359183510364074.
15. Roland Barthes, *The Fashion System*, trans. Matthew Ward and Richard Howard (New York: Hill and Wang, 1983).
16. Elizabeth Vlossak, *Marianne or Germania? Nationalizing Women in Alsace, 1870–1946* (Oxford: Oxford University Press, 2010), 5.
17. Alfred Wahl, *Confession et comportement dans les campagnes d'Alsace et de Bade, 1871–1939: catholiques, protestants et juifs: démographie, dynamisme économique et social, vie de relation et attitude politique* (Strasbourg: Editions Coprur, 1980), 30.
18. Vlossak, *Marianne or Germania*, 4.
19. Alfred Wahl, *L'option et l'émigration des Alsaciens-Lorrains, 1871–1872* (Paris: Ophrys, 1974).
20. Vlossak, *Marianne or Germania*, 7.
21. Vlossak, *Marianne or Germania*, 7.
22. These tensions eventually culminated in the episode known as the Zabern Affair, so-called for the German name of the city where it took place, now known in French as Saverne. A significant amount has been written on this event with the standard accounts being: David Schoenbaum, *Zabern 1913: Consensus Politics in Imperial Germany* (London; Boston: George Allen & Unwin, 1982); Dan P. Silverman, *Reluctant Union; Alsace-Lorraine and Imperial Germany, 1871–1918* (University Park: Pennsylvania State University Press, 1972); Hans Ulrich Wehler, "Der Fall Zabern von 1913/14 Als Verfassungskrise Des Wilhelminischen Kaiserreichs," in *Krisenherde Des Kaiserreichs. 1871–1918. Studien z. Dt.Sozial- u. Verfassungsgeschichte* (Göttingen: Vandenhoeck u. Ruprecht, 1970), 70–80.
23. Roland Schwab, "La grande mutation des campagnes alsaciennes (1871–1960)," in *Histoire de l'Alsace rurale*, ed. Jean-Michel Boehler, Dominique Lerch, and Jean Vogt, Collection "Grandes publications" t. 24 (Strasbourg: ISTRA, 1983), 363.

Chapter 1

1. Lynne Hume, *The Religious Life of Dress: Global Fashion and Faith*, Dress, Body, Culture (New York: Bloomsbury Academic, 2013).
2. Bernard Vogler, "En Alsace: orthodoxie et territorialisme," in *Histoire des protestants en France*, ed. Robert Mandrou (Toulouse: Privat, 1977), 182.
3. The Alsatian Anabaptists were joined in the eighteenth century by Swiss Anabaptists who fled persecution. Jean Séguy, "Quatre siècles et demi d'histoire: Les anabaptistes," in *Les Anabaptistes Mennonites d'Alsace: Destin d'une minorité*, ed. Saisons D'Alsace. Nouvelle série 76 (Strasbourg: Librairie Istra, 1981), 10–11.

4 Claude Muller, *Églises mixtes: du Kochersberg, du pays de Hanau et de l'Alsace bossue: 1802–1914*, ed. Pays d'Alsace. Série Recherches (Saverne: Société d'histoire et d'archéologie de Saverne et environs, 1983), 58–63.
5 Alfred Wahl, *Confession et comportement dans les campagnes d'Alsace et de Bade, 1871–1939: catholiques, protestants et juifs: démographie, dynamisme économique et social, vie de relation et attitude politique* (Strasbourg: Editions Coprur, 1980), 28.
6 Wahl, 30.
7 Vogler, "En Alsace: orthodoxie et territorialisme," 162.
8 Joëlle Callot Burnouf, ed., *Le Kochersberg: histoire et paysages* (Strasbourg: Publitotal, 1980), 5.
9 Charles Emrich, *Collection de six costumes nationaux Alsaciens et Badois* (Strasbourg, 1834).
10 The reference by Gatineau in an image caption is typical of the explanation of this image in the secondary literature when she says the plates "témoignent de la différenciation confessionnelle dans le costume féminin dans la région du Kochersberg." There is no indication on the original plate that one is Catholic and the other Protestant. Barbara Gatineau, "Preface," in *Costumes et coutumes d'Alsace*, ed. Anselme Laugel, Nouv. éd. (Nancy: Place Stanislas, 2008), caption on p. 20.
11 Anselme Laugel and Charles Spindler, *Costumes et coutumes d'Alsace*, Nouv. éd. (Nancy: Place Stanislas, 2008), 113.
12 Vogler, "En Alsace: orthodoxie et territorialisme," 156.
13 Heinz Schmitt, "Die Bollenhuttracht: Entwicklung, Pflege, Vermarktung," *Die Ortenau: Zeitschrift des Historischen Vereins für Mittelbaden*, no. 69 (1989): 441.
14 Hugh McLeod, *Secularization in Western Europe, 1848–1914* (New York: St. Martin's Press, 2000), 19.
15 Ralph Gibson, *A Social History of French Catholicism, 1789–1914*, Christianity and Society in the Modern World (London; New York: Routledge, 1989), 174–6.
16 Caroline Ford, "Religion and the Politics of Cultural Change in Provincial France: The Resistance of 1902 in Lower Brittany," *The Journal of Modern History* 62, no. 1 (1990): 2–33.
17 Patrick Young, "Of Pardons, Loss, and Longing: The Tourist's Pursuit of Originality in Brittany, 1890–1935," *French Historical Studies* 30, no. 2 (Spring 2007): 269–304.
18 Bernard Vogler, *Histoire des chrétiens d'Alsace des origines à nos jours* (Paris: Desclée, 1994), 282.
19 Christian Roy, *Traditional Festivals a Multicultural Encyclopedia* (Santa Barbara, CA: ABC-CLIO, 2005), 77–80.
20 Mairie de Geispolsheim, *Geispolsheim: gare et village, une histoire*, Mémoire de vies (Strasbourg: Carré blanc, 2006), 32.
21 Mairie de Geispolsheim, *Geispolsheim*, 66.
22 Philomène Buntz, trans. Lucette Rudloff, March 31, 2009.
23 Mairie de Geispolsheim, *Geispolsheim*, 22.

24 Joëlle Chabart, ed., *Schleithal: le village le plus long d'Alsace*, [Monographies des villages d'Alsace] 64 (Strasbourg: Coprur, 1999), 186, 190. In 1905 there were 1852 Catholics and 91 Protestants in Schleithal.
25 Chabart, *Schleithal*, 10.
26 Chabart, *Schleithal*, 122.
27 Oliver Zimmer, "Beneath the 'Culture War': Corpus Christi Processions and Mutual Accommodation in the Second German Empire," *The Journal of Modern History* 82, no. 2 (June 1, 2010): 299.
28 Caroline Ford, *Creating the Nation in Provincial France: Religion and Political Identity in Brittany* (Princeton: Princeton University Press, 1993), 71–2.
29 Jean-Pierre Gonidec, *Costume et société: Le monde de Douarnenez, Ploaré vu à travers ses modes vestimentaires* (Spezet: Coop Breizh, 2000).
30 Ellen Badone, "Pardons, Pilgrimage and the (Re-) Construction of Identities in Brittany," in *Gender, Nation and Religion in European Pilgrimage*, ed. Willy Jansen and Catrien Notermans (Surrey: Ashgate, 2012), 148–9.
31 Christian Kempf and Michel Loetscher, *Une Alsace 1900* (Nancy: Place Stanislas, 2007), 88–9.
32 Philippe Legin, *Coutumes et costumes alsaciens*, ed. Toute l'Alsace (Ingersheim: Editions S.A.E.P., 1993), 52.
33 Lucien Blumer, 1930s, Photograph, 1930s, 1 Fi 189, AVES. It is possible that the men and women traveled to the church separately but during the procession away from the church they left as couples. The photographs are not labeled in any way except for notes identifying the village.
34 Anthony J. Steinhoff, "Building Religious Community: Worship Space and Experience in Strasbourg after the Franco-Prussian War," in *Protestants, Catholics, and Jews in Germany, 1800–1914*, ed. Helmut Walser Smith (Oxford; New York: Berg, 2001), 268.
35 Séguy, "Quatre siècles et demi d'histoire: Les anabaptistes," 15.
36 Alfred Michiels, *Les anabaptistes des Vosges* (Paris: Poulet-Malassis et de Broise, 1860), 27.
37 Jan Lewicki, *Costumes d'Alsace et de Bade* (Strasbourg: E. Simon fils, 1834).
38 Lewicki.
39 Paula Hyman, *The Emancipation of the Jews of Alsace: Acculturation and Tradition in the Nineteenth Century* (New Haven: Yale University Press, 1991), 12.
40 Astrid Starck, "Alsatian Yiddish Theater at the Turn of the Century," in *Insiders and Outsiders: Jewish and Gentile Culture in Germany and Austria*, ed. Dagmar C. G. Lorenz and Gabriele Weinberger (Detroit: Wayne State University Press, 1994), 100.
41 Hyman, *The Emancipation of the Jews of Alsace*, 13.
42 Quoted in Alfred Rubens, *A History of Jewish Costume* (New York: Crown, 1973), 7. (NSRV: You shall not round off the hair on your temples or mar the edges of your beard.)

43 Jean-Louis Fesquet, "Département du Bas-Rhin," in *Voyage de Paris à Strasbourg, et principalement dans tout le Bas-Rhin [...]* (s.n., 1801), 8.
44 1 Cor. 11:4-6 American Standard Version.
45 Rubens, *A History of Jewish Costume*, 92–7.
46 The illustrations by Bernard Picart include one entitled "Nuptial Ceremony of the German Jews" in which most of the people depicted wear fashionable early eighteenth century dress. Bernard Picart, *The Ceremonies and Religious Customs of the Various Nations of the Known World: Together with Historical Annotations, and Several Curious Discourses Equally Instructive and Entertaining* (London: Printed by W. Jackson, for Claude Du Bosc, 1733).
47 David-Léon Cahun, *La vie juive* (Paris: E. Monnie, de Brunhoff, 1886), 10, 34, 66.
48 Vicki Caron, *Between France and Germany: The Jews of Alsace-Lorraine, 1871–1918* (Stanford, CA: Stanford University Press, 1988), 168.
49 Cahun, *La vie juive*, 7.
50 Daniel Stauben, *Scènes de la vie Juive en Alsace* (Paris: Michel Lévy Frères, 1860), 11–12.
51 Cahun, *La vie juive*, 104.
52 Freddy Raphaël and Robert Weyl, *Regards nouveaux sur les juifs d'Alsace* (Strasbourg: Librairie Istra: Éditions des dernières nouvelles d'Alsace, 1980), 75.
53 Freddy Raphaël, "Juifs et Mennonites en Alsace," in *Les Anabaptistes Mennonites d'Alsace: Destin d'une minorité*, ed. Saisons D'Alsace. Nouvelle série 76 (Strasbourg: Librairie Istra, 1981), 83.
54 Michiels, *Les anabaptistes des Vosges*, 49–50.
55 Séguy, "Quatre siècles et demi d'histoire: Les anabaptistes." It was the custom of shunning that was at the heart of the seventeenth-century schism between followers of Jacob Amman who became Amish and the other Anabaptists who would be called Mennonites. The majority of Anabaptists in Alsace followed Amman in adopting strict practices of excommunication. However, the strictest followers ultimately emigrated to the United States largely over their refusal to serve in the military.
56 Quoted in Raphaël, "Juifs et Mennonites en Alsace," 84; Cited by P. Leulliot, "Les anabaptistes alsaciens sous le Second Empire," *Revue d'Alsace* 87 (1947): 207–11.
57 Stauben, *Scènes de la vie Juive en Alsace*, 11.
58 Stauben, *Scènes de la vie Juive en Alsace*, 11.
59 Stauben was actually the pseudonym of Auguste Widal, born in Wintzenheim in the Haut-Rhin near Colmar in 1822. He left Alsace for Paris to attend first the Lycée Charlemagne then the École Normale Supérieure. Ultimately he had a career as a literature professor. Maurice Samuels, *Inventing the Israelite: Jewish Fiction in Nineteenth-Century France* (Stanford, CA: Stanford University Press, 2009), 195–6.
60 *Seebach* (Strasbourg: Edition Coprur, 1983), 75–113.
61 *Seebach*, 88.
62 One method of assembling the *coiffe* was shown to me by Jean-Luc Neth, a collector and expert on Alsatian costumes.

63 Raphaël and Weyl, *Regards nouveaux sur les juifs d'Alsace*, 73.
64 Mairie de Geispolsheim, *Geispolsheim*, 31.
65 American fashion periodicals did not include communion dresses.
66 Commune de Bouxwiller, *Bouxwiller: Imbsheim, Riedheim/Griesbach-le-Bastberg: autour du Bastberg*, ed. Mémoire de Vie (Strasbourg: Carré blanc, 2007), 73.
67 Commune de Bouxwiller, 59. The numbers arrived at by simply counting the children in the pictures have been supplemented with a chart showing the number of boys and girls confirmed in roughly five-year intervals between 1925 and 2005. The numbers do not begin to consistently decline until the 1970s.
68 Mairie de Geispolsheim, *Geispolsheim*, 60.
69 *Grand'Messe pontificale, dimanche matin, 21 July 1935*, 1935, Photograph, 1935, 1 Fi 2, AVES.
70 Margaret Lavinia Anderson, "The Limits of Secularization: On the Problem of the Catholic Revival in Nineteenth-Century Germany," *The Historical Journal* 38, no. 3 (September 1, 1995): 662–3.
71 Heinrich Hansjakob, *Unsere Volkstrachten: ein Wort zu ihrer Erhaltung* (Freiburg im Breisgau; München: Herder, 1892).
72 Heinz Schmitt, *Volkstracht in Baden: ihre Rolle in Kunst, Staat, Wirtschaft und Gesellschaft seit zwei Jahrhunderten* (Karlsruhe: Badenia Verlag, 1988), 64.
73 Richard Nuzinger, *Die Erhaltung der Volkstrachten: Eine Warnung* (Heidelberg Evang: Verlag, 1897); quoted by Schmitt, *Volkstracht in Baden*, 67.
74 Schmitt, *Volkstracht in Baden*, 66–7.
75 August Kassel, *Über elsaessische Trachten* (Strassburg: Du Mont-Schauberg, 1907), 39.
76 August Kassel, *Messti und Kirwe im Elsass* (Strassburg: J.H. Ed. Heitz, 1908).
77 Kassel, *Messti und Kirwe*, 35–6.
78 Gibson, *French Catholicism*, 143.
79 Gibson, *French Catholicism*, 140–1.
80 Hyman, "The Social Contexts of Assimilation: Village Jews and City Jews in Alsace," in *Assimilation and Community: The Jews in Nineteenth-Century Europe*, ed. Jonathan Frankel and Steven J. Zipperstein (Cambridge and New York: Cambridge University Press, 1992), 110–29.

Chapter 2

1 Roland Barthes, *The Fashion System*, trans. Matthew Ward and Richard Howard (New York: Hill and Wang, 1983).
2 Frédéric Maguet, "De la série éditoriale dans l'imagerie: L'exemple des costumes régionaux," *Ethnologie française*, nouvelle serie 24, no. 2 (April 1, 1994): 226–7.

3   Léone Prigent, "La vision des Strasbourgeoises dans les recueils de costumes du XVIIIe siecle: une image plurielle," in *Les costumes régionaux entre mémoire et histoire*, ed. Jean-Pierre Lethuillier (Rennes: Presses universitaires de Rennes, 2009), 203–15; Daniel Roche, *La culture des apparences: une histoire du vêtement (XVIIe-XVIIIe siècle)* (Paris: Fayard, 1989), 20.

4   Nicole Pellegrin, "Une géographie pour les filles? Les recueils de costumes français de Jacques Grasset de Saint-Sauveur au tournant des XVIIIe et XIXe siècles," in *Les costumes régionaux entre mémoire et histore*, ed. Jean-Pierre Lethuillier (Rennes: Presses universitaires de Rennes, 2009), 223.

5   Jacques Grasset de Saint-sauveur, *Encyclopédie des voyages, contenant l'abrégé historique des moeurs, usages, habitudes domestiques, religions, fêtes, supplices, funérailles, sciences, arts et commerce de tous les peuples: et la collection complette de leurs habillemens civils, militaires, religieux et dignitaires, dessines d'après nature, gravés avec soin et coloriés à l'aquarelle*, vol. Europe (Paris: author (Grasset), 1796), 5.

6   Annemarie Kleinert, *Le "Journal des dames et des modes" ou la conquête de l'Europe féminine (1797–1839)* (Stuttgart: Jan Thorbecke Verlag, 2001), 13.

7   Maguet, "De la série éditoriale dans l'imagerie," 228.

8   While Lanté did many of the illustrations for this series, the illustrator Horace Vernet provided some of them as well. Louis-Marie Lanté and Georges-Jacques Gatine, *Costumes de divers pays* (Paris: [s.n], 1827).

9   Jan Lewicki, *Costumes d'Alsace et de Bade* (Strasbourg: E. Simon fils, 1834); Charles Emrich, *Collection de six costumes nationaux Alsaciens et Badois* (Strasbourg, 1834).

10 Celia Applegate, *A Nation of Provincials: The German Idea of Heimat* (Berkeley: University of California Press, 1990); Alon Confino, *The Nation as a Local Metaphor: Württemberg, Imperial Germany, and National Memory, 1871–1918* (Chapel Hill: University of North Carolina Press, 1997).

11 Peter Sahlins, "The Nation in the Village: State-Building and Communal Struggles in the Catalan Borderland during the Eighteenth and Nineteenth Centuries," *The Journal of Modern History* 60, no. 2 (1988): 234–63.

12 "Polski Drukarz w Lizbonie—Ojciec Litografii Portugalskiej," accessed March 5, 2017, http://www.mariolasocha.republika.pl/lewicki.htm.

13 Kleinert, *Journal des dames et des modes*, 39.

14 Kleinert, *Journal des dames et des modes*, 40–1.

15 Émile de la Bédollierre, "L'Alsacien," in *Les Français peints par eux-mêmes: encyclopédie morale du dix-neuvième siècle*, vol. 8, 9 vols. (Paris: L. Curmer, 1842), 145–52, https://books.google.com/books?id=tdxAAQAAMAAJ&printsec=frontcover&source=gbs_ge_summary_r&cad=0#v=onepage&q&f=false.

16 "Serien—Universität Regensburg," accessed December 3, 2016, http://www.uni-regensburg.de/bibliothek/bilderbogen/muenchener-bilderbogen/serien/index.html.

17 Louis Braun, *Zur Geschichte der Kostüme* (München: Braun & Schneider; New York: E. Weye, 1898).

18 Paul Ristelhuber, *Galerie universelle des peuples. Alsace* (Strasbourg: Lallemand & Hart, 1865). Lallemand was the draughtsman while Ludovic Hart was the photographer. "L'Alsace dans la Galerie internationale des peuples–Fonds-alsacien-presentation.pdf," accessed January 16, 2014, http://www.culture.gouv.fr/documentation/phocem/Albums/Fonds-alsacien-presentation.pdf.

19 Charles Lallemand and Ludovic Hart, *Deutsche Volkstrachten* (Basel: A Varady & Co., 1865). Several stereoscopic slides from the series published by A Varady belonged to the artist, Charles Spindler and were consulted by the author in his studio. This German version of the series does not contain any identifying information on the slides including the names of the artists and the village in the photographs.

20 According to a handwritten note on the copy at Spindler's atelier, this photograph is of Blaesheim. Other publications of the photographs identify Blaesheim as one of the villages where the photographs were taken.

21 Maureen C. O'Brien, "The Influence of Contemporary French Painting," in *Image and Enterprise: The Photographs of Adolphe Braun*, ed. Mary Bergstein and Maureen C. O'Brien (London: Thames & Hudson in association with Museum of Art, Rhode Island School of Design, 2000), 85.

22 Christian Kempf, "Adolphe Braun's Photographic Enterprise," in *Image and Enterprise: The Photographs of Adolphe Braun*, ed. Mary Bergstein and Maureen C. O'Brien (London: Thames & Hudson in association with Museum of Art, Rhode Island School of Design, 2000), 24.

23 Kempf, 87.

24 Raymond Grew, "Picturing the People: Images of the Lower Orders in Nineteenth-Century French Art," *The Journal of Interdisciplinary History* 17, no. 1 (1986): 206, https://doi.org/10.2307/204131.

25 Michael Fried, "The Structure of Beholding in Courbet's 'Burial at Ornans,'" *Critical Inquiry* 9, no. 4 (1983): 635–83.

26 Timothy J. Clark, *Image of the People: Gustave Courbet and the 1848 Revolution* (Berkeley: University of California Press, 1999).

27 Patricia Mainardi, *The End of the Salon: Art and the State in the Early Third Republic* (Cambridge: Cambridge University Press, 1993), 15.

28 Patricia Mainardi, *Art and Politics of the Second Empire: The Universal Expositions of 1855 and 1867* (New Haven: Yale University Press, 1987), 190.

29 Gabriel Weisberg, *The Realist Tradition: French Painting and Drawing, 1830–1900* (Cleveland: Cleveland Museum of Art, 1980), 89.

30 Annette Bourrut Lacouture, *Jules Breton, Painter of Peasant Life* (New Haven: Yale University Press in association with the National Gallery of Ireland, Dublin, 2002), 103.

31 Bourrut Lacouture, *Jules Breton*, 99.
32 Bourrut Lacouture, *Jules Breton*, 17.
33 Bourrut Lacouture, *Jules Breton*, 154.
34 Weisberg, *The Realist Tradition*, 276.
35 Frédéric Théodore Piton, *Strasbourg illustré ou Panorama pittoresque, historique et statistique de Strasbourg et de ses environs: Promenades dans les faubourgs, déscription des environs* (Strasbourg: printed by the author, 1855), 183.
36 Piton, *Strasbourg illustré*, plate between pages 182–3.
37 Piton, *Strasbourg illustré*; Jacques Baquol and Paul Ristelhuber, *L'Alsace ancienne et moderne: ou Dictionnaire topographique, historique et statistique du Haut et du Bas-Rhin*, 3rd ed. (Strasbourg: Salomon, 1865).
38 Jacques Longchamp, *Marc Louis Benjamin Vautier (dit l'ancien)* (Geneva: Editions Slatkine, 2015), 52.
39 Jean-Pierre Klein, *Un romantique alsacien: Théophile Schuler: 1821–1878* (Strasbourg: Château de Rohan, 1979), 16.
40 Klein, *Un romantique alsacien*, 18.
41 Klein, *Un romantique alsacien*, 20.
42 Eric Zafran, Robert Rosenblum, and Lisa Small, *Fantasy and Faith: The Art of Gustave Doré* (New York: Dahesh Museum of Art; New Haven: Yale University Press, 2007), 14.
43 Zafran, Rosenblum, and Small, 113–15.
44 Jean-Jacques Henner, *L'Alsace. Elle Attend*, 1871, Oil on canvas, 60 cm × 30 cm, 1871, Musée Jean-Jacques Henner (Paris).
45 "L'Alsace. Elle Attend (Alsace. She Waits) | Musée National Jean-Jacques Henner," accessed February 21, 2021, https://www.musee-henner.fr/en/collections/l-alsace-elle-attend-alsace-she-waits.
46 Michel Loetscher, "L'Âge d'or d'un peuple et d'un artiste," in *L'âge d'or d'un artiste en Alsace: mémoires inédits 1889–1914*, by Charles Spindler (Nancy: Place Stanislas, 2009), 9.
47 Loetscher, "L'Âge d'or d'un peuple et d'un artiste," 9–10.
48 Schuler was a Romantic artist who was a native of Alsace known for his illustrations of popular works of literature including those of Jules Verne, Victor Hugo, and Erckmann-Chatrian as well as for a series of studies of Alsatian folk costumes. René Metz, "Schuler Jules Théophile," in *Nouveau dictionnaire de biographie alsacienne* (Strasbourg, France: Fédération des sociétés d'histoire et d'archéologie d'Alsace, 2006 [1982]).
49 Loetscher, "L'Âge d'or d'un peuple et d'un artiste," 10.
50 Spindler reports that Laugel was born in 1852, a date that is contradicted by the editors of his memoire in the caption on the same page. Charles Spindler, *L'âge d'or d'un artiste en Alsace: mémoires inédits 1889–1914* (Nancy: Place Stanislas, 2009), 23. Gatineau also indicates that his birth was in 1851. Barbara Gatineau, "Preface," in *Costumes et coutumes d'Alsace*, by Anselme Laugel, Nouv. éd. (Nancy: Place Stanislas, 2008).

51 Biographical information about Laugel from Gatineau, "Preface," 16.
52 Spindler, *Mémoires*, 71.
53 Spindler, *Mémoires*, 133.
54 Spindler, *Mémoires*, 119.
55 Étienne Martin, "Charles Spindler und der Kreis von St. Léonard: Regionalismus und Moderne um 1900 im Elsass," in *Jugendstil am Oberrhein: Sonderausstellung des Badischen Landesmuseums Karlsruhe 18.4-9.8.2009* ed. Elisabeth Gurock (Karlsruhe: DRW-Verlag Weinbrenner: G. Braun Buchverlag, 2009); Christian Kempf and Michel Loetscher, *Une Alsace 1900* (Nancy: Place Stanislas, 2007); Michel Loetscher and Jean-Charles Spindler, *Charles, Paul, Jean-Charles Spindler: un siècle d'art en Alsace* (Strasbourg: Nuée bleue, 2005).
56 Detmar Klein, "Folklore as a Weapon: National Identity in German-Annexed Alsace, 1890-1914," in *Folklore and Nationalism in Europe during the Long Nineteenth Century*, ed. Timothy Baycroft and David Hopkin (Leiden: BRILL, 2012), 161–91; James Wilkinson, "The Uses of Popular Culture by Rival Elites: The Case of Alsace, 1890–1914," *History of European Ideas* 11 (1989): 605–18, https://doi.org/10.1016/0191-6599(89)90247-7; Simone Orzechowski, "La Revue Alsacienne Illustrée (1898–1914): L'art, paravent de la lutte contre la germinisation," in *Le Problème de l'Alsace-Lorraine vu par les périodiques (1871–1914) = Die Elsass-Lothringische Frage im Spiegel der Zeitschriften (1871–1914)*, ed. Michel Grunewald, Convergences; 7 (Bern; New York: P. Lang, 1998).
57 Klein, "Folklore as a Weapon," 165–6.
58 Piton, *Strasbourg illustré*; Baquol and Ristelhuber, *L'Alsace ancienne et moderne*; Lewicki, *Costumes d'Alsace et de Bade*; Emrich, *Collection de six costumes nationaux Alsaciens et Badois*.
59 Spindler, *Mémoires*, 27.
60 Quoted by Michel Loetscher, "Planète lumière, ou l'image habitée," in *Une Alsace 1900* (Nancy: Place Stanislas, 2007), 10.
61 Loetscher, 10.
62 Spindler, *Mémoires*, 61.
63 Kempf and Loetscher, *Une Alsace 1900*, 12–15.
64 Spindler, *Mémoires*, 65.
65 Ristelhuber, *Galerie universelle des peuples*.
66 Anselme Laugel and Charles Spindler, *Costumes et coutumes d'Alsace*, Nouv. éd. (Nancy: Place Stanislas, 2008), 41.
67 Laugel and Spindler, *Costumes et coutumes d'Alsace*, 41.
68 Spindler, *Mémoires*, 61.
69 Spindler, *Mémoires*, 67.
70 Spindler, *Mémoires*, 89–101; More information about the magazine's origins and political leanings can be found in Georges Klein and Musée Alsacien, *La Naissance*

Du Musée Alsacien et La Revue Alsacienne Illustrée: Strasbourg, Musée Alsacien, 29 Juin-29 Septembre 1985 (Strasbourg: Le Musée alsacien, 1985); Orzechowski, "La Revue Alsacienne Illustrée (1898–1914): L'art, paravent de la lutte contre la germinisation."

71 Benoît Bruant, *Hansi: l'artiste tendre et rebelle* (Strasbourg: Nuée Bleue, 2008), 157.

72 Elizabeth Vlossak, *Marianne or Germania? Nationalizing Women in Alsace, 1870–1946* (Oxford: Oxford University Press, 2010), 190–3.

73 Sara Hume, "Between Fashion and Folk: Dress Practices in Alsace during the First World War," in *Fashion, Society and the First World War: International Perspectives*, ed. Maude Bass-Krueger, Hayley Edwards-Dujardin, and Sophie Kurkdjian (London: Bloomsbury, 2021), 117–18.

74 Laugel and Spindler, *Costumes et coutumes d'Alsace*, 57–8.

75 Laugel and Spindler, *Costumes et coutumes d'Alsace*, 183.

Chapter 3

1 *Wedding Dress*, 1903, Silk faille, jet beads, 1903, 66.2008.10.1-2, Musée Alsacien.

2 Musée Alsacien, 66.003.0.115.

3 ADBR, 7E59/52, IAD for wife of Kilian Triebel, May 19, 1880.

4 ADBR, 7E59/80, IAD for Maria-Magdalena-Leonie Kieffer, February 11, 1896.

5 The first issue of the Vogesen-Club's *Jahrbuch für Geschichte, Sprache und Literatur Elsass-Lothringens* was published in 1885.

6 ADBR, 7E59/53, IAD for Margaretha Lapp, February 9, 1881.

7 ADBR, 7E59/44, IAD for Ludwig Hammacher, July 21, 1875.

8 Out of a sample size of twenty-six men's wardrobes, four were below 10 M, four were above 30 M, and the remaining eighteen were within the range.

9 Out of a sample size of twenty-six women's wardrobes seven were below 10 M, nine were above 30 M, and ten were within the range.

10 ADBR, 7E59/80, IAD for Anna Brucker, April 13, 1896.

11 ADBR, 7E59/78, IAD for Margaretha Berst, February 27, 1895.

12 ADBR, 7E59/53, IAD for Margaretha Lapp, February 9, 1881.

13 ADBR, 7E59/79, IAD for Maria Josephina Heydmann, June 12, 1895.

14 Philippe Legin, *Coutumes et costumes alsaciens*, Toute l'Alsace (Ingersheim: Editions S.A.E.P., 1993), 56. Legin puts the date for wedding photography to the 1880s.

15 *Berstett: un village pittoresque du Kochersberg* (Strasbourg: Editions Coprur, 1993), 161.

16 A selection of wedding photographs has been published in books about the local history of villages such as *Berstett*; Joëlle Callot Burnouf, ed., *Le Kochersberg: histoire et paysages* (Strasbourg: Publitotal, 1980); Commune de Bouxwiller, *Bouxwiller: Imbsheim, Riedheim/Griesbach-le-Bastberg: autour du Bastberg*, Mémoire de vie (Strasbourg: Carré blanc, 2007); Mairie de Geispolsheim, ed., *Geispolsheim: gare et village, une histoire*, Mémoire de vies (Strasbourg: Carré blanc, 2006).

17 Tim Coles, "Department Stores as Retail Innovations in Germany: A Historical-Geographical Perspective on the Period 1870 to 1914," in *Cathedrals of Consumption: The European Department Store, 1850–1939*, ed. Geoffrey Crossick and Serge Jaumain, The History of Retailing and Consumption (Aldershot, Hants, England; Brookfield, VT: Ashgate, 1999), 75.

18 Coles, "Department Stores as Retail Innovations in Germany," 73.

19 Coles, "Department Stores as Retail Innovations in Germany," 77.

20 Coles, "Department Stores as Retail Innovations in Germany," 73.

21 Uwe Westphal, *Berliner Konfektion und Mode: die Zerstörung einer Tradition, 1836–1939*, Stätten der Geschichte Berlins; Bd. 14 (Berlin: Edition Hentrich, 1986), 21.

22 Westphal, 21.

23 Barbara Franzoi, *At the Very Least She Pays the Rent: Women and German Industrialization, 1871–1914* (Westport, CT: Greenwood Press, 1985), 26–27.

24 ADBR, 79 J 959.

25 Jean-Paul Sartre, *War Diaries: Notebooks from a Phoney War, November 1939–March 1940* (London: Verso, 1999), 157.

26 AVES, 1 ALS 37.

27 *Modèles des costumes et confections pour enfants*, Au Bon Marché, Été 1879.

28 *Weissenburger Wochenblatt* (October 14, 1882).

29 ADBR, 7 E 59/74.

30 (December 2, 1882, a similar ad also runs October 30, 1886 and December 7, 1887).

31 Stéphane Jonas, "Strasbourg 1900: Une ville de frontière et d'innovation (1890–1918)," *Revue des sciences sociales* 19 (1991): 13–30.

32 AVES, 720 W 138 Letter from Kaufhaus Modern to the Bürgermeisteramt, March 12, 1915.

33 AVES, 720 W 142.

34 AVES, 5 MW 283.

35 Kreisdirektor, "Letter regarding Home Industry in the district of Erstein," April 30, 1897, 193 D 153, ADBR.

36 Jean-Louis Humbert, "La Constitution des entreprises de la confection aux 19ème et 20ème siècles: ouvrières, ouvriers, patrons," in *Approche comparative des entreprises en France et en Allemagne: le déclin de l'empire des aiguilles*, ed. Jan Spurk, Collection Dynamiques d'entreprises; Variation: Dynamiques d'entreprises. (Paris: Harmattan, 1997), 81.

37 ADBR, 193 D 153, 154.
38 Franzoi, *At the Very Least She Pays the Rent*, 24.
39 ADBR, 27 AL 1107. "Commission für das Handwerk," *Strassburger Post*, September 18, 1896.
40 ADBR, 27 AL 1107. "Kommission für das Handwerk," *Strassburger Correspondenz*, September 30, 1897, Nr. 105.
41 "Einbeziehung der Handwerkerinnen in die Organisation der Handwerkskammer," 1912 in ADBR, 193 D 150/1.
42 "Bekanntmachung betreffend die Erfordernisse für die Meisterprüfung in den weiblichen Berufen der Schneiderinnen, Putzmacherinnen und Friseusen." 11 May 1913 in ADBR, 193 D 150/1.
43 *Amtliche nachrichten für Elsass-Lothringen: Verordnungen und bekanntmachungen des general-gouverneurs, des civil-commissars und des ober-präsidenten, August 1870 bis ende März 1879*, 1879, 111–12.
44 Katherine Kennedy, "Domesticity (Hauswirtschaft) in the Volkschule," *Internationale Schulbuchforschung: Zeitschrift Des Georg-Eckert-Instituts Für Internationale Schulbuchforschung* 13, no. 1 (1991): 5–21.
45 Kennedy, "Domesticity (Hauswirtschaft) in the Volkschule," 12.
46 Kennedy, "Domesticity (Hauswirtschaft) in the Volkschule," 13.
47 Gérard Bodé, "État français—état allemand: l'enseignement technique mosellan entre deux modèles nationaux, 1815–1940," *Histoire de l'éducation*, no. 66 (May 1, 1995): 109–36.
48 Elizabeth Vlossak, *Marianne or Germania? Nationalizing Women in Alsace, 1870–1946* (Oxford: Oxford University Press, 2010), 94–7.
49 Fräulein L. Otto, *Prospect der Frauen-Industrie- und Fortbildungs-Schule des Vaterländischen Frauen-Vereins zu Strassburg im Elsass* (Strassburg: Strassburger Neueste Nachrichten, 1903).
50 Otto.
51 Chambre de Métiers d'Alsace et de Lorraine, "Compte-rendu de la XXXVe Séance plénière tenue le 29 décembre 1921 dans la grande salle de Séance de la Chambre de Métiers," December 29, 1921, 286 D 64, ADBR. *Le Tailleur et la Tailleuse d'Alsace*, January 25, 1928.
52 Chambre de Métiers d'Alsace et de Lorraine, *Annuaire de la Chambre de Metiers d'Alsace et de Lorraine 1918/19* (Strasbourg: Imprimerie des Dernières Nouvelles, 1919), 22.
53 Chambre de Métiers d'Alsace et de Lorraine, *Annuaire*, 28.
54 Chambre de Métiers d'Alsace et de Lorraine, *Annuaire*, 30.
55 Chambre de Métiers d'Alsace, "Rapport moral et administrative 1930," *Procès Verbal de la Chambre de métiers d'Alsace*, 1931.
56 Chambre de Métiers d'Alsace, "Liste des artisans," 1939 1920, 1713 W 191-4, ADBR.

57 Chambre de Métiers d'Alsace et de Lorraine, *Annuaire 1918/19*, 22.
58 Conseil Général département du Bas-Rhin, "Extrait des déliberations du Conseil Général," April 25, 1934, 258 D 301, ADBR.
59 Conseil Général département du Bas-Rhin.
60 Emilie Hahn, *Zwei Schweschtere. Komödie in elsässischer Mundart in zwei Akten*, Le Roux elsässisches Vereinstheater 27 (Strasbourg: F.X. Le Roux & Cie., 1926).
61 Hahn, 13.
62 A. Seyller, *D'Hochzittshose. Schwank in 1 Akt*, Salvator-Theater Sammlung Ernster und Heiterer Theaterstücke 127 (Mulhausen: Salvator-Verlag, 1932).

Chapter 4

1 Société du Musée Alsacien, "Statuts" (C. Müh & Cie, 1902), 5 MW 275, AVES.
2 Isabelle Collet, "Les premiers musées d'ethnographie régionale en France," in *Muséologie et ethnologie*, Notes et documents des musées de France 16 (Paris: Editions de la Réunion des musées nationaux, 1987), 73. Several authors repeat the chronology Collet identifies including Bjarne Stoklund, "The Role of the International Exhibitions in the Construction of National Cultures in the 19th Century," *Ethnologia Europaea* 24 (1994): 39; Lou Taylor, *Establishing Dress History*, Studies in Design (Manchester; New York: Manchester University Press, 2004).
3 Martin Wörner, "Chapter 6 'Kulturmuseum der Menschheit' - Weltausstellung und Museumswesen," in *Vergnügung und Belehrung: Volkskultur auf den Weltausstellungen, 1851–1900* (Münster; New York: Waxmann, 1999), 237–84.
4 Taylor, *Establishing Dress History*, 217, fn 56 traces it to; Malou Schneider, *Le Musée alsacien, Strasbourg*, Kaléidoscope d'Alsace (Strasbourg: La Nuée bleue, Impr. SAG, 1995); Also James Wilkinson, "The Uses of Popular Culture by Rival Elites: The Case of Alsace, 1890–1914," *History of European Ideas* 11, nos. 1–6 (January 1989): 605–18, https://doi.org/10.1016/0191-6599(89)90247-7.
5 Stoklund, "International Exhibitions," 39.
6 Stoklund, "International Exhibitions," 39.
7 Edward N. Kaufman, "The Architectural Museum from World's Fair to Restoration Village," *Assemblage*, no. 9 (June 1, 1989): 22–3, https://doi.org/10.2307/3171150.
8 Kaufman, "The Architectural Museum from World's Fair to Restoration Village," 24.
9 Stoklund, "International Exhibitions," 43.
10 Bjarne Stoklund, "Between Scenography and Science: Early Folk Museums and Their Pioneers," *Ethnologia Europaea* 33, no. 1 (2003): 24; Daniel DeGroff, "Ethnographic Display and Political Narrative: The Salle de France of the Musée d'Ethnographie Du Trocadéro," in *Folklore and Nationalism in Europe during the Long Nineteenth Century*, ed. Timothy Baycroft and David Hopkin (BRILL, 2012), 115.

11 Nélia Dias, "Vers l'archivage des objets: la naissance du Musée d'ethnographie du Trocadéro," *Bulletin d'information de l'Association des Bibliothècaires Français*, no. 138 (1er trimestre 1988): 29.
12 Nélia Dias, *Le musée d'ethnographie du Trocadéro : (1878-1908) : anthropologie et muséologie en France* (Paris: Ed. du Centre National de la Recherche Scientifique, 1991), 187.
13 Dias, *Le musée d'ethnographie du Trocadéro*, 189.
14 Dias, *Le musée d'ethnographie du Trocadéro*, 190.
15 This quotation appears in DeGroff, "Ethnographic Display," 121. The translation is that of DeGroff.
16 Andrew Zimmerman, "Anti-Semitism as Skill: Rudolf Virchow's 'Schulstatistik' and the Racial Composition of Germany," *Central European History* 32, no. 4 (1999): 409-29.
17 Stoklund, "Between Scenography and Science," 31.
18 Stoklund, "Between Scenography and Science," 30.
19 A floor plan for the museum is included in François Igersheim, "Robert Forrer et le premier 'Musée alsacien' à Berlin en 1889," *Cahiers alsaciens d'archéologie d'art et d'histoire* LI (2008): 132.
20 "Chronique d'Alsace-Lorraine," *Revue alsacienne illustrée*, 1900.
21 "Chronique d'Alsace-Lorraine," *Revue alsacienne illustrée*, 1903.
22 Thiébaut Flory, *Le Mouvement régionaliste français, sources et développements* (Paris: Presses universitaires de France, 1966), 31-4.
23 Maurice Barrès, "La Genèse d'une oeuvre: Comment aimer notre terre et nos morts—Le musée d'Arles. Une lettre de Mistral," *Revue alsacienne illustrée = Illustrirte elsässische Rundschau*, 1902.
24 Frederic Mistral in letter dated Maillane (Bouches-du-Rhone), November 12, 1900 quoted by Barrès, 36.
25 Barrès, "La Genèse d'une oeuvre," 33.
26 Igersheim, "Robert Forrer," 131.
27 Bernadette Schnitzler, *Robert Forrer (1866-1947): archéologue, écrivain et antiquaire*, Publications de la Société Savante d'Alsace; Collection "Recherches et documents"; 65 (Strasbourg: Soc. Savante d'Alsace, 1999), 23.
28 Igersheim, "Robert Forrer," 132-3.
29 Société du Musée Alsacien, "Statuts."
30 Liste des Sociétaires of the Musée Alsacien, no date, 5 MW 283, Archives de Strasbourg.
31 Société du Musée Alsacien, "Statuts." Ultimately on the eve of World War I, the museum was liquidated and the building and collections transferred to the city of Strasbourg.
32 Charles Spindler, *L'âge d'or d'un artiste en Alsace: mémoires inédits 1889-1914* (Nancy: Place Stanislas, 2009), 187.

33 Excerpt from the mortgage for the Musée Alsacien, February 8–9, 1904, 5 MW 278, Archives de Strasbourg.
34 "Le musée Alsacien : un lieu authentique et pittoresque - Musées de Strasbourg," accessed April 8, 2020, https://www.musees.strasbourg.eu/web/musees/musee-alsacien-lieu-authentique-et-pittoresque.
35 Mortgage, 5 MW 278, AVES.
36 Spindler, *Mémoires*, 187.
37 Société du Musée Alsacien, "Rapport des Gérants sur l'activité de la société pendant les années 1906, 1907 et 1908," 1908, 5 MW 275, AVES.
38 Spindler, *Mémoires*, 187.
39 Spindler, *Mémoires*, 189.
40 Spindler, *Mémoires*, 189.
41 Mark B. Sandberg, *Living Pictures, Missing Persons: Mannequins, Museums, and Modernity* (Princeton, NJ: Princeton University Press, 2003), 148.
42 Sandberg, *Living Pictures, Missing Persons*, 151.
43 Spindler, *Mémoires*, 189.
44 Spindler, *Mémoires*, 191.
45 "Chronique d'Alsace-Lorraine," 1903.
46 Dias, *Le musée d'ethnographie du Trocadéro*, 188.
47 Armand Landrin and Paul Sébillot, "Instructions sommaires relatives aux collections provinciales d'objets Ethnographiques," in *La tradition au pays basque: Ethnographie, folklore, art populaire, histoire, hagiographie*, by Gustave Boucher (Paris: Aux bureaux de la Tradition nationale, 1899), 585–95; Paul Sébillot, "L'Ethnographie traditionelle et les musées cantonaux," *Annuaire des musées cantonaux* (1886–87): 9–20.
48 Landrin and Sébillot, "Instructions sommaires," 591.
49 Emile Marignan, *Instructions pour la récolte des objets d'ethnographie du pays arlésien* (Arles: ed. Jouve, 1896); reference found in Marie-France Noël, "Du musée d'ethnographie du Trocadéro au Musée National des Arts et traditions populaires," in *Muséologie et ethnologie*, Notes et documents des musées de France (Paris: Editions de la Réunion des musées nationaux, 1987), 149.
50 Charles Galtier, Maurice Rouquette Laroche, and Museon Arlaten, *La Provence et Frédéric Mistral au Museon arlaten* (Paris: J. Cuénot, 1977), 9.
51 Museon Arlaten, "La Collecte - Museon Arlaten," accessed February 27, 2014, http://www.museonarlaten.fr/museon/CG13/cache/offonce/pid/7;jsessionid=2798F88299AABA6B783FBE06F2DE9084.
52 Gesine Schulz-Berlekamp, "Mönchgut: Entdeckung einer Tracht," in *Kleidung zwischen Tracht + Mode: aus der Geschichte des Museums 1889–1989*, ed. Ulrich Reuter and Museum für Volkskunde (Berlin: Staatliche Museen zu Berlin, 1989), 49.

53 Heidi Müller, "Die Sammlungskonzeption des Museums für Deutsche Volkskunde von der Gründung 1889 bis Zum Ersten Weltkrieg," *Jahrbuch der Berliner Museen* 34 (1992): 186.
54 Ulrich Steinmann, "Gründer und Förderer des Berliner Volkskunde-Museums. Rudolf Virchow, Ulrich Jahn, Alexander Meyer Cohn, Hermann Sökeland, James Simon," *Forschungen und Berichte* 9 (January 1, 1967): 84, https://doi.org/10.2307/3880592.
55 Igersheim, "Robert Forrer," 131.
56 Société du Musée Alsacien, "Rapport des Gérants," 8, 11.
57 Schnitzler, *Robert Forrer*, 165.
58 Quoted in Céline Edel and Musée alsacien, *Ça décoiffe … : centenaire du Musée alsacien* (Strasbourg: Les Musées de la Ville de Strasbourg, 2007), 17.
59 Spindler, *Mémoires*, 67.
60 Barbara Gatineau, "Preface," in *Costumes et coutumes d'Alsace*, by Anselme Laugel, Nouv. éd (Nancy: Place Stanislas, 2008), 34.
61 August Kassel, *Über elsaessische Trachten* (Strassburg: Du Mont-Schauberg, 1907).
62 Gatineau, "Preface," 31.
63 Quoted in Gatineau, "Preface," 31.
64 Inventory of the Musée alsacien, record for MAL 3392.
65 Stoklund, "Between Scenography and Science," 26.
66 Société du Musée Alsacien, "Rapport des Gérants," 4. AVES 5 MW 275.
67 Société du Musée Alsacien, "Rapport des Gérants," 4, 5.
68 Société du Musée Alsacien, "Rapport des Gérants," 6–7.
69 Société du Musée Alsacien, "Rapport des Gérants," 6.
70 Pierre Bucher to Charles Spindler, 14 June [?], Private Collection.
71 Bucher to Spindler, 14 June.
72 Georges Klein and Musée alsacien, *La Naissance Du Musée Alsacien et La Revue Alsacienne Illustrée : Strasbourg, Musée Alsacien, 29 Juin-29 Septembre 1985* (Strasbourg: Le Musée, 1985), 29.
73 Société du Musée Alsacien, "Rapport des Gérants," 18.
74 Klein and Musée alsacien, *La Naissance Du Musée Alsacien*, 29.
75 Klein and Musée alsacien, *La Naissance Du Musée Alsacien*, 30.
76 Société du Musée Alsacien, "Rapport des Gérants," 18.
77 Société du Musée Alsacien, "Rapport des Gérants," 16.
78 Société du Musée Alsacien, "Rapport des Gérants," 16.
79 Société du Musée Alsacien, "Rapport des Gérants," 17.
80 Société du Musée Alsacien, "Rapport des Gérants," 17.
81 Société du Musée Alsacien, "Rapport des Gérants," 14.
82 Armand Landrin, "Anciens Costumes Populaires français au Palais du Trocadéro," *La Nature. Revue des sciences et de leurs applications aux arts et à l'industrie* 17 (1889): 295; Quoted in DeGroff, "Ethnographic Display," 125.

83 Charles Spindler, "Réflexion sur le costume alsacien," in *Costumes et coutumes d'Alsace*, by Anselme Laugel and Charles Spindler, Nouv. éd. (Nancy: Place Stanislas, 2008), 366.

Chapter 5

1. An excellent summary of the development of scholarship on folklorism is in Regina Bendix, "Folklorism: The Challenge of a Concept," *International Folklore Review* 6 (1988): 5–15; Guntis Šmidchens, "Folklorism Revisited," *Journal of Folklore Research* 36, no. 1 (1999): 51–70.
2. Hugh Trevor-Roper, "The Invention of Tradition: The Highland Tradition of Scotland," in *The Invention of Tradition*, ed. Eric Hobsbawm and Terence Ranger, Past and Present Publications (Cambridge: Cambridge University Press, 1983), 15–41; Malcolm Chapman, "'Freezing the Frame': Dress and Ethnicity in Brittany and Gaelic Scotland," in *Dress and Ethnicity*, ed. Joanne B. Eicher, Ethnicity and Identity (Oxford: Berg, 1995), 7–28.
3. Chapman, "Freezing the Frame."
4. For a definition and explanation of folklorism as well as a review of the literature, see Bendix, "Folklorism," 5.
5. For the French case the conventional view of centralization developed out of Eugen Weber, *Peasants into Frenchmen: The Modernization of Rural France, 1870–1914* (Stanford, CA: Stanford University Press, 1976); Anne-Marie Thiesse, *Ils apprenaient la France : l'exaltation des régions dans le discours patriotique*, vol. 17 (Paris: Editions de la Maison des sciences de l'homme, 1997); Celia Applegate, *A Nation of Provincials: The German Idea of Heimat* (Berkeley: University of California Press, 1990); Alon Confino, *The Nation as a Local Metaphor: Württemberg, Imperial Germany, and National Memory, 1871–1918* (Chapel Hill: University of North Carolina Press, 1997).
6. Gerda Möhler, *Das Münchner Oktoberfest: Brauchformen des Volksfestes zwischen Aufklärung und Gegenwart*, Miscellanea Bavarica Monacensia; Heft 100; Neue Schriftenreihe des Stadtarchivs München 100 (München: Kommissionsbuchhandlung R. Wölfe, 1980), 245.
7. Gustav Kraus, *Festzug zur Feyer der Jubel Ehe I.I.M.M. des Königs Ludwig und der Königin Therese zu München am 4ten October 1835* (München: J. C. Hochwind, 1836). Similar terminology was used a decade earlier in the collection of images of regional dress in Felix Joseph Lipowsky, *Sammlung Bayerischer National-Costume* (München: Hermann & Barth, 1820).
8. Heinz Schmitt, *Volkstracht in Baden: ihre Rolle in Kunst, Staat, Wirtschaft und Gesellschaft seit zwei Jahrhunderten* (Karlsruhe: Badenia Verlag, 1988), 28.

9 Quoted in Schmitt, *Volkstracht in Baden*, 28–9.
10 Schmitt, *Volkstracht in Baden*, 30.
11 Martyn Lyons, *Reading Culture and Writing Practices in Nineteenth-Century France* (Toronto: University of Toronto Press, 2008), 101.
12 Frédéric Théodore Piton, *Strasbourg illustré ou Panorama pittoresque, historique et statistique de Strasbourg et de ses environs: Promenades dans les faubourgs, déscription des environs* (Strasbourg: printed by the author, 1855), plate between pages 182–3.
13 Piton, *Strasbourg illustré*, 183.
14 Gustav Kraus, *Festzug der 35 Brautpaare zur Vermählungsfeyer Seiner Königlichen Hoheit des Kronprinzen Maximilian von Bayern und Ihrer Königlichen Hoheit der Kronprinzeß Marie von Bayern im Vorbeiziehen vor dem Königszelt bey dem Octoberfeste in München den 16ten October 1842* (G. Kraus, 1842).
15 Möhler, *Das Münchner Oktoberfest*; Heft 100; Neue Schriftenreihe des Stadtarchivs München 100, 263.
16 Möhler, *Das Münchner Oktoberfest*, 265.
17 "Messti et Messtizug: La Kermesse et son cortège," *Schilick Infos*, Juillet/Août 2009, 9.
18 Schilkemer Messti, *Festschrift und Fuehrer durch die Industrie- und Gewerbeausstellung* (Schiltigheim: J. Schneider, 1895), 42.
19 Mayor of Strasbourg, "Letter to the Bezirkspräsident," July 13, 1895, 69 AL 455, ADBR.
20 August Kassel, *Nachklaenge zum Trachtenfest in der Strassburger Ausstellung am 8. September 1895. Eine volkstuemliche Plauderei* (Brumath: Buchdruckerei des "Neuen Zornthal Boten," 1895).
21 Möhler, *Das Münchner Oktoberfest*, 282.
22 Maximilian Schmidt, *Meine Wanderung durch 70 Jahre. Zweiter Teil*, Gesammelte Werke 22 (Reutlingen: Ensslin & Laiblin, 1902), 259, http://libsysdigi.library.uiuc.edu/OCA/Books2010-10/3502318/3502318_2/3502318_2.pdf.
23 Schmidt, *Meine Wanderung durch 70 Jahre*, 248.
24 Jules Charles-Roux and Frédéric Mistral, *Le costume en Provence: Période moderne* (Paris: A. Lemerre, 1907), 196.
25 Charles-Roux and Mistral, *Le costume en Provence*, 200.
26 Patrick Young, *Enacting Brittany: Tourism and Culture in Provincial France, 1871–1939* (Paris: Routledge, 2017), 76–7.
27 Young, *Enacting Brittany*, 78.
28 Young, *Enacting Brittany*, 81.
29 Anselme Laugel and Charles Spindler, *Costumes et coutumes d'Alsace*, Nouv. éd. (Nancy: Place Stanislas, 2008), 184.
30 Laugel and Spindler, *Costumes et coutumes d'Alsace*, 185.
31 Charles Spindler, *L'âge d'or d'un artiste en Alsace: mémoires inédits 1889–1914* (Nancy: Place Stanislas, 2009), 63.

32 Spindler, *L'âge d'or d'un artiste en Alsace*, 65.
33 Céline Edel and Musée Alsacien, *Ça décoiffe … : centenaire du Musée alsacien* (Strasbourg: Les Musées de la Ville de Strasbourg, 2007), 24–5.
34 Alfeld, *Kaiser Wilhelm in Elsass-Lothringen: 1.-9. Mai 1877* (Strassburg: J. Schneider, 1877), 30.
35 Bernhard Rogge, *Kaiserbüchlein: 1797–1888. Zur Erinnerung an Deutschlands Heldenkaiser Wilhelm I* (Bielefeld: Velhagen & Klasing, 1888), 63.
36 Kassel, *Nachklaenge zum Trachtenfest*, 10.
37 Anna Christien Piebenga, "Us keninginnen yn 'e pronk," in *Klederdracht en kleedgedrag: het kostuum harer majesteits onderdanen, 1898–1998*, ed. Dolly Verhoeven (Nijmegen: SUN, 1998), 85.
38 Piebenga, "Us keninginnen yn 'e pronk", 85–6.
39 Mairie de Geispolsheim, ed., *Geispolsheim: gare et village, une histoire*, Mémoire de vies (Strasbourg: Carré blanc, 2006), 41.
40 Mathilde Joseph, "Le poilu de music-hall. L'image du poilu dans les music-halls parisiens pendant la Grande Guerre," *Guerres mondiales et conflits contemporains* no. 197 (March 1, 2000): 22.
41 Maurice Agulhon, *Marianne into Battle: Republican Imagery and Symbolism in France, 1789–1880* (Cambridge; New York: Cambridge University Press, 1981), 21.
42 Elizabeth Vlossak, *Marianne or Germania? Nationalizing Women in Alsace, 1870–1946* (Oxford: Oxford University Press, 2010), 138–9.
43 Edel and Musée alsacien, *Ça décoiffe*, 22–3.
44 "Exposition de Nancy: Le village alsacien et les fêtes alsaciennes," *Revue alsacienne illustrée* 11 (1909): 36.
45 1 ALS 37 AVES.
46 Michel Brumpter, "L'Harmonie de Furdenheim (1920–1972)," *Kochersbari* 38 (Hiver 1998): 58–65.
47 Brumpter, "L'Harmonie de Furdenheim (1920–1972)," 58.
48 Brumpter, "L'Harmonie de Furdenheim (1920–1972)," 58–9.
49 Fédération pour la conservation du costume paysan alsacien, "Statuts" (Imp. Nouv. Journal, n.d.), 3, 1 ALS 4, AVES.
50 Gustave Stoskopf, "Letter to the Chairman of the Schweizerisch Trachtenvereinigung," March 23, 1936, Gustave Stoskopf private archives.
51 "Zur Geschichte der Weissenburger Pferdrennen. Ein Fest der elsässischen Bauerntrachten.," *Neueste Nachrichten*, May 13, 1934, Gustave Stoskopf private archives.
52 Gustave Stoskopf, "Letter to Madame Caillau," February 20, 1939, Gustave Stoskopf private archives.
53 Fédération pour la conservation du costume paysan alsacien, "Rapport de la Fédération pour la conservation du costume paysan alsacien," probably 1936, Gustave Stoskopf private archives.

54 Manifest of the FRF: "Par un choix intelligent dans les traditions, par l'enseignement de l'histoire locale et du folklore, par le respect des parlers locaux, rattacher l'enfant à ses ancêtres et lui donner l'orgueil du sol natal." Thiébaut Flory, *Le Mouvement régionaliste français, sources et développements* (Paris: Presses universitaires de France, 1966), 111–12.

55 Quoted in Shanny Peer, *France on Display: Peasants, Provincials, and Folklore in the 1937 Paris World's Fair* (Albany: State University of New York Press, 1998), 62.

56 Peer, *France on Display*, 62.

57 Peer, *France on Display*, 1.

58 "Trachten-Vereine," *Elsass-Lothringer Zeitung*, November 25, 1936, Gustave Stoskopf private archives.

59 "La pittoresque fête du Costume alsacien à Wissembourg s'est déroulée dans un cadre ravissant et en présence d'une foule enthousiaste," *Les Dernières nouvelles d'Alsace et de Lorraine*, June 7, 1936, Gustave Stoskopf private archives.

60 "Instructions sur la tenue des Groupes" (Fédération des Groupes Folkloriques des Provinces Françaises, 1936), Gustave Stoskopf private archives.

61 Ernst Laur, "Letter to Gustave Stoskopf from the Chairman of the Schweizerische Trachtenvereinigung," January 7, 1936, Gustave Stoskopf private archives.

62 Schmitt, 68.

63 Hitler, Mein Kampf (München, Eher, 1933), 151 quoted in Hermann Bausinger, "Nazi Folk Ideology and Folk Research," in *The Nazification of an Academic Discipline: Folklore in the Third Reich*, Folklore Studies in Translation (Bloomington: Indiana University Press, 1994), 18.

64 Hans Strobel, "Tracht und Mode," *Nationalsozialistische Monatshefte* 8, no. 92 (November 1937): 977.

65 Irene Guenther, *Nazi Chic?: Fashioning Women in the Third Reich* (Oxford; New York: Berg, 2004), 111.

66 Guenther, *Nazi Chic?* 110–12.

67 Guenther, *Nazi Chic?* 113.

68 Strobel, "Tracht und Mode," 981.

69 Henry Amard, "De Wissembourg à Strasbourg L'Alsace, hier a acclamé de Gaulle," *Dernière Nouvelles d'Alsace*, October 5, 1945, 235 MW 145, AVES.

70 "Les Fêtes de Strasbourg," *Illustration*, March 30, 1946, 235 MW 143, AVES.

71 A. Schmitt, Adjoint, "Rapport pour Monsieur le Maire, Objet: Spectacles folkloriques," June 27, 1963, 54 W 767, AVES.

72 "Du folklore pour les touristes," *Dernière Nouvelles du Lundi*, July 8, 1963, 54 W 767, AVES.

73 "Letter from the Mayor of Strasbourg to Monsieur Gugumus," February 6, 1964, 54 W 767, AVES.
74 "Note, Objet: Spectacles folkloriques sur les places publiques," March 15, 1968, 54 W 767, AVES.
75 "Note, Objet: Spectacles folkloriques sur les places publiques."
76 "Groupe folklorique du Pays de Hanau de Bouxwiller - Présentation," accessed March 11, 2014, http://hanau.folklore.free.fr/folk/?presentation~fr.
77 This text appears in the English-language section of the group's website. "The Bouxwiller Folk Dance Group of Pays de Hanau," accessed March 11, 2014, http://hanau.folklore.free.fr/accueil_en.html.

Conclusion

1 "La Fête Dieu, Épisode 1," accessed January 15, 2021, https://www.francebleu.fr/emissions/le-patrimoine-alsacien-par-emilienne-kauffmann/elsass/la-fete-dieu-episode-1.
2 "Le Marché de l'Oncle HANSI," accessed March 12, 2014, http://www.hansi.fr/.
3 "Vor 65 Jahren: Emilie Bouwman alias 'Frau Antje' geboren," *WDR*, November 11, 2008, https://www1.wdr.de/stichtag/stichtag3430.html.
4 "Trachten kaufen für die ganze Familie | MOSER Trachten," Moser: Bayerns Grösster Trachtenausstatter, accessed January 17, 2021, https://trachten.de/.
5 "La Maison Bossert au fil du temps," Maison Bossert, spécialiste des costumes d'Alsace, accessed January 31, 2014, http://www.maison-bossert.fr/maison-bossert.html.
6 Charles Spindler, "Réflexion sur le costume alsacien," in *Costumes et coutumes d'Alsace*, by Anselme Laugel and Charles Spindler, Nouv. éd (Nancy: Place Stanislas, 2008), 362.
7 Interview with Marie Rose Allard at Maison Bossert, August 9, 2007.
8 "La Maison Bossert au fil du temps."
9 "Village De Poul Fetan," Office de Tourisme de Pontivy Communauté, accessed January 18, 2021, https://en.tourisme-pontivycommunaute.com/Fiche/Detail/11826/Things-to-see-and-do~Sport-and-Nature/VILLAGE-DE-POUL-FETAN.
10 "Fierce Protests Mar NATO Summit as Anarchists Storm Hotel and Start Torching Buildings," Mail Online, accessed March 12, 2014, http://www.dailymail.co.uk/news/article-1167205/Fierce-protests-mar-Nato-summit-anarchists-storm-hotel-start-torching-buildings.html.

Bibliography

Primary Sources

Archives départementales du Bas-Rhin (ADBR)

27 AL 1107 Bureau des Statthalters in Elsass-Lothringen: Organisation des Handwerks 1896–1913
69 AL 455 Ministerium für Elsass-Lothringen: Volkstrachtenfest, 1895
193 D 150/1 Erneuerungs-und Ergaenzungswahlen zur Handwerkskammer, 1912–1918
193 D 153 Hausarbeit, 1897–1915
193 D 154 Hausarbeit Generalia, 1913–1917
193 D 157 Handwerkskammer-Angelegenheiten—Meister und Gesellenpruefungen (Verschiedenes), 1907–1915
258 D 301 Artisanat rural: Récompenses: Bourses d'apprentissage, 1933
286 D 64 Chambres de métiers d'Alsace et de Lorraine: séances; correspondance generale (1920–1927)
7 E 59/40 - 7 E 52/93 Actes notaires: Truchtersheim, 1869–1907
7 E 67.2/171 - 7 E 67.2/263 Actes notaires: Wissembourg 1, 1870–1894
7 E 67.3/69 - 7 E 67.3/127 Actes notaires: Wissembourg 2, 1869–1897
79 J 374 Hausirhandel, Detailreisen, 1879–1909
79 J 378 Warenhäuser, 1898–1916
79 J 813 Kaufmännisches Unterrichtswesen in Strassburg für weibliche Angestellte, 1900–1918
79 J 959 Reichsbekleidungs-Ordnung II, 1916–1918
79 J 973 Städtische Nähereibetrieb, 1914–1915
1713 W 191 Liste des Artisans: Strasbourg-Ville, 1920–1939
1713 W 192 Liste des Artisans: Strasbourg-Campagne, 1920–1939
1713 W 194 Liste des Artisans: Arrondissement de Saverne, 1920–1939
1713 W 195 Liste des Artisans: Arrondissement de Wissembourg, 1920–1939

Archives de Strasbourg (AVES)

1 ALS 4 Differents programmes et invitations de Sociétés chorales et musicales, 1856–1935
1 ALS 37 Fêtes et manifestations
1 Fi 1 1919–1935
1 Fi 2 1935–1937
1 Fi 3 1937

1 Fi 6 1938–1939
1 Fi 7 1939
1 Fi 179 Lucien Blumer, Photographies de la procession de Geispolsheim et costumes traditionels alsaciens
1 Fi 189 Lucien Blumer, Photographies de Schleithal et Seebach
5 MW 275, 276, 278, 279, 280, 283 Musée Alsacien
234 MW 264 Trachtenfest, 1895
235 MW 143 Visite de M. Félix Gouin 24 mars 1946
54 W 767 Concerts et spectacles folkloriques sur les places publiques (1965–68)
54 W 768 Concerts et spectacles folkloriques sur les places publiques (1969–1970)
54 W 775 Flâneries nocturnes: Organisation d'une Fête Folklorique internationale
720 W 138–142 Records for 34, rue du 22 Novembre (Magasins Modernes)
845 W 3–9 Records for 1-5 rue de la Haute-Montée (Grandes Galéries)

Private Collections

Photographs and letters of Charles Spindler in private collection
Files and newspaper clippings of Gustave Stoskopf in private collection

Museum Objects

Dresses and bodices in the collection of the Musée Alsacien
Coiffes, aprons, casaquins, corselets, and shawls in the collection of the Musée d'Art et d'Histoire de Saverne
Coiffes and archives of the Musée du Pays de Hanau

Newspapers

Anzeiger für die Kantone Landau, Annweiler und Bergzabern
Buchsweiler Kantons-Blatt
Elsässische Nachrichten
Gewerbezeitung für Elsass-Lothringen
Strassburger Neueste Nachrichten
Strassburger Post
Weissenburger Wochenblatt

Periodicals

(Bibliothèque nationale et universitaire Strasbourg)

Album de la Mode et Linge
Elsass-Lothringer Mode-Journal

Das Heim: illustrierte Familienzeitschrift
Jahrbuch für Geschichte, Sprache und Literatur Elsass-Lothringens
Revue alsacienne illustrée
Le Tailleur et la tailleuse d'Alsace et de Lorraine

Mail Order Catalogues (Bibliothèque nationale de France Département des Estampes et de la photographie)

Au Bon Marché
La Belle Jardinière
Grands Magasins
Grands Magasins du Louvre

Published Sources

Agulhon, Maurice. *Marianne into Battle: Republican Imagery and Symbolism in France, 1789-1880.* Cambridge [Eng.]; New York: Cambridge University Press, 1981.

Alfeld. *Kaiser Wilhelm in Elsass-Lothringen: 1.-9. Mai 1877.* Strassburg: J. Schneider, 1877.

Anderson, Margaret Lavinia. "The Limits of Secularization: On the Problem of the Catholic Revival in Nineteenth-Century Germany." *The Historical Journal* 38, no. 3 (September 1, 1995): 647–70.

Applegate, Celia. *A Nation of Provincials: The German Idea of Heimat.* Berkeley: University of California Press, 1990.

Badone, Ellen. "Pardons, Pilgrimage and the (Re-) Construction of Identities in Brittany." In *Gender, Nation and Religion in European Pilgrimage*, edited by Willy Jansen and Catrien Notermans, 145–61. Surrey: Ashgate, 2012.

Baquol, Jacques, and Paul Ristelhuber. *L'Alsace ancienne et moderne: ou Dictionnaire topographique, historique et statistique du Haut et du Bas-Rhin.* 3rd ed. Strasbourg: Salomon, 1865.

Barrès, Maurice. "La Genèse d'une oeuvre: Comment aimer notre terre et nos morts— Le musée d'Arles. Une lettre de Mistral." *Revue alsacienne illustrée = Illustrirte elsässische Rundschau* IV(1902): 33–8.

Barthes, Roland. *The Fashion System.* Translated by Matthew Ward and Richard Howard. New York: Hill and Wang, 1983.

Bausinger, Hermann. "Nazi Folk Ideology and Folk Research." In *The Nazification of an Academic Discipline: Folklore in the Third Reich*, 11–33. Folklore Studies in Translation. Bloomington: Indiana University Press, 1994.

Bédollierre, Émile de la. "L'Alsacien." In *Les Français peints par eux-mêmes: encyclopédie morale du dix-neuvième siècle*, 8: 145–52. Paris: L. Curmer, 1842.

Bendix, Regina. "Folklorism: The Challenge of a Concept." *International Folklore Review* 6 (1988): 5–15.

Bendix, Regina. "Diverging Paths in the Scientific Search for Authenticity." *Journal of Folklore Research* 29, no. 2 (1992): 103–32.

Berstett: *un village pittoresque du Kochersberg*. Strasbourg: Editions Coprur, 1993.

Bodé, Gérard. "État français - état allemand: l'enseignement technique mosellan entre deux modèles nationaux, 1815–1940." *Histoire de l'éducation*, no. 66 (May 1, 1995): 109–36.

Bourrut Lacouture, Annette. *Jules Breton, Painter of Peasant Life*. New Haven: Yale University Press in association with the National Gallery of Ireland, Dublin, 2002.

Braun, Louis. *Zur Geschichte der Kostüme*. München: Braun & Schneider; New York: E. Weye, 1898.

Bruant, Benoît. *Hansi: l'artiste tendre et rebelle*. Strasbourg: Nuée Bleue, 2008.

Brumpter, Michel. "L'Harmonie de Furdenheim (1920–1972)." *Kochersbari* 38 (Hiver 1998): 58–65.

Burnouf, Joëlle Callot, ed. *Le Kochersberg: histoire et paysages*. Strasbourg: Publitotal, 1980.

Cahun, David-Léon. *La vie juive*. Paris: E. Monnie, de Brunhoff, 1886.

Caron, Vicki. *Between France and Germany: The Jews of Alsace-Lorraine, 1871–1918*. Stanford, CA: Stanford University Press, 1988.

Chabart, Joëlle, ed. *Schleithal: le village le plus long d'Alsace*. [Monographies des villages d'Alsace] 64. Strasbourg: Coprur, 1999.

Chapman, Malcolm. "'Freezing the Frame': Dress and Ethnicity in Brittany and Gaelic Scotland." In *Dress and Ethnicity*, edited by Joanne B. Eicher, 7–28. Ethnicity and Identity. Oxford: Berg, 1995.

Charles-Roux, Jules, and Frédéric Mistral. *Le costume en Provence: Période moderne*. Paris: A. Lemerre, 1907.

Clark, Timothy J. *Image of the People: Gustave Courbet and the 1848 Revolution*. Berkeley: University of California Press, 1999.

Coles, Tim. "Department Stores as Retail Innovations in Germany: A Historical-Geographical Perspective on the Period 1870 to 1914." In *Cathedrals of Consumption: The European Department Store, 1850–1939*, edited by Geoffrey Crossick and Serge Jaumain, 72–96. The History of Retailing and Consumption. Aldershot, Hants, England; Brookfield, VT: Ashgate, 1999.

Collet, Isabelle. "Les premiers musées d'ethnographie régionale en France." In *Muséologie et ethnologie*. Notes et documents des musées de France 16. Paris: Editions de la Réunion des musées nationaux, 1987.

Commune de Bouxwiller. *Bouxwiller: Imbsheim, Riedheim/Griesbach-le-Bastberg: autour du Bastberg*. Mémoire de vie. Strasbourg: Carré blanc, 2007.

Confino, Alon. *The Nation as a Local Metaphor: Württemberg, Imperial Germany, and National Memory, 1871–1918*. Chapel Hill: University of North Carolina Press, 1997.

DeGroff, Daniel. "Ethnographic Display and Political Narrative: The Salle de France of the Musée d'Ethnographie Du Trocadéro." In *Folklore and Nationalism in Europe during the Long Nineteenth Century*, edited by Timothy Baycroft and David Hopkin, 113–36. Leiden: BRILL, 2012.

Dias, Nélia. *Le musée d'ethnographie du Trocadéro: (1878–1908): anthropologie et muséologie en France*. Paris: Ed. du Centre National de la Recherche Scientifique, 1991.

Dias, Nélia. "Vers l'archivage des objets: la naissance du Musée d'ethnographie du Trocadéro." *Bulletin d'information de l'Association des Bibliothècaires Français*, no. 138 (1er trimestre 1988): 28–31.

Doerflinger, Marguerite. *Découverte des costumes traditionnels en Alsace*. Colmar: Editions S. A. E. P., 1979.

Edel, Céline, and Musée alsacien. *Ça décoiffe. ... : centenaire du Musée alsacien*. Strasbourg: Les Musées de la Ville de Strasbourg, 2007.

Emrich, Charles. *Collection de six costumes nationaux Alsaciens et Badois*. Strasbourg, 1834.

Faraut, François. *Histoire de La Belle Jardinière*. Modernités XIXe–XXe. Paris: Belin, 1987.

Fesquet, Jean-Louis. "Département du Bas-Rhin." In *Voyage de Paris à Strasbourg, et principalement dans tout le Bas-Rhin [...]*. s.n., 1801.

Flory, Thiébaut. *Le Mouvement régionaliste français, sources et développements*. Paris: Presses universitaires de France, 1966.

Ford, Caroline. *Creating the Nation in Provincial France: Religion and Political Identity in Brittany*. Princeton: Princeton University Press, 1993.

Ford, Caroline. "Religion and the Politics of Cultural Change in Provincial France: The Resistance of 1902 in Lower Brittany." *The Journal of Modern History* 62, no. 1 (1990): 2–33.

Franzoi, Barbara. *At the Very Least She Pays the Rent: Women and German Industrialization, 1871–1914*. Westport, CT: Greenwood Press, 1985.

Fried, Michael. "The Structure of Beholding in Courbet's 'Burial at Ornans.'" *Critical Inquiry* 9, no. 4 (1983): 635–83.

Galtier, Charles, Maurice Rouquette Laroche, and Museon arlaten. *La Provence et Frédéric Mistral au Museon arlaten*. Paris: J. Cuénot, 1977.

Gatineau, Barbara. "Preface." In *Costumes et coutumes d'Alsace*, by Anselme Laugel, Nouv. éd. Nancy: Place Stanislas, 2008.

Gerson, Stéphane. *The Pride of Place: Local Memories and Political Culture in Nineteenth-Century France*. Ithaca: Cornell University Press, 2003.

Gibson, Ralph. *A Social History of French Catholicism, 1789–1914*. Christianity and Society in the Modern World. London; New York: Routledge, 1989.

Gonidec, Jean-Pierre. *Costume et société: Le monde de Douarnenez, Ploaré vu à travers ses modes vestimentaires*. Spezet: Coop Breizh, 2000.

Grasset de Saint-Saveur, Jacques. *Encyclopédie des voyages, contenant l'abrégé historique des moeurs, usages, habitudes domestiques, religions, fêtes, supplices, funérailles, sciences, arts et commerce de tous les peuples: et la collection complette de leurs habillemens civils, militaires, religieux et dignitaires, dessines d'après nature, gravés avec soin et coloriés à l'aquarelle*. Paris: l'auteur, 1796.

Green, Nancy L. *Ready-to-Wear and Ready-to-Work: A Century of Industry and Immigrants in Paris and New York*. Comparative and International Working-Class

History; Variation: Comparative and International Working-Class History. Durham: Duke University Press, 1997.

Grew, Raymond. "Picturing the People: Images of the Lower Orders in Nineteenth-Century French Art." *The Journal of Interdisciplinary History* 17, no. 1 (1986): 203–31.

Guenther, Irene. *Nazi Chic?: Fashioning Women in the Third Reich.* Oxford; New York: Berg, 2004.

Hahn, Emilie. *Zwei Schweschtere. Komödie in elsässischer Mundart in zwei Akten.* Le Roux elsässisches Vereinstheater 27. F.X. Le Roux & Cie., 1926.

Hansjakob, Heinrich. *Unsere Volkstrachten: ein Wort zu ihrer Erhaltung.* Freiburg im Breisgau; München: Herder, 1892.

Harvey, David. *Paris, Capital of Modernity.* New York: Routledge, 2006.

Haupt, Heinz-Gerhard, and Jürgen Kocka, eds. *Comparative and Transnational History: Central European Approaches and New Perspectives.* New York: Berghahn Books, 2009.

Hobsbawm, Eric, and Terence Ranger, eds. *The Invention of Tradition.* Past and Present Publications. Cambridge: Cambridge University Press, 1983.

Honeyman, Katrina. *Well Suited: A History of the Leeds Clothing Industry, 1850–1990.* Pasold Studies in Textile History 11. Oxford; New York: Oxford University Press, 2000.

Humbert, Jean-Louis. "La Constitution des entreprises de la confection aux 19ème et 20ème siècles: ouvrières, ouvriers, patrons." In *Approche comparative des entreprises en France et en Allemagne: le déclin de l'empire des aiguilles*, edited by Jan Spurk. Collection Dynamiques d'entreprises; Variation: Dynamiques d'entreprises. Paris, France: Harmattan, 1997.

Hume, Lynne. *The Religious Life of Dress: Global Fashion and Faith.* Dress, Body, Culture. New York: Bloomsbury Academic, 2013.

Hume, Sara. "Between Fashion and Folk: Dress Practices in Alsace during the First World War." In *Fashion, Society and the First World War: International Perspectives*, edited by Maude Bass-Krueger, Hayley Edwards-Dujardin, and Sophie Kurkdjian 110–23. London: Bloomsbury, 2021.

Hume, Sara. "Charles Frederick Worth: A Study in the Relationship between the Parisian Fashion Industry and the Lyonnais Silk Industry 1858–1889." Fashion Institute of Technology, 2003.

Hyman, Paula. *The Emancipation of the Jews of Alsace: Acculturation and Tradition in the Nineteenth Century.* New Haven: Yale University Press, 1991.

Hyman, Paula. "The Social Contexts of Assimilation: Village Jews and City Jews in Alsace." In *Assimilation and Community: The Jews in Nineteenth-Century Europe*, edited by Jonathan Frankel and Steven J. Zipperstein, 110–29. Cambridge and New York: Cambridge University Press, 1992.

Igersheim, François. "Robert Forrer et le premier 'Musée alsacien' à Berlin en 1889." *Cahiers alsaciens d'archéologie d'art et d'histoire.* LI (2008): 131–4.

Jonas, Stéphane. "Strasbourg 1900: Une ville de frontière et d'innovation (1890–1918)." *Revue des sciences sociales* 19 (1991): 13–30.

Jones, Siân. "Negotiating Authentic Objects and Authentic Selves: Beyond the Deconstruction of Authenticity." *Journal of Material Culture* 15, no. 2 (June 2010): 181–203. https://doi.org/10.1177/1359183510364074.

Joseph, Mathilde. "Le poilu de music-hall. L'image du poilu dans les music-halls parisiens pendant la Grande Guerre." *Guerres mondiales et conflits contemporains*, no. 197 (March 1, 2000): 21–41.

Kassel, August. *Messti und Kirwe im Elsass*. Strassburg: J.H. Ed. Heitz, 1908.

Kassel, August. *Nachklaenge zum Trachtenfest in der Strassburger Ausstellung am 8. September 1895. Eine volkstuemliche Plauderei*. Brumath: Buchdruckerei des "Neuen Zornthal Boten," 1895.

Kassel, August. *Über elsaessische Trachten*. Strassburg: Du Mont-Schauberg, 1907.

Kaufman, Edward N. "The Architectural Museum from World's Fair to Restoration Village." *Assemblage*, no. 9 (June 1, 1989): 21–39.

Kempf, Christian. "Adolphe Braun's Photographic Enterprise." In *Image and Enterprise: The Photographs of Adolphe Braun*, edited by Mary Bergstein and Maureen C. O'Brien, 9–29. London: Thames & Hudson in association with Museum of Art, Rhode Island School of Design, 2000.

Kempf, Christian, and Michel Loetscher. *Une Alsace 1900*. Nancy: Place Stanislas, 2007.

Kennedy, Katherine. "Domesticity (Hauswirtschaft) in the Volkschule." *Internationale Schulbuchforschung: Zeitschrift Des Georg-Eckert-Instituts Für Internationale Schulbuchforschung* 13, no. 1 (1991): 5–21.

Klein, Detmar. "Folklore as a Weapon: National Identity in German-Annexed Alsace, 1890–1914." In *Folklore and Nationalism in Europe during the Long Nineteenth Century*, edited by Timothy Baycroft and David Hopkin, 161–91. Leiden: BRILL, 2012.

Klein, Georges, and Charles Woehly. *Costume d'Alsace: matières, travaux d'aiguille*. Strasbourg: Musée alsacien, 1979.

Klein, Georges, and Musée alsacien. *La Naissance Du Musée Alsacien et La Revue Alsacienne Illustrée: Strasbourg, Musée Alsacien, 29 Juin-29 Septembre 1985*. Strasbourg: Le Musée, 1985.

Klein, Jean-Pierre. *Un romantique alsacien: Théophile Schuler: 1821–1878*. Strasbourg: Château de Rohan, 1979.

Kleinert, Annemarie. *Le "Journal des dames et des modes" ou la conquête de l'Europe féminine (1797–1839)*. Stuttgart: Jan Thorbecke Verlag, 2001.

Kraus, Gustav. *Festzug zur Feyer der Jubel Ehe I.I.M.M. des Königs Ludwig und der Königin Therese zu München am 4ten October 1835*. München: J. C. Hochwind, 1836.

Kraus, Gustav. *Festzug der 35 Brautpaare zur Vermählungsfeyer Seiner Königlichen Hoheit des Kronprinzen Maximilian von Bayern und Ihrer Königlichen Hoheit der Kronprinzeß Marie von Bayern im Vorbeiziehen vor dem Königszelt bey dem Octoberfeste in München den 16ten October 1842*. G. Kraus, 1842.

Lallemand, Charles, and Ludovic Hart. *Deutsche Volkstrachten*. Basel: A Varady & Co., 1865.

Landrin, Armand. "Anciens costumes populaires français au Palais du Trocadéro." *La Nature. Revue des sciences et de leurs applications aux arts et à l'industrie* 17, no. 853 (October 5, 1889): 295–8.

Landrin, Armand, and Paul Sébillot. "Instructions sommaires relatives aux collections provinciales d'objets ethnographiques." In *La tradition au pays basque: Ethnographie, folklore, art populaire, histoire, hagiographie*, edited by Gustave Boucher, 585–95. Paris: Aux bureaux de la Tradition nationale, 1899.

Lanté, Louis-Marie, and Georges-Jacques Gatine. *Costumes de divers pays*. Paris, 1827.

Lanté, Louis-Marie, and Georges-Jacques Gatine. *Costumes des femmes du Pays de Caux, et de plusieurs autres parties de l'ancienne province de Normandie*. Paris: Pierre de la Mésangère, 1827.

Laugel, Anselme, and Charles Spindler. *Costumes et coutumes d'Alsace*. Nouv. éd. Nancy: Place Stanislas, 2008.

Legin, Philippe. *Coutumes et costumes alsaciens*. Toute l'Alsace. Ingersheim: Editions S.A.E.P., 1993.

Leulliot, P. "Les anabaptistes alsaciens sous le Second Empire." *Revue d'Alsace* 87 (1947): 207–11.

Lewicki, Jan. *Costumes d'Alsace et de Bade*. Strasbourg: E. Simon fils, 1834.

Lipowsky, Felix Joseph. *Sammlung Bayerischer National-Costume*. München: Hermann & Barth, 1820.

Loetscher, Michel. "L'Âge d'or d'un peuple et d'un artiste." In *L'âge d'or d'un artiste en Alsace: mémoires inédits 1889–1914*, by Charles Spindler, 9–17. Nancy: Place Stanislas, 2009.

Loetscher, Michel. "Planète lumière, ou l'image habitée." In *Une Alsace 1900*, 10–11. Nancy: Place Stanislas, 2007.

Loetscher, Michel, and Jean-Charles Spindler. *Charles, Paul, Jean-Charles Spindler: un siècle d'art en Alsace*. Strasbourg: Nuée bleue, 2005.

Longchamp, Jacques. *Marc Louis Benjamin Vautier (dit l'ancien)*. Geneva: Editions Slatkine, 2015.

Lyons, Martyn. *Reading Culture and Writing Practices in Nineteenth-Century France*. Toronto: University of Toronto Press, 2008.

Maguet, Frédéric. "De la série éditoriale dans l'imagerie: L'exemple des costumes régionaux." *Ethnologie française*, nouvelle serie 24, no. 2 (April 1, 1994): 226–41.

Mainardi, Patricia. *Art and Politics of the Second Empire: The Universal Expositions of 1855 and 1867*. New Haven: Yale University Press, 1987.

Mainardi, Patricia. *The End of the Salon: Art and the State in the Early Third Republic*. Cambridge: Cambridge University Press, 1993.

Mairie de Geispolsheim, ed. *Geispolsheim: gare et village, une histoire*. Mémoire de vies. Strasbourg: Carré blanc, 2006.

Marignan, Emile. *Instructions pour la récolte des objets d'ethnographie du pays arlésien*. Arles: ed. Jouve, 1896.

Martin, Étienne. "Charles Spindler und der Kreis von St. Léonard: Regionalismus und Moderne um 1900 im Elsass." In *Jugendstil am Oberrhein: Sonderausstellung des*

Badischen Landesmuseums Karlsruhe 18.4-9.8.2009, edited by Elisabeth Gurock. Karlsruhe: DRW-Verlag Weinbrenner: G. Braun Buchverlag, 2009.

McLeod, Hugh. *Secularization in Western Europe, 1848–1914*. New York: St. Martin's Press, 2000.

Michiels, Alfred. *Les anabaptistes des Vosges*. Paris: Poulet-Malassis et de Broise, 1860.

Möhler, Gerda. *Das Münchner Oktoberfest: Brauchformen des Volksfestes zwischen Aufklärung und Gegenwart*. Miscellanea Bavarica Monacensia; Heft 100; Neue Schriftenreihe des Stadtarchivs München 100. München: Kommissionsbuchhandlung R. Wölfe, 1980.

Muller, Claude. *Églises mixtes: du Kochersberg, du pays de Hanau et de l'Alsace bossue: 1802–1914*. Pays d'Alsace. Série Recherches. Saverne: Société d'histoire et d'archéologie de Saverne et environs, 1983.

Müller, Heidi. "Die Sammlungskonzeption des Museums für Deutsche Volkskunde von der Gründung 1889 bis Zum Ersten Weltkrieg." *Jahrbuch der Berliner Museen* 34 (1992): 185–94.

Noël, Marie-France. "Du musée d'ethnographie du Trocadéro au Musée national des Arts et Traditions populaires." In *Muséologie et ethnologie*, 140–51. Notes et documents des musées de France. Paris: Editions de la Réunion des musées nationaux, 1987.

Nuzinger, Richard. *Die Erhaltung der Volkstrachten: Eine Warnung*. Heidelberg: Evangelischer Verlag, 1897.

O'Brien, Maureen C. "The Influence of Contemporary French Painting." In *Image and Enterprise: The Photographs of Adolphe Braun*, edited by Mary Bergstein and Maureen C. O'Brien, 67–91. London: Thames & Hudson in association with Museum of Art, Rhode Island School of Design, 2000.

Orzechowski, Simone. "La Revue Alsacienne Illustrée (1898–1914): L'art, paravent de la lutte contre la germinisation." In *Le Problème de l'Alsace-Lorraine vu par les périodiques (1871–1914) = Die Elsass-Lothringische Frage im Spiegel der Zeitschriften (1871–1914)*, edited by Michel Grunewald. Convergences; 7. Bern; New York: P. Lang, 1998.

Otto, Fräulein L. *Prospect der Frauen-Industrie- und Fortbildungs-Schule des Vaterländischen Frauen-Vereins zu Strassburg im Elsass*. Strassburg: Strassburger Neueste Nachrichten, 1903.

Peer, Shanny. *France on Display: Peasants, Provincials, and Folklore in the 1937 Paris World's Fair*. Albany: State University of New York Press, 1998.

Pellegrin, Nicole. "Une géographie pour les filles? Les recueils de costumes français de Jacques Grasset de Saint-Sauveur au tournant des XVIIIe et XIXe siècles." In *Les costumes régionaux entre mémoire et histoire*, 217–33. Rennes: Presses universitaires de Rennes, 2009.

Picart, Bernard. *The Ceremonies and Religious Customs of the Various Nations of the Known World: Together with Historical Annotations, and Several Curious Discourses Equally Instructive and Entertaining*. London: Printed by W. Jackson, for Claude Du Bosc, 1733.

Piebenga, Anna Christien. "Us keninginnen yn 'e pronk." In *Klederdracht en kleedgedrag: het kostuum harer majesteits onderanen, 1898–1998*, edited by Dolly Verhoeven. Nijmegen: SUN, 1998.

Piton, Frédéric Théodore. *Strasbourg illustré ou Panorama pittoresque, historique et statistique de Strasbourg et de ses environs: Promenades dans les faubourgs, déscription des environs*. Strasbourg: printed by the author, 1855.

Prigent, Léone. "La vision des Strasbourgeoises dans les recueils de costumes du XVIIIe siecle: une image plurielle." In *Les costumes régionaux entre mémoire et histoire*, edited by Jean-Pierre Lethuillier, 203–15. Rennes: Presses universitaires de Rennes, 2009.

Raphaël, Freddy. "Juifs et Mennonites en Alsace." In *Les Anabaptistes Mennonites d'Alsace: Destin d'une minorité*, 77–104. Saisons D'Alsace. Nouvelle série 76. Strasbourg: Librairie Istra, 1981.

Raphaël, Freddy, and Robert Weyl. *Regards nouveaux sur les juifs d'Alsace*. Strasbourg: Librairie Istra: Éditions des dernières nouvelles d'Alsace, 1980.

Ristelhuber, Paul. *Galerie universelle des peuples. Alsace*. Strasbourg: Lallemand & Hart, 1865.

Roche, Daniel. *La culture des apparences: une histoire du vêtement (XVIIe–XVIIIe siècle)*. Paris: Fayard, 1989.

Rogge, Bernhard. *Kaiserbüchlein: 1797–1888. Zur Erinnerung an Deutschlands Heldenkaiser Wilhelm I*. Bielefeld: Velhagen & Klasing, 1888.

Roy, Christian. *Traditional Festivals a Multicultural Encyclopedia*. Santa Barbara, CA: ABC-CLIO, 2005.

Rubens, Alfred. *A History of Jewish Costume*. New York: Crown, 1973.

Sahlins, Peter. "The Nation in the Village: State-Building and Communal Struggles in the Catalan Borderland during the Eighteenth and Nineteenth Centuries." *The Journal of Modern History* 60, no. 2 (1988): 234–63.

Samuels, Maurice. *Inventing the Israelite: Jewish Fiction in Nineteenth-Century France*. Stanford, CA: Stanford University Press, 2009.

Sandberg, Mark B. *Living Pictures, Missing Persons: Mannequins, Museums, and Modernity*. Princeton, NJ: Princeton University Press, 2003.

Sartre, Jean-Paul. *War Diaries: Notebooks from a Phoney War, November 1939–March 1940*. London: Verso, 1999.

Schilkemer Messti. Festschrift und Fuehrer durch die Industrie- und Gewerbeausstellung. Schiltigheim: J. Schneider, 1895.

Schlagdenhauffen, Jean-Marc Auteur. *Le costume paysan*. Uhrwiller: Association culturelle Uhrwiller, 1992.

Schmidt, Maximilian. *Meine Wanderung durch 70 Jahre. Zweiter Teil*. Gesammelte Werke 22. Reutlingen: Ensslin & Laiblin, 1902.

Schmitt, Heinz. "Die Bollenhuttracht: Entwicklung, Pflege, Vermarktung." *Die Ortenau: Zeitschrift des Historischen Vereins für Mittelbaden*, no. 69 (1989): 440–58.

Schmitt, Heinz. *Volkstracht in Baden: ihre Rolle in Kunst, Staat, Wirtschaft und Gesellschaft seit zwei Jahrhunderten*. Karlsruhe: Badenia Verlag, 1988.

Schneider, Malou. *Le Musée alsacien, Strasbourg*. Kaléidoscope d'Alsace. Strasbourg: La Nuée bleue, Impr. SAG, 1995.

Schnitzler, Bernadette. *Robert Forrer (1866–1947): archéologue, écrivain et antiquaire*. Publications de la Société Savante d'Alsace; Collection "Recherches et documents"; 65. Strasbourg: Soc. Savante d'Alsace, 1999.

Schoenbaum, David. *Zabern 1913: Consensus Politics in Imperial Germany*. London; Boston: George Allen & Unwin, 1982.

Schulz-Berlekamp, Gesine. "Mönchgut: Entdeckung einer Tracht." In *Kleidung zwischen Tracht + Mode: aus der Geschichte des Museums 1889–1989*, edited by Ulrich Reuter and Museum für Volkskunde, 49–59. Berlin: Staatliche Museen zu Berlin, 1989.

Schwab, Roland. "La grande mutation des campagnes alsaciennes (1871–1960)." In *Histoire de l'Alsace rurale*, edited by Jean-Michel Boehler, Dominique Lerch, and Jean Vogt, 363–86. Collection "Grandes publications" t. 24. Strasbourg: ISTRA, 1983.

Sébillot, Paul. "L'Ethnographie traditionelle et les musées cantonaux." *Annuaire des musées cantonaux*, 1886–87: 9–20.

Seebach. Strasbourg: Edition Coprur, 1983.

Séguy, Jean. "Quatre siècles et demi d'histoire: Les anabaptistes." In *Les Anabaptistes Mennonites d'Alsace: Destin d'une minorité*, 7–24. Saisons D'Alsace. Nouvelle série 76. Strasbourg: Librairie Istra, 1981.

Seyller, A. *D'Hochzittshose. Schwank in 1 Akt*. Salvator-Theater Sammlung Ernster und Heiterer Theaterstücke 127. Mulhausen: Salvator-Verlag, 1932.

Silverman, Dan P. *Reluctant Union; Alsace-Lorraine and Imperial Germany, 1871–1918*. University Park: Pennsylvania State University Press, 1972.

Šmidchens, Guntis. "Folklorism Revisited." *Journal of Folklore Research* 36, no. 1 (1999): 51–70.

Spindler, Charles. *L'âge d'or d'un artiste en Alsace: mémoires inédits 1889–1914*. Nancy: Place Stanislas, 2009.

Spindler, Charles. "Réflexion sur le costume alsacien." In *Costumes et coutumes d'Alsace*, by Anselme Laugel and Charles Spindler, 357–66, Nouv. éd. Nancy: Place Stanislas, 2008.

Starck, Astrid. "Alsatian Yiddish Theater at the Turn of the Century." In *Insiders and Outsiders: Jewish and Gentile Culture in Germany and Austria*, edited by Dagmar C. G. Lorenz and Gabriele Weinberger. Detroit: Wayne State University Press, 1994.

Stauben, Daniel. *Scènes de la vie Juive en Alsace*. Paris: Michel Lévy Frères, 1860.

Steinhoff, Anthony J. "Building Religious Community: Worship Space and Experience in Strasbourg after the Franco-Prussian War." In *Protestants, Catholics, and Jews in Germany, 1800–1914*, edited by Helmut Walser Smith, 267–96. Oxford; New York: Berg, 2001.

Steinmann, Ulrich. "Gründer und Förderer des Berliner Volkskunde-Museums. Rudolf Virchow, Ulrich Jahn, Alexander Meyer Cohn, Hermann Sökeland, James Simon." *Forschungen und Berichte* 9 (January 1, 1967): 71–T27.

Stoklund, Bjarne. "Between Scenography and Science: Early Folk Museums and Their Pioneers." *Ethnologia Europaea* 33, no. 1 (2003): 21–36.

Stoklund, Bjarne. "The Role of the International Exhibitions in the Construction of National Cultures in the 19th Century." *Ethnologia Europaea* 24 (1994): 35–44.

Strobel, Hans. "Tracht und Mode." *Nationalsozialistische Monatshefte* 8, no. 92 (November 1937): 970–84.

Taylor, Lou. *Establishing Dress History. Studies in Design*. Manchester; New York: Manchester University Press, 2004.

Thiesse, Anne-Marie. *Ils apprenaient la France : l'exaltation des régions dans le discours patriotique*. Vol. 17. Paris: Editions de la Maison des sciences de l'homme, 1997.

Trevor-Roper, Hugh. "The Invention of Tradition: The Highland Tradition of Scotland." In *The Invention of Tradition*, edited by Eric Hobsbawm and Terence Ranger, 15–41. Cambridge: Cambridge University Press, 1983.

Vlossak, Elizabeth. *Marianne or Germania? Nationalizing Women in Alsace, 1870–1946*. Oxford: Oxford University Press, 2010.

Vogler, Bernard. "En Alsace: orthodoxie et territorialisme." In *Histoire des protestants en France*, edited by Robert Mandrou, 151–87. Toulouse: Privat, 1977.

Vogler, Bernard. *Histoire des chrétiens d'Alsace des origines à nos jours*. Paris: Desclée, 1994.

Wahl, Alfred. *Confession et comportement dans les campagnes d'Alsace et de Bade, 1871–1939: catholiques, protestants et juifs: démographie, dynamisme économique et social, vie de relation et attitude politique*. Strasbourg: Editions Coprur, 1980.

Wahl, Alfred. *L'option et l'émigration des Alsaciens-Lorrains, 1871–1872*. Paris: Ophrys, 1974.

Wahl, Alfred, and Jean-Claude Richez. *L'Alsace entre France et Allemagne: 1850–1950*. Vol. 1. Paris: Hachette, 1993.

Weber, Eugen. *Peasants into Frenchmen: The Modernization of Rural France, 1870–1914*. Stanford, CA: Stanford University Press, 1976.

Wehler, Hans Ulrich. "Der Fall Zabern von 1913/14 Als Verfassungskrise des Wilhelminischen Kaiserreichs." In *Krisenherde des Kaiserreichs. 1871–1918. Studien z. dt. Sozial- u. Verfassungsgeschichte*, 70–80. Göttingen: Vandenhoeck u. Ruprecht, 1970.

Weisberg, Gabriel. *The Realist Tradition: French Painting and Drawing, 1830–1900*. Cleveland: Cleveland Museum of Art, 1980.

Westphal, Uwe. *Berliner Konfektion und Mode: die Zerstörung einer Tradition, 1836–1939*. Stätten der Geschichte Berlins; Bd. 14. Berlin: Edition Hentrich, 1986.

Wilkinson, James. "The Uses of Popular Culture by Rival Elites: The Case of Alsace, 1890–1914." *History of European Ideas* 11, nos. 1–6 (January 1989): 605–18.

Wörner, Martin. "Chapter 6 'Kulturmuseum der Menschheit'—Weltausstellung und Museumswesen." In *Vergnügung und Belehrung: Volkskultur auf den Weltausstellungen, 1851–1900*, 237–84. Münster; New York: Waxmann, 1999.

Young, Patrick. *Enacting Brittany: Tourism and Culture in Provincial France, 1871–1939*. London: Routledge, 2017.

Young, Patrick. "Of Pardons, Loss, and Longing: The Tourist's Pursuit of Originality in Brittany, 1890–1935." *French Historical Studies* 30, no. 2 (Spring 2007): 269–304.

Zafran, Eric, Robert Rosenblum, and Lisa Small. *Fantasy and Faith: The Art of Gustave Doré*. New York: Dahesh Museum of Art; New Haven: Yale University Press, 2007.

Zimmer, Oliver. "Beneath the 'Culture War': Corpus Christi Processions and Mutual Accommodation in the Second German Empire." *The Journal of Modern History* 82, no. 2 (June 1, 2010): 288–334.

Zimmerman, Andrew. "Anti-Semitism as Skill: Rudolf Virchow's 'Schulstatistik' and the Racial Composition of Germany." *Central European History* 32, no. 4 (1999): 409–29.

Index

advertisement 114–21, 203, 205, 209
Alsace 1–4, 22–3, 172, 182, 204
   department stores 119–21
   integration 191
   political contest 9, 20, 136, 139, 208
   population of 3, 9, 10, 16, 19
   religious conflicts in 49
   retail in 112–19
   rural 7, 8, 10, 12, 16, 18, 37, 43, 83, 91, 98, 103, 110, 132, 133, 135, 143, 150, 179, 190, 208
   symbol of 93–5
   Upper and Lower 9–11, 27, 35, 121, 142, 175, 181, 205
Alsace (Doré) 79
Alsace-Lorraine 8–9, 80, 117, 124, 128, 186
"Alsacien et Alsacienne" 64–5
Alsacienne 79, 80, 93–5, 106, 159, 203, 204
Alsatian
   Awakening *(reveil alsacien)* 12, 80–3
   costume 16, 58, 76, 79, 87, 92, 116, 130, 141, 161, 179, 186, 188
   culture 9, 10, 12, 18, 80, 83, 91, 116, 135, 136, 141, 144, 145, 149–51, 158, 203
   festival 52, 187
   history 8–13
   Jews 35, 37–41, 44
   newspapers 117–19
   rural 10, 12, 19, 27, 44, 49, 53, 99, 100–4, 106, 110, 121, 189, 206
   Volksschulen 125
Anabaptists 15–17, 32–6, 41, 43, 53, 54, 64
Ant and the Grasshopper, The (Doré) 77–9
Anthropological Society *(Anthropolgischen Gesellschaft)* 147
apprenticeships 125, 127–30
Arles 140, 141, 151, 177
Armbruster, L. 188, 190, 193
Art Nouveau 80–3
Aryan-Nordic type 193

Au Bon Marché 117
Augsburg 17
authenticity 5–7, 161, 188, 190

Baden 51, 62, 63, 66, 141, 171, 172, 191, 208
Barrès, M. 140, 141, 145
Barthes, R. 57
Bas-Rhin 43, 81, 130, 142
Bastille Day 182–4, 187
Bavaria 125, 169–73, 176, 177, 191, 202, 205, 208
Bavarian Oktoberfest 171
Bendix, R. 6, 168
Berlin 13, 81, 113, 114, 118, 133, 139, 141, 150, 204, 205
Berst, T. 143
Bible Reading. Protestant Interior in Alsace (Brion) 70–1
Blessing of the Wheat in Artois, The (Breton) 72
Blumer, L. 25, 27, 28, 31
bombasin 161
Botrel, T. 177
Braun, A. 68, 69, 96
Braun & Schneider 65, 66
Breton, J. 22, 27, 58, 65, 71–3, 138, 146, 177, 198, 202
Brion, G. 70–6, 96
Brittany 22, 27, 54, 72, 138, 146, 167, 177, 191, 202, 203, 206–8
Bucher, P. 94, 135, 140, 141, 143, 145, 150, 157, 158, 165
Bückeburger Flügelhaube (winged bonnet) 193–4
Burial at Ornans (Courbet) 70

Cahun, D. -L. 37–42
Calvinism 17
casaquin 101, 102, 104
Catholic Church 2, 22, 49, 50, 52
Catholicism 17, 23–7, 54, 156, 202, 203

Catholics and Protestants 9, 15–19, 22, 23, 27, 34, 35, 40, 41, 43, 44, 47, 51, 192
Cercle St.-Léonard 81, 82, 94, 135, 142, 149, 150, 159
Chamber of Artisans 100, 124–9, 133
Chapman, M. 167
Charles-Brun, J. 188
Charles-Roux, J. 177
Christian
  and Anabaptists 34
  denominations 15
  humility 32
  and Jewish practices 36–7
  processions 45
church suit (*Kirchenanzug*) 105
clothing 7, 85, 100, 146, 147
  ability of 11
  choices 50–1
  Jews and Anabaptists 15
  people and 8
  production 12, 97, 99, 100, 113, 114, 119, 121, 124, 129, 131–3
  quantity and value of 107–10
  rural 11, 97, 101, 103, 106, 107, 110, 111
  style 3, 6, 12, 19, 23, 44, 47, 64, 97, 104, 106, 193
coiffe 29, 31, 40, 43, 45, 72, 80, 100, 112, 215 n.62
consumerism 97, 109, 116
Corpus Christi 23, 24, 202
Cortège nuptial (Brion) 73, 74
Costume de divers pays (Lanté and Gatine) 61–2
costume de fête 156
Costume et Coutumes d'Alsace 178
Costumes d'Alsace et de Bade (Lewicki) 33–4, 62
Costumes de divers pays (Lanté and Gatine) 63
Costumes et coutumes d'Alsace 89, 95, 150
Courbet, G. 70–2
craftspeople, education and apprenticeship 124–9

DeGroff, D. 139
department stores 3, 5, 12, 97, 98, 112–14, 116, 117, 119–21, 124, 127, 129, 132, 133, 135, 165, 209
Deutsche Volkstrachten (Lallemand and Hart) 66, 87

D'Hochzittshose 132
Dollinger, L. 140, 162, 165, 187
Doré, G. 11, 77–80, 96
dressmaking 128–33
Dutch Dairy Organization (NZB) 204
Dutch Girl 204

Ecomusée d'Alsace 206–7
education
  and apprenticeship 124–9
  elementary 126
  primary 125, 126
Elsässische Landestrachten 116
Elsässische Nachrichten 118
Elsässisches Stube 141
Elsass-Lothringer Zeitung 189
Emrich, C. 18, 19, 25, 62–4, 146
Encyclopédie des voyages (Grasset) 59, 60, 65
Eucharistic Congress (1927) 49
everyday suit (*Alltagskleid*) 105

fantaisiste costumes 188
Fashion System, The (Barthes) 57
feast day dress (*Festtagskleid*) 106
Fédération des Groupes Folkloriques des Provinces Françaises 188, 191
Fédération régionaliste française (FRF) 188
festivals
  Breton 202
  folk 51, 169, 175, 176, 189–91, 203
  in France 178
  non-religious 169–72
  turn-of-the-century 174–8
Festo Virginienco (Virginal Festival) 177
Fête des Fleurs 177, 178, 191
Fête des Provinces Françaises 187
Fête-Dieu 23, 25–7, 32, 49, 84, 95, 178–80, 198, 201, 202
Fêtes des Provinces 191
field guide 58–66
First World War 8, 12, 54, 83, 94, 96, 114, 116, 119, 124, 128, 132, 133, 158, 182, 195, 198, 203, 208
Foch, M. 185
folk dress 6, 10, 11, 16, 52, 53, 57, 80, 95, 112, 116, 135, 139, 166–8, 171, 180–6, 196, 198, 205, 209

folk groups 1–2, 13, 167, 168, 196, 198, 199, 201, 202, 205–8, 210
  development of 191
  establishment of 189
  history of 168–9
  organization of 176, 186–91
folklore 72, 137, 167, 168
  Nazi influence on 192–5
  Nazism and 168
  re-emergence of interest 195–8
folklorism 167, 168
Forrer, R. 141, 148–51, 165
Fortbildungsschule 126, 127
Francophiles 165
Franco-Prussian War 8, 9, 11, 58, 69, 78, 79, 81–3, 96, 113
Franzoi, B. 124
Frauen-Industrie und Fortbildungs-Schule 126
French Revolution 2, 22, 35, 60
Fresquet, J. -L. 36

Gatineau, B. 213 n.10, 219 n.50
Gatine, G. -J. 60–4
Gavarni, P. 62
Gebirgstrachtenerhaltungsvereine 176
Geispolsheim 23–6, 39, 47–50, 84, 95, 102, 103, 153, 178, 179, 182, 187, 201, 202, 207
Gerson, S. 4
Gesellschaft mit beschränkter Haftung (GmbH) 142, 143
Gibson, R. 52
Gouin, F. 195
Grande Kermesse Alsacienne 187
Grande Percée 119
grand'messe pontificale 50
Grand Pardon 177–8
Grands Magasins du Louvre 117
Grasset de Saint-Sauveur, J. 59–61, 69, 71, 96
Great Pilgrimage in Brittany, A (Breton) 72
Grew, R. 70
Groupe folklorique du Pays de Hanau de Bouxwiller (GFPHB) 196, 197, 208
Gugumus, M. 195

Handwerkskammer. *See* Chamber of Artisans

Hansi 94, 95, 186, 203
Hansjakob, H. 51
Hart, L. 66–8, 87, 88, 98
Harvey, D. 3
Hazelius, A. 137, 139, 144, 206
Heil, M. 130
Hemd (shirts) 101
Henner, J. -J. 11, 79–80, 94, 96, 186
Hobsbawm, E. 5
Hugo, V. 76
human life *(la vie humaine)* 146, 147
Hume, L. 15

"image clothing" 57, 58
Images du Musée Alsacien 158–61
industrial production 121–4
Invention of Tradition, The (Hobsbawm and Ranger) 5
inventories 4, 12, 100, 101, 104–10, 148

Jews 15, 16, 32, 35–41, 43, 44, 46, 53, 54, 193
Jones, S. 6
Judenhut 37
Jugendstil 82

Kaseweck 102, 104
Kassel, A. 52, 150–1, 165, 175, 181, 186
Kaufhaus Louvre 119, 120
Kaufhaus Modern 119–21
Kennedy, K. 125
Ketuboth (7:6) 36
kippah 41, 46
kippot 37, 46
Kleid/Anzug 105
Klein, D. 83
Kochersberg 18, 19, 21, 33–5, 45, 63, 64, 66, 75, 100, 112, 155, 187
Kochloeffel de Souffelweyersheim 207
Kraus, G. 169, 170, 173, 174

Labrousse, L. F. 61
La Foire aux servantes (Marchal) 73, 74
Lallemand, C. 66–9, 87, 88, 218 n.18
L'Alsace. Elle Attend (Henner) 79, 80, 185–6
L'Alsace Meutrie (Doré) 78–9
Landrin, A. 138–40, 146, 151
Lanté, L. -M. 60–4, 66, 71, 217 n.8

Laugel, A. 80–3, 89, 91, 95, 140, 150, 178, 179, 219 n.50
Les français peints par eux-mêmes (Bédollierre) 64–5
Le Tailleur et la Tailleuse d'Alsace 128
Lévy, A. 37–42, 53
Lewicki, J. 33–4, 62, 64, 68, 146
Lix, F. 92, 146
Loferl 205
Lorraine (Doré) 78
Louis XIV 17
Lutherans 17

Magasins Modernes 119, 120
Maguet, F. 58–9
Maison Bossert 205, 206
Marchal, C. -F. 73, 74
Mariage Protestante en Alsace (Brion) 76
Marignan, E. 147, 151
Mary, statue of 24–6, 201
men
　Hemd (shirt) 101
　Jewish dress practice 36
　in Kochersberg 112
　in Wissembourg 149
messtis 52, 84, 163, 174, 175, 182, 183
minority religions 41–4
minority religious groups 32–41
Mistral, F. 140, 141, 144, 177
modernization 2–4, 6, 7, 15, 48, 97–9, 116, 210
Munich Oktoberfest. *See* Oktoberfest
Musée Alsacien 13, 94, 98–9, 101–2, 135–6, 140, 164–6, 180, 201, 206
　collection and acquisition 145–53
　displays 153–7
　folk museums 136–40
　founding 140–5
　kermesse 162–4
　traditional culture 157–62
Musée d'Art et d'Histoire de Saverne 102
Musée d'ethnographie du Trocadéro 138, 147
Museon Arlaten 13, 144, 147, 177
museum 12–13. *See also* Musée Alsacien
　ethnographic 135, 136, 138, 139
　folk 135–40, 146–8
　French 139
　German 139
　idea of 135
　limitations of 157
　national 136–9, 147, 164
　open-air 144, 206, 207
　Provençal 147
　wax 154
Museum für deutsche Volkstrachten 141
Museum für Volkstrachten und Erzeugnisse des Hausgewerbes 139, 147, 150

national dress 170
nationalism 2, 4, 57, 62, 82, 98, 133, 136, 140, 145, 164, 165, 168, 198, 199, 209, 210
Nationaltracht 170
Nazism 168, 195
Neueste Nachrichten 194, 195
Nuzinger, R. 51

Obama, B. 208
Oberseebach 20–2, 27, 28, 31, 45, 66, 76, 155, 156, 186
Oktoberfest 169–71, 173, 174, 176, 178, 181, 198, 209
Oppenheim, M. 41, 42
outfits 19, 26, 47, 61, 104–7, 109, 203
Outre-Forêt 9, 17–21, 24, 27, 45, 67, 76, 85, 88, 115, 156, 195

Pannemaker, A. F. 77
pardons 22, 27, 72, 198, 202, 203
Pays de Hanau 9, 18, 19, 45–7, 175, 196, 208
photography 12, 26–31, 45, 47–50, 57, 58, 66–9, 80, 83–5, 87–9, 91–3, 98, 100, 103, 105, 110–12, 115, 121, 122, 158, 160, 174, 175, 182, 183, 185, 189, 194, 195, 203
Piton, F. 75, 173
poilu 183–5
political
　ideology 140, 149, 165, 178
　parades 4, 193
　propaganda 57, 58
　rallies 167, 180–6
　situation 136
　symbolism 4, 80, 178, 182
politicization 168, 180
politics 58, 81, 82, 138, 209
Première École de coupe et de couture 127–8

processions 23–7, 29–32, 43, 45, 49, 54, 72, 84, 95, 161, 169–74, 177–81, 201, 202
Protestantism 9, 15–19, 22, 23, 27–32, 34, 35, 41, 43, 44, 47, 52, 192
Provence 13, 138, 141, 147, 177

Rajon, P. 76
Ranger, T. 5
Rapport des Gérants 148, 154, 156, 160, 162
ready-to-wear 97, 98, 112, 118–20, 127, 129, 130, 133, 205
realism 69–74
red bows 19, 22, 25, 95, 179, 201, 202, 207
regional culture 12, 13, 22, 82, 91, 135–8, 141, 143, 157–62, 167, 168, 177, 189, 199, 209
regional dress 1–7, 10, 11, 168–78, 180–3
　characterization of 57
　decline of 12
　deployment of 198, 205
　diversity of 92
　emergence of 63
　evolution of 3, 6
　fashion and 192
　history of 57
　photography of 66–9
　preservation of 51
　realism and 69–74
　religion and 54–5
　and religious observance 47–53
　and religious practice 48–9
　women's 27, 45, 185
regional identity 4, 7, 16, 62, 169, 176, 201, 203, 209
regionalism 4, 57, 82, 119, 137, 140, 168, 188, 199, 209
Reichsland 9, 10, 80, 133
religion
　and dress 16–23, 32, 54
　legal status of 3
　minority 41–4
　and regional dress 54–5
　significance of 22
Religious Life of Dress, The (Hume) 15
religious observance 3, 4, 11, 16, 22, 27, 32, 35, 37, 47–55, 72, 164, 198, 201, 202
Revue Alsacienne Illustrée 93, 94, 140–2, 146, 159, 187

Riefenstahl, L. 193
ritual 24, 26, 27, 29, 31, 32, 41, 45–7, 50, 54, 55, 72, 84, 179
Rivet, P. 189
Rivière, G.-H. 189
Robertsau 172
Rock 101
rural dress 12, 54, 57, 66, 80, 99, 100, 105, 106, 148, 165, 193, 199

Salle de France 138, 139, 224 n.10
Scènes de la vie Juive en Alsace (Stauben) 43–4
scheitel 41
Schleithal 20, 21, 23–6, 39, 76, 84, 155, 156, 186
Schlumberger, P. 149
Schmidt, M. 176, 177
Schmid, W. 83
Schmitt, O. 98–100
Schulé-Klopfer (synagogue knocker) 44
Schuler, T. 20, 21, 58, 76–8, 81, 96, 146, 149, 219 n.48
Second World War 168, 194, 208
simultaneum 17
Société à responsabilité limitée (SARL) 142
Société du Musée alsacien 142, 144–6, 157
Söderman, C. A. 154
Soir en Alsace (Doré) 78
special occasion dress 3, 15, 18, 25, 32, 41, 43, 48, 52, 53, 105, 106, 109–112, 206
Speer, A. 193
Spezialgeschäft 113
Spindler, C. 12, 27–30, 58, 80–2
　Alsatian museum 145
　and Bucher 94
　ceremony and 179–80
　photographer and ethnologue 83–93
Spindler, P. -L. 81
Stauben, D. 40, 43–4, 53, 215 n.59
Steinhoff, A. 31
Stein, M. 205
Stoklund, B. 137
Stoskopf, G. 149, 187, 188, 190, 191
Strasbourg illustré (Piton) 75
streimel 38
Strobel, H. 192, 193
Stube 154

Stubenprinzip 154
Sunday dress 26, 106
Sunday suit *(Sonntagskleid)* 105, 106

tailoring 128–33
Tanzpause auf einer elsässischen Bauernhochzeit (Vautier) 73
Touchemolin, A. 75, 173, 181
Tracht 116, 168, 175, 176, 191–4
Trachtenfest 175, 176, 186
tradition
 clothing 97
 France and Germany 146
 goods 161–2
 and industrial culture 137
 and modernity 209
 and modern society 3
 survival of 129–30
Trevor-Roper, H. 5
Truchtersheim 100–1, 106, 108

Vaterländischen Frauenverein (VFV) 126
Vautier, B. 72, 73, 75–6
Verne, J. 76
villageoise 162
Virchow, R. 139, 147, 148
Vlossak, E. 94
Vogtsbauernhof 207
Volkskunde 192
Volksschulen 125

wardrobes 4, 91, 100–10
Weber, E. 2–4
wedding 29–31, 45, 54, 74, 75, 84, 98, 100, 105, 111, 112, 132, 169, 173–4
Weissenburger Wochenblatt 114, 117
Westercamp, P. 149, 150
Wolff, A. 205–6
women
 Catholic 19, 21, 34
 clothing 8, 104, 129, 156
 costumes 29, 34, 44, 147, 156, 182
 inclusion of 185
 Jewish 36, 37, 40, 41
 men and 1, 4, 7, 8, 10, 30, 36, 44, 72, 101, 108, 109, 112, 129, 156, 170, 171, 173, 181, 193, 202
 Protestant 8, 19, 21, 22
workday suit
 (Werktagsanzug/Werktagskleid) 105
World's Fairs 13, 82, 135–8, 140, 144, 145, 154, 162, 165, 168, 188, 189
"written clothing" 57, 58

Young Communicants at Courrieres (Breton) 72

Zittelkatalog 152
Zur Geschichte der Kostüme (Braun) 65
Zwei Schweschtere 131, 132

Plate 1 Members of the Groupe folklorique du Pays de Hanau de Bouxwiller perform in Strasbourg's Place Gutenberg in summer 2007. Photograph by author.

Plate 2 Fête-Dieu procession in Geispolsheim, 1908 from *Images du Musée Alsacien*. Coll. et photogr. Bibliothèque nationale et universitaire, Strasbourg.

Plate 3 Charles Emrich, "Paysanne de Kochersberg" [Catholic] from *Collection de six costumes nationaux alsaciens et badois*, 1834. Coll. et photogr. BNU, Strasbourg.

Plate 4 Charles Emrich, "Paysanne de Kochersberg" [Protestant] from *Collection de six costumes nationaux alsaciens et badois*, 1834. Coll. et photogr. BNU, Strasbourg.

Plate 5 Jan Lewicki, "Paysans du Kochersberg, jeunes gens" from *Costumes d'Alsace et de Bade*, 1834. Coll. et photogr. BNU, Strasbourg.

Plate 6 Louis Marie Lanté and Georges Jacques Gatine, "Paysanne alsacienne de Kochersberg" from *Costumes de divers pays*, 1827. Coll. et photogr. BNU, Strasbourg.

Plate 7 Gustave Courbet, *Burial at Ornans (Un enterrement à Ornans)*, 1849–50. Paris, Musée d'Orsay, accepté par l'Etat à titre de don de Mlle Juliette Courbet en 1881.

Plate 8 Gustave Brion, *Cortège nuptial*, 1873. Musée des Beaux-Arts de Strasbourg, Photo Musées de Strasbourg, A. Plisson.

Plate 9 Gustave Doré, *Soir en Alsace*, 1869. Musée d'Art Moderne et Contemporain de Strasbourg, Photo Musées de Strasbourg, A. Plisson.

Plate 10 Jean-Jacques Henner, *Alsace. Elle attend*, 1871. Paris, Musée National Jean-Jacques Henner. Photo © RMN-Grand Palais/Franck Rau.

Plate 11 Hansi, Pages d'Album, 1916, Gravure no. 53/150. Coll. et photogr. BNU, Strasbourg.

Plate 12 Bodice of wedding dress of Odile Schmitt, 1903. Collection of the Musée Alsacien de Strasbourg.

Plate 13 Purple silk bodice from Geispolsheim. Collection of the Musée Alsacien de Strasbourg.

Plate 14 Courtyard of Musée Alsacien. Photograph by author.

Plate 15 Gustav Kraus, Procession celebrating the wedding of King Ludwig and Queen Therese in Munich on October 4, 1835. Münchner Stadtmuseum, Sammlung Graphik/Gemälde.

Plate 16 Gustav Kraus, Procession celebrating the wedding of King Ludwig and Queen Therese in Munich on October 4, 1835. Münchner Stadtmuseum, Sammlung Graphik/Gemälde.

Plate 17 Frédéric-Emile Simon, Cultivators from the Industrial Parade in Strasbourg June 25, 1840. Coll. et photogr. BNU, Strasbourg.

Plate 18 Frédéric-Emile Simon, Inhabitants of the Robertsau from the Industrial Parade in Strasbourg June 25, 1840. Coll. et photogr. BNU, Strasbourg.

Plate 19 Fête-Dieu procession in Geispolsheim, 2009, Photograph by author.

Plate 20 Corpus Christi procession in Seehausen, Bavaria, June 2015. Photo by Carsten Koall/Getty Images.

Plate 21 The character of Frau Antje created to promote the dairy products in the Netherlands. Dutch Dairy Association.

Plate 22 President Barack Obama and German Chancellor Angela Merkel are welcomed by girls in traditional Black Forest dress in Baden Baden, April 3, 2009. Photo by Alex Grimm/Getty Images.

www.ingramcontent.com/pod-product-compliance
Lightning Source LLC
Chambersburg PA
CBHW052217300426
44115CB00011B/1728